New Philosophy of Social Science

New
Philosophy
of Social
Science

Problems of Indeterminacy

James Bohman

The MIT Press
Cambridge, Massachusetts

ISBN 0–262–02343–1

Library of Congress Catalog Card Number 91–62790

Typeset in 10.5 on 12 pt Sabon
by Graphicraft Typesetters Ltd., Hong Kong
Printed in Great Britain by T. J. Press, Padstow, Cornwall

Contents

Preface

Philosophers and methodologists have tried for decades to unify the complex and diverse activities called "social science," without much success. At the one extreme, naturalistic philosophers of science have demanded that the social sciences imitate the natural sciences. But the social sciences have never achieved much in the way of predictive general laws – the hallmark of naturalistic knowledge – and so have often been denied the honorific status of "sciences." From the opposite end of the spectrum, advocates of the "human sciences" have placed interpretation and meaning at the center of the social sciences; their methods were to serve higher, moral purposes. Fortunately, these have not been the only views. There has also been a long history of attempts to incorporate features from both sides, to see mixtures of both explanations and interpretations as the hallmark of social science. Max Weber and, more recently, Jürgen Habermas are among those who have persuasively argued for this irreducible methodological complexity. This book is an attempt to develop the latter tradition in a comprehensive fashion, now that "new" post-empiricist philosophy of science has given it better tools and concepts and now that "new," more complex forms of explanation have emerged in social theory. Where the old logic of the social sciences sought unity, the new logic finds complexity; where the old logic sought idealized reconstructions, the new logic begins from the actual practices of the social sciences.

The main argument of this book is that social phenomena are shot through with indeterminacy and open-endedness, and that good explanations in vital research programs must find ways to deal with the problems that this indeterminacy raises. In the philosophy of science, post-empiricism has undermined the view that there is something determinate which everyone can agree to call scientific knowledge and explanation. Against "the received view" and its idealized picture of science, post-empiricism has counselled us to look at the history and practices of the various sciences; for that reason, this book draws all of its examples from actual social science. In fact, the turn to history and to practices has placed the social sciences at the center of contemporary epistemology and philosophy of science. All sciences are now rightly regarded as historical, social and self-reflective practices, including those social sciences from which the concept of a social practice itself derives. However, from this assumption many post-empiricists and sociologists of science draw the unwarranted conclusion that the "new" philosophy of science can no longer be normative. One of the goals of this book is to dispute the interpretation of post-empiricism that underlies this position and to offer a different version of the turn to social practice.

Certainly, the "new" philosophy of science cannot legislate for the practices that it reflects upon by simply referring to some idealized, supposedly universal features of knowledge. Rather, it starts from the assumption that there is no royal road to scientific knowledge. But it must still be normative, now in a different way: it must develop critical standards for self-reflection with which to compare various explanatory strategies and patterns; it must elucidate the goals and purposes of new social theories and judge how well they fulfill them; and it must find criteria of adequacy within indeterminacy, criteria that help research programs evaluate the success of their explanations. Above all, it must help change our conception of science from one in which an individual knower faces a neutral world of facts to one in which knowledge is seen as an ongoing social and historical accomplishment. Such changes are already being shaped by recent sociologies of scientific knowledge.

My major aim is to provide a synthetic treatment of the main issues of the philosophy of social science from a post-empiricist perspective, including causality, rules, interpretation, holism, and social criticism. Such an attempt is also a case study in developing the normative epistemology of social practices, a project that can be completed only in cooperation with the social sciences. My view is that the skeptical conclusions that many post-empiricist philosophers draw from this involvement in practices are the result of their faulty use of the categories and results of the social sciences. These false skeptical inferences can be corrected by a closer examination of the social sciences that reveals the standards of adequacy and evaluation already operating within them. This anti-skeptical conclusion can best be established by looking at research programs in the social sciences that take the knowledgeable social actor as their starting point: rational choice theory, ethnomethodology, and the theory of communicative action. Most of my examples will be drawn from these research programs, although I discuss recent "postmodern" ethnography in the chapter on interpretation and sociology and ethnography of science throughout. In keeping with the self-reflective character of post-empiricist social science, some of the debates considered here will be about the social character of science itself; indeed, both the social and the natural sciences are themselves the subject of some of the best current social scientific research within these programs. In order to test my claims, I will relate each problem discussed in this book to actual debates within the social sciences themselves. Hence, they will serve as "case studies" with which to test my philosophic claims and arguments. These case studies will include theoretical, empirical, and methodological controversies in current sociology, economics, and anthropology.

Apart from this normative yet post-empiricist perspective, the conclusions of this book do not reflect a commitment to any one theoretical tradition. If its central problem is to develop comprehensive standards of comparison between theories, such a normative account of explanation must recognize the possibility of multiple valid explanations even of the same phenomena. Certain theoretical programs in the social sciences have already tried to incorporate many different types of explanation and theory into a coherent and comprehensive whole. Besides Weber, perhaps the best example of a comprehensive theory is the program of "interdisciplinary materialism" espoused by the Frankfurt School in the 1930s and continued today in the work of Jürgen Habermas. While I may or may not accept any of their substantive theories or views on the sciences, I accept this program as the proper direction for a philosophy of social science. Both Habermas and the Frankfurt School are also instructive in that they have tried to incorporate various forms of empirical social research into their comprehensive explanatory theories; they have therefore had to deal with questions of judging among and reconciling various competing theoretical and explanatory claims.

No work of this sort would be possible without the support of various institutions and individuals. I would like to thank the Alexander von Humboldt-Stiftung for a research grant that helped bring the work to completion. I would also like to thank St. Louis University both for several summer research grants and for a course reduction to give me time to complete the work. A Summer Institute sponsored by the National Endowment for the Humanities entitled "Interpretation and the Human Sciences" helped to clarify many of the issues discussed here. I would like to thank its directors, Bert Dreyfus and David Hoy, as well as all the participants for their lively discussion. Many people too numerous to mention have helped as well. I would especially like to thank Jürgen Habermas and Thomas McCarthy for their criticisms and advice. I would also like to thank Michael Barber for reading several drafts, William Charron for his assistance in the sections on rational choice theory, Paul Roth for his criticisms of the section on interpretation, and Bill Caspary for reading parts of the manuscript. All of them made many helpful suggestions.

Most of all, I want to thank Gretchen Arnold for her support, companionship, criticism, editorial advice and just about everything else. I dedicate the book to her.

Introduction
Post-Empiricism, Indeterminacy, and the Social Sciences

In sociology we have, up until now, no clear trend of hypotheses.
Otto Neurath, *Foundations of the Social Sciences*

When these philosophers and their principles each had their day, and the latter were found inadequate to generate the nature of things, it was once again necessary to inquire into the next kind of cause.
Aristotle, *Metaphysics*

The quotations above represent two different reactions to a certain type of disciplinary perplexity. In the first statement, Neurath was waiting for a unifying trend in sociology that would end its immaturity and put it on the secure path of cumulative growth. In the second passage, Aristotle described the development of natural philosophy in his day as discontinuous; his lesson was not to seek unity but instead to multiply the meanings of the explanatory term, "cause," which provides the answer to any "why" question. Neurath was, of course, a member of the Vienna Circle and a positivist. Aristotle opposed the Platonic unification of the sciences and was in effect a post-empiricist *avant la lettre*, at least in this passage. In this book, I will follow the second rather than the first strategy and argue that methodological legislation and unity should be replaced by self-reflection on the history and explanatory practice of the social sciences.

In the beginning of that history, the social sciences were not as epistemologically perplexing to philosophers as they were to Neurath. In early modernity, when social reformers and engineers hoped that the social sciences could solve emerging social problems, few doubted the character of knowledge they produced. The social sciences could simply emulate the successful sciences of the day: Hobbes saw classical mechanics as supplying the proper "abstractive" method, while Durkheim preferred the holistic features of biology. This assumption of a unity of method in the sciences, however, later proved to be the source of both hope and despair about the social sciences. On the one hand, reformers placed hope in the ability of technical knowledge to solve problems. Critics, on the other hand, saw such knowledge as turning people into objects of control by experts and argued for a model of social science that viewed beings as self-interpreting, autonomous subjects. This dispute about the methods and purposes of social science gave rise to nineteenth century debates about some essential distinction between the natural and human sciences, the *Natur-* and the *Geisteswissenschaften*. From this distinction between different types of science followed a host of other distinctions that have become part of the traditional subject matter of the philosophy of social science: in method, between explanation and understanding; in domain, between objects and subjects, or nature and culture; in purpose, between technical control and increased understanding. Even the opponents of the naturalistic conception of social science accepted it as accurate for the parts of science they rejected as models for the human sciences. In any case, both sides of the debate – the naturalistic and positivist approaches on the one hand and the hermeneutic approaches on the other – flourished in the heyday of methods. Each was sure that its methods had the distinctive features that were to define their privileged place in producing the proper knowledge for the study of human beings.

Though the philosophical debate continued all the while naturalism prevailed in scientific institutions, it took on new life in the late 1960s and early 1970s as the strong and essentialistic distinctions between human and natural science began to break down for different reasons.[1] Surprisingly, perhaps, the impetus came first from the side of the natural sciences, in the challenges to the "received view" of naturalism by post-empiricist philosophers of science like Thomas Kuhn, Mary Hesse and Paul Feyerabend.[2] The standard list of contrasts between the natural and human sciences had all derived from a positivist and empiricist view of scientific knowledge: the neutrality of observation and the givenness of experience; the ideal of a univocal language and the independence of data from theoretical interpretation; the belief in the universality of conditions of knowledge and criteria for theory choice. After Kuhn, many of these views and the distinctions that upheld them collapsed. With the rejection of positivism and its thesis of the "unity of method," many of the historic reasons for defending the sharp distinction between the sciences have simply disappeared. Newer versions of the methodological distinctiveness of the human sciences, like those of Taylor and Dreyfus, have more to do with moral and political issues than with epistemological and scientific ones.[3] Regardless of how much such attempts contribute to our understanding of politics and morals, they do not contribute much to a post-empiricist understanding of the social sciences, or to clarifying the moral and political purposes of natural science.

In many respects, post-empiricism has removed the social sciences from their contentious and peripheral status and placed them directly in the center of some new epistemological debates. In one such debate, the "old logic" of the sciences is exemplified in Hempel's deductive–nomological reconstruction of all adequate explanations. In light of this reconstruction, Hempel thought he could show why some explanations in the social sciences, such as functionalism, fail and why other cases are successful, including "rational explanations" using "laws" of utility maximization (discussed in chapter 1 below). In place of such highly idealized and ahistorical reconstructions, post-empiricism has turned to the actual practices and histories of various sciences. This historical approach has led to an anti-essentialist view of what counts as scientific knowledge, one that denies that any single universal and necessary set of features qualifies a practice to be scientific or an explanation to be adequate. This historicism and anti-essentialism directs post-empiricism to local and situational features of scientific practices. Such features are often sociological, as can be seen by the first major post-empiricist work, Thomas Kuhn's *Structure of Scientific Revolutions*.

In this work, Kuhn described the history of science in terms of long periods of "normal science" at work on problem solving within a "paradigm," punctuated by revolutionary periods of theory change. As opposed to Hempel's account of single explanations or the empiricist appeal to privileged representations, post-empiricism places theories and disciplines in larger social and historical contexts in which they are applied, change and develop. Imre Lakatos called these larger units "research programmes" and judged their success pragmatically, in terms of whether or not they were "fruitfully" solving problems or "degenerating" into *ad hoc* defenses of core hypotheses. Such a contrast between degenerating and fruitful research programs signaled one of the first post-empiricist attempts to reintroduce normative and rational criteria for deciding between competing theories and visions of scientific practice. Still, it is not altogether clear that science ever developed in this way, raising questions about "rationality and relativism" that have raged in the philosophy of science since Kuhn.[4]

In these debates, two problems emerged that were related to historicism and anti-essentialism. First, with larger units like theories and paradigms, the problem of incommensurability concerns just how local and contextual our descriptions of scientific practice should be; if they are too local, then no comparison and evaluation seem possible. Does the turn to practice make normative epistemological judgments merely local? Second, anti-essentialism further undermines the possibility of rethinking the normative component of rational reconstruction. Does the lack of a definite list of universal features of explanation or scientific knowledge make it impossible to distinguish between better and worse explanations? The main unresolved problem of post-empiricism has therefore been how to derive standards for the comparison and evaluation of competing explanations and research programs without falling back into an ahistorical and essentialist epistemology.

In the "old" philosophy of science, such questions concerned claims about the objectivity of science and could be settled by sure appeals to methodological standards of deductive reasoning and empirical proof. Under post-empiricist assumptions, objectivity now concerns the choice of a research program and of its standards of evaluation, which can be settled only by appealing to weaker forms of theoretical justification and assessment. As Habermas points out, "The approval of a procedure or the acceptance of a norm can be supported or weakened by argument; it can at least be rationally assessed.... This is precisely the task of critical theoretical thought."[5]

The analyses in this book attempt to fulfill the task of developing forms of rational assessment for the explanatory power of theories produced by various ongoing research programs: rational choice, ethnomethodology, interpretive social science, and the theory of communicative action. I have chosen these particular theories because of their continuing fruitfulness and the range of explanations that have been produced by them; they also lend themselves to inter-theoretical comparison, sharing certain minimal assumptions about knowledgeable social actors and their capacity to generate and maintain social life. Each begins with the problem of action and takes the intentional perspective of actors to be a necessary ingredient of good social science explanation, while differing significantly about what reasons and beliefs are and how they play an explanatory role.

The book starts with problems of the theory of action as conceived by the "old" logic of explanation. I will criticize Hempel's and Parsons' attempts to determine general and necessary features of rational and social action. Then, I will attempt to reconstruct the forms of explanation that are typical in specific research programs and compare them on a significant issue in social theory: the explanatory importance of rules and norms. While Hempel and Parsons did not succeed in discovering universal features and laws of all social action, it is possible to do a more historically oriented rational reconstruction of a specific research program; in doing so, it becomes possible to assess the structure and scope of explanations within it. The result of such a reconstruction is what I will call an explanatory pattern: a list of statements that are necessary conditions for an adequate explanation within a certain research program. These conditions can be used as a standard or norm: explanations which lack one or more of such statements or premises are incomplete and hence inadequate. Each type and pattern of explanation can best be discovered by examining not only the writings of major theorists in each program, but also by looking at paradigmatic cases of good explanation taken from its research practice. I view these patterns not so much as rigorous logical inferences but more as Kuhnian exemplars: they are "paradigmatic" cases that exhibit the general features of an adequate and complete explanation of a certain type (chapter 2).[6] Similar patterns can be reconstructed for functionalist and macro-structural explanations (chapter 4) and for critical social science (chapter 5), although exemplars of explanations of these latter types are not confined to particular research programs. As exemplars, these patterns represent the distillation of successful cases which form the "core" of the program and can then be extended to include other sorts of cases, so long as they have similar features.[7] This process of extension can also show the limits of the research program, as, for example, in the consistent application of the core case of rational choice theory, maximizing behavior; while many activities fit the pattern surprisingly well, many more obvious cases of rational action, such as voting, do not fit it at all. One of the primary benefits of these reconstructions is that they provide a form of reflection that is neither general nor local. According to the view of explanation developed in this book, wherever there is such a reconstructible pattern, standards of adequacy can be established. Such a method of middle-range reconstruction is nonetheless post-empiricist, since it sees the role of the philosophy of social science to be reflection upon scientific practice, which is itself varied, self-reflective and normative.[8]

One self-reflective aspect of any scientific practice is that it offers different explanations of the same phenomenon by rival theories.

In the social sciences, this feature is particularly accentuated, since there are many competing theoretical orientations (due more often to fashion than anything else). If we accept with post-empiricism that there are no invariant features of explanations and theories, how can we judge between them? Is this possible at all, if the theories do not agree even about the goals of social science? The theories discussed here do agree that the social sciences should be empirical in the broad sense of being verified or falsified by evidence. But in the absence of neutral description, establishing the data and explaining them often go hand in hand, as Donald Davidson has pointed out for intentional explanations.[9] Rather than implying a lack of criteria, such circularity presents the problem of too many criteria, none of which are determining or definitive. In light of such problems of evidence, post-modern skeptics abandon the search for even weak standards as being so much fruitless metatheorizing about local and indeterminate phenomena.[10]

My argument is that such skepticism is unfounded, even if we accept that there may not be a lot that we can say about "science" in general that will resolve the problem. Theories can still be judged in terms of the various purposes they avow, often in common with other theories. In chapter 5, I argue that any explanatory pattern can be employed for the purpose of social criticism. However, not all of them are particularly suited to that purpose, nor are they all sufficiently reflective. Jon Elster has proposed two general criteria of theoretical adequacy in the social sciences relative to the purpose of prediction: theories may be inadequate or indeterminate. Whereas a theory is inadequate when its theories fail, it is indeterminate "when and to the extent to which it fails to yield unique predictions."[11] Elster admits that a theory has explanatory power even if it is not fully determinate; determinacy is, however, a proper evaluative feature of explanations. But not all theories can be evaluated relative to the purpose of prediction, even in the natural sciences. Like Hempel's reconstructions, Elster presupposes too strong a connection between explanation and prediction, one which would fail to obtain for just about every theory in the social sciences. Even the weaker criterion of determinateness does not decide between very many theories. The social sciences are indeed "sciences of indeterminacy" whose theories do not succeed by predicting unique and determinate outcomes. My hypothesis is that even on post-empiricist assumptions it is possible to show how indeterminacy excludes neither rigorous theorizing nor the search for evidence. The proper form of explanation in the social sciences is both non-reductionist and non-determinist, treating phenomena that are not only diverse and irregular, but intentional and complex. The main problem of this book is to show how explanatory rigor is possible without necessity or determinacy.

Since predictive success requires determinacy, empiricist philosophy of social science has long tried to discover general laws and powerful formal models. After reconstructing Hempel's account of rational explanation as a form of causal explanation, in chapter 1 I will show the failure of all such attempts to make reasons into determinate causes, including notions of the internalization of norms in Parsons' theory of social order and explanations of scientific beliefs in the so-called "strong programme" in the sociology of science. Both try to overcome the indeterminate character of intentions and beliefs through various ideas of causality; social causality becomes either overly singular or ill-defined: it is either the basic mechanism for the social integration of action ("internalized norms"), or it is seen as some general influence of society that operates independently from the content of the actors' beliefs ("interests"). With the failure of both these strategies to replace intentional determinacy, I will turn to explanations which take the indeterminacy of intentional social action as their starting point and build into their patterns of explanation ways in which indeterminacy is recognized and rigorously explained.

The explanation of social action is a convenient starting point for a post-empiricist philosophy of social science, not only because of its indeterminacy but because it is the starting point for the research programs examined in this book. All these programs hold that actions are doubly indeterminate: they are performed by reflective and knowledgeable actors in interaction with other reflective and knowledgeable social actors. If this is true, explanations of action do not fail predictively because their theoretical laws or models are weak, but for the opposite reason: the rigidity of their explanatory premises fixes agents' purposes and goals, making them into "judgmental dopes" or "rational fools," to borrow apt characterizations of the failures of Parsonian sociology and rational choice theories. Indeed, the very identification of an intentional action is indeterminate, as can be seen in Ryle's discussion of the differences between a twitch and a wink.[12] Agents' own self-descriptions enter in, but there are also acts that must be identified as such by others, like insults and warnings. While Davidson has argued that this indeterminacy establishes that we must use the same means to interpret ourselves as we would the most distant culture, it surely also means that actions are open to multiple interpretations, contextual variations and forms of failure. Each research program tries to build in interpretive and contextual components, integrating interpretive indeterminacy into a theoretical framework that makes it comprehensible. In this sense, too, such theories are Weberian, insofar as they fulfill the demands of "explanatory understanding"[13] and escape the old dichotomies of the natural and the human sciences, like hybrid theories since Marx and Freud attempted. These explanations are evidence that the old dichotomies no longer serve any methodological purpose but only help to obscure the indeterminacy of social phenomena in two opposite ways: by denying it, as do the natural science models; or making it into an insuperable limit on explanation, as do traditional human sciences.

Problems of indeterminacy arise in quite diverse contexts, and the chapter headings denote one such context, each with its own form of indeterminacy: causality, rules, interpretation, the micro–macro link, and social criticism. I regard these traditional categories of philosophy of social science as problems that different social theories have to solve: to discover and explain regularities in society, to understand common frames of reference and expectations, to understand things from an agent's point of view, to grasp phenomena of large scope and scale, and to criticize beliefs and structures in a society. Because the research programs examined here are all comprehensive, their styles of explanation have been employed for all of these purposes. Each chapter begins by developing alternative theoretical approaches to these problems and then turns to case studies that illuminate the fundamental difficulties in resolving each type of indeterminacy. As opposed to many other books in the philosophy of social science, my case studies are taken primarily from actual explanations, most of them from sociology, and are meant to contrast successes with failures. While many of my discussions are critical, each chapter includes a success story of an actual explanation which is adequate to the various purposes of social science. In the rest of the introduction, I will give a general indication of the problems and results of each chapter. If the reader does not wish a summary without the accompanying argumentation, she may go ahead to the discussion of the concept of indeterminacy that closes the introduction.

Chapter 1 takes up problems of causality related to explanations of social action. No causal account offered so far yields anything like predictions: causal theories are neither adequate with respect to the diversity of social actions, nor true with respect to their general laws. Reasons cannot be determinate causes that would fulfill the requirements for ad quate causal explanation in my two case studies in this chapter: (1) Durkheim's explanations of the relation between collective moral beliefs and suicide rates and (2) the explanations of scientific beliefs in the strong programme, in particular Paul Forman's analysis of the influence of Weimar culture on quantum physics. Once the assumption of causal determinacy is abandoned, successful explanations can appeal to mechanisms which specify how the context in which social action occurs influences practices of belief formation.

The various explanatory patterns developed in chapter 2 result from abandoning the methodological assumptions of determinacy and generality; each theoretical approach develops core cases of explanations based on distinct features of social action: choice under constraint (rational choice theory), reflective accountability to other actors (ethnomethodology), and communicative interaction (the theory of communicative action). In light of these patterns for explaining action, different forms of indeterminacy with regard to rules and rule following can be addressed: frequent exceptions and free rider problems in choice situations constrained by sanctions; the indeterminacy in the elaborative and *ad hoc* application and employment of rules; and the failure of an action to fulfill normative expectations. My view is that rule following does not constitute the basis for a distinct approach in the social sciences, but makes sense only in the context of other theories that both explain rule following and use rules as explanatory terms. By employing the resources of each pattern, this indeterminacy does not exclude the possibility of both explaining rules and using rules in adequate explanations, despite the fact that they do not predict any unique outcomes or have a fixed reference in actual behavior.

Chapter 3 deals with the source of much indeterminacy in the social sciences: the problem of interpretation. Many argue that post-empiricism and the end of the natural–human science dichotomy together imply that "everything is interpretation" or that, in Stanley Fish's phrase, "interpretation is the only game in town." Charles Taylor has described this view as the "pleasing fantasy" of "old guard Diltheyeans," their shoulders hunched from years-long resistance to positivism, who now "suddenly pitch forward on their faces as all opposition ceases to the reign of universal hermeneutics."[14] I will argue that the claim that "everything is interpretation" arises only because of the holistic character of current theories of interpretation. On this account, interpretation always takes place within a certain background or context of relations (such as the webs of beliefs or the practices of a form of life).

Moreover, interpretation is circular and hence can be evaluated only in light of other interpretation; there is no escape from the hermeneutic circle. While such holistic constraints on determinate interpretation do hold for the social sciences, I argue that skeptical conclusions about explanation do not follow from them. My case studies in this chapter focus on the role of interpretation in debates engendered by two skeptical social scientific analyses of "representation": James Clifford's analysis of cultural anthropology and Steve Woolgar's sociology of science. Even if interpretation is unavoidably indeterminate, it follows only that there is no unique best interpretation, not that there is no way to distinguish better from worse interpretations. Such comparative distinctions can be made in two ways: in light of available evidence, but also in light of the moral responsibility to the other in the dialogical situation that characterizes acts of interpretation. The appeal to evidence and responsibility imply that questions of interpretation can be settled without semantic theory. Social theories inform our interpretation by putting them in larger contexts of evidence and responsibility, not by avoiding interpretive indeterminacy altogether.

In chapter 4, I consider what these larger contexts might be by discussing the problem of explanation in macrosociology. In general, debates between individualists and holists are another legacy of the demarcation problem in the social sciences. Individualists have tended to use natural scientific models and holists have used interpretive models.[15] Holism has also demarcated the social sciences from psychology and has been used to resist reductionism with regard to social facts. Indeed, "classical social theory" often claimed to be able to formulate explanations of practices and even of individual actions and beliefs in terms of properties of society as a whole. Functionalist explanations, for example, explain a practice or a set of beliefs in terms of some social purpose or benefit for society as a whole, as in the case of the integrating effects of rituals. Objections to such explanations typically trade on explanatory indeterminacy: many different practices, actions or beliefs could have fulfilled the same purpose in a different way; conversely, any practice or belief can be said to provide some benefit or another. This indeterminacy has led some to argue that holistic explanations tend to be vacuous and that whatever explanatory force they have is carried by the actions or interactions of individuals which they imply. However, the best current macro-level explanations are neither collective nor individualist; rather, they seek to integrate micro- and macro-levels of explanation. I will argue that such linkages can go in either direction: micro-level explanations can be extended into macro-level contexts and structures; and macro-level structures must be translated into micro-level realizations in actions and interactions. Without such linkages, both micro- and macro-level explanations remain incomplete and inadequate, with little explanatory power. Case studies in this chapter deal with successful and unsuccessful micro–macro links, including debates about functionalism, Marxist base–superstructure explanations, and Habermas's system–lifeworld reformulations.

In chapter 5, I argue that any valid pattern of explanation can be put to use in critical social science. Even interpretations may be employed by social critics, so long as they depart sufficiently from generally accepted ones. Despite its large resources, critical social science shares the indeterminacy of all the forms of explanation discussed previously, including problems of interpretive correctness when criticizing beliefs and desires. But by attempting to be critical, explanations accept the burden of normative–practical criteria of adequacy, as well as further burdens of the indeterminacy of criticism itself. Criticism raises fundamental questions about the pragmatic character of social scientific knowledge; if the description given in this book is correct, then it is a decidedly practical and reflective form of knowledge, rather than a technical and an objective one. Indeed, one of the outmoded dichotomies of the natural–human science controversy – namely, that between "facts" and "values" – is blurred and is no longer the logical distinction modern philosophers have thought it to be. What is "fact" and what is "value" is itself indeterminate, dependent upon the reflective status of norms and of knowledge claims in the theory employed by the critic. Once social science begins to explain and interpret norms and practices, there is no theory-neutral way to assign statements to either side of the distinction. But rather than being a threat to the possibility of critical social science, the collapse of this distinction undermines many of the standard objections to it: it undermines claims to ethical neutrality as in Weber's account of values, as well as the force of the naturalistic fallacy (that is, that critical social science confuses is and ought).

Even without the comfort of the distinction between facts and values, critical social science must not simply assume its standards of criticism but must instead develop them out of its successful forms of explanation. Nor can it claim the status of "objective" knowledge typical of some forms of orthodox Marxism. There are problems of indeterminacy related to the act of criticism itself: problems related to the applicability of the critic's standards, of the direction and consequences of the critic's acts of communication with those criticized, and of the availability of alternative practices and ideals necessary for effective criticism. In this chapter, I will take the goals of Marx's critique of ideology as an exemplar of critical social science, and my case studies will concern various attempts to reformulate its theoretical basis: Elster's conception of social irrationality; Woolgar and Latour's criticism of the "ideology of representation" in science; and Habermas's idea of ideology as distorted communication, or communication distorted by power and domination. As in the micro–macro link, the best criticisms are the most complete, and fulfill a number of criteria: they are based on adequate explanations; they point in an emancipatory direction and provide agents with insights into the forces and restrictions operative in their lives; and they are practical in that they suggest alternatives to the practices which they negatively evaluate. It is clear from these case studies that certain critical theories can perform some but not all of these tasks: while both make similar criticisms, feminist criticisms of science are more adequate *qua* critical social science than current "ethnographies of science." They not only develop a more adequate critical framework, but suggest persuasive alternatives to current concepts and practices and give indications of how such social realities might be changed and who might change them. Hence, the theoretical goals and practical purposes of social critics establish the characteristics of theories that help to change people's beliefs and attitudes, to transform existing practices and to formulate alternative ones.

For all these reasons, the concept of indeterminacy can serve a number of different purposes in this book: it can serve as a critical foil for older criteria of adequacy, illustrate the basic problems of a post-empiricist philosophy of social science and reveal a new logic for the rational reconstruction of actual explanatory practice. Given its organizing role in this book, perhaps it is important to distinguish the use of the term here from other current ones. Indeterminacy here has nothing to do with "indeterminism," the doctrine that free actions must be uncaused; it also is not directly related to chance or randomness. Nor does it have anything to do with the special conditions of knowledge governing quantum mechanics. Furthermore, Quine's argument for the "indeterminacy of translation" makes a stronger case for the undecidability between alternatives than I want to make here, again because of the special conditions governing radical translation and theories of meaning that are not applicable here. In order to make the indeterminacy of translation more than a case of the underdetermination of empirical theories, Quine argues that competing translation manuals can be consistent with all the available evidence and inconsistent with each other.[16] But social science is not like radical translation: social scientists have various theories as resources and sources of evidence.[17] Unlike translation, in the social sciences there is no intrinsic limit on what counts as evidence, although they are similar to the extent that no particular type of evidence is decisive or neutral enough to decide the matter between competing alternatives in advance. Rather than having any of these meanings, the variety of forms of indeterminacy in the social sciences discussed above all derive from special problems concerning the role of agency in explanations. Despite all the theories to the contrary, social actors are not simply the passive bearers of social forces or judgemental dopes within a cultural order. Equipped with capacities for knowledge and reflection, agents may alter their circumstances and conditions of the social life. If this is the case, then the social sciences face deeper problems of indeterminacy than their failure to yield unique predictions like the natural sciences (as Elster has argued). If agents become aware of and change the conditions under which they act, no factor or set of factors can fully or determinately explain a social event or action. By becoming aware of social influences on them, agents may undermine their causal efficacy. Causal explanations in the social sciences, then, cannot be expressed in terms of universal, and hence determinate, laws. Or, to use an example from the cultural order, a rule or norm never fully implies how it must be carried out or can be applied in various situations. Nor do functional or structural explanations determinately describe recurrent patterns of action, since the same structure or function may be maintained by an indefinite number of other actions or behaviours. Thus, the protean character of reflective, social agency evades all attempts to discover some determinate theoretical use of all such explanatory terms in the social sciences.

But this recognition of the inevitability of indeterminacy in social scientific explanations does not, I will argue, exclude the possibility of constructing adequate and fruitful explanations that can fulfill a variety of purposes. How the social sciences can operate within the constraints of indeterminacy and still offer a whole range of explanations is one of the basic themes of this book. In each chapter, I will begin by developing the problem of indeterminacy for each type of explanation; I will then state as precisely as possible its scope and criteria of adequacy. These reconstructions of various types of explanations will take the form of the full statement of a "pattern" or scheme for the use of various indeterminate, yet explanatory, terms. The statements of the pattern make up the conditions of application of the term in an adequate explanation. I will also try to show that it is precisely by recognizing such indeterminacy that the social sciences can perform their practical tasks, such as interpreting other cultures, explaining scientific knowledge, or criticizing social institutions.

As these last remarks reveal, for all its emphasis on indeterminacy and its post-empirical orientation, this book is profoundly anti-skeptical. I take both indeterminacy and post-empiricism to be primarily negative theses: the former criticizes inadequate accounts of explanation in the social sciences, while the latter undermines older forms of the logic of explanation. Both simply serve as starting points, in that they do not contribute much in the way of positive proposals other than that the social sciences must recognize agency and that epistemology must be socialized and historicized. Instead of skepticism, they only require that we change what normative questions we ask and that we broaden what counts as science or explanation. Under post-empiricist assumptions, the philosophy of any science must at least understand its current practice and past history. It cannot be in the business of deciding once and for all what is scientific and what is not; such considerations are generally irrelevant to actual practice.[18] Since the practice of a science is quite varied, philosophical self-reflection should not take upon itself the authority to eliminate alternative directions and theories. Instead, it should take up a comparative but no less normative role, judging research programs and their typical explanations to be better in some respects and worse in others. While such comparative criteria of evaluation are not strong enough for many epistemologies, they are sufficiently normative for the social sciences and the practical knowledge that they warrant. They may also provide solutions to the problems of indeterminacy, to the extent that they can be resolved.

With the turn to history and practice, post-empiricism places the philosophy of social science at the center of epistemology. I hope that this book can help to define its new normative role in developing a logic for making comparative judgments of adequacy between competing claims and approaches according to practical criteria. Certainly, there are unresolved problems with the theories and research programs examined here. But philosophical reflection on them will succeed if it is like the theories it studies, that is, if it is critical, practical and self-reflective in its understanding of knowledge as a social–historical endeavor. Its success depends upon the extent to which new forms of explanation are now in a position to develop a new logic of social scientific practice. The new approaches in the social sciences are now the proper context to ask some of the important philosophical questions about reason, action, and the good life, as they emerge in attempts to interpret, explain and criticize the social–cultural world. At least from the side of philosophy, the first step toward such a cooperative relation will have been taken when it sees social scientific research and theorizing for what it already is. The main contribution of post-empiricism is to get us started: it replaces Neurath's expectation of determinacy and unity with Aristotle's recognition of indeterminacy and multiplicity.

1

The Old Logic of
Social Science:
Action, Reasons, and Causes

For the greater part of this century, up until the recent rise of "post-empiricism," the philosophy of science attempted to identify those distinguishing criteria and features of knowledge which qualify it as scientific. Accounts of this kind usually designated "explanation" to be the distinguishing feature of such knowledge, regardless of the type of explanation it might be. Thus, the analysis of scientific knowledge entailed a "logic" of explanation, that is, an analysis of the relationship between two sets of assertions: the set of statements which does the explaining (the *explanans*) and the statement which describes the phenomenon to be explained (the *explanandum*). In the various forms of positivism and neo-positivism, this relation was considered to be one of entailment (the logical implication of a conclusion by its premises) specified by some basic inferential rule or set of rules or patterns. These rules, it was thought, differ in particular cases, but only according to possible variations of basic logical relationships: some explanatory inferences are inductive and hence probabilistic, while others are deductive and hence determinate. For some philosophers of science, the inference rules were quite particular in scope, applying to explanations of particular events or domains of events, while for others they were thought to apply to theories as a whole or to crucial statements of the theory which warrant explanations until they are "falsified." But for all these differences, the idea of a logic of scientific explanation remained the same: it required the discovery of a set of general methodological rules or forms of inference which would be the same for all the sciences, natural and social. The belief that such a rule exists is responsible not only for the thesis of the "unity of science" but also for attempts to demarcate the natural and the human sciences, as well as to separate science from the rest of culture. The interrelated errors of positivist and hermeneutic claims about social science and about strong distinctions of explanation and understanding were discussed in the introduction to this book. "Post-empiricism" signifies a loss of faith in this essentialist epistemology as the proper guide in the philosophy of science, calling into question the very idea of such a "logic," as well as all those distinctions – hermeneutic or positivist – which rested upon it.

Of course, neither the actual practice of science nor good cases of successful explanation always fit these rules or follow their logic (even in the case favored as a paradigm, causal explanation). This fact, so the positivists argued, did not invalidate their formal results. The goal was not an accurate description of how science worked but instead what Carnap called a "rational reconstruction," an ideal theory of scientific knowledge on a par with the grammar of a language never strictly adhered to by any of its speakers. Even while post-empiricism demands the rejection of not only the conclusions but also the goals of such a "logic" of explanation, by itself the idea of a rational reconstruction is quite useful and need not be abandoned too quickly, although it may not fit the original purpose for which it was intended. In the next chapter, I shall employ the method of "rational reconstruction" not to discover the basic features of scientific knowledge in general but to make explicit the different explanatory practices in various ongoing research programs in the social sciences. Originally, however, reconstruction was supposed to yield a solution to the "demarcation problem," that is, to distinguish science from non-science by appealing to exclusive methodological rules and forms of inference.

In the philosophy of the social sciences, this logic could be used to distinguish explanation from interpretation and other modes of non-scientific, common sense or folk knowledge, all of which at best are as yet unformalized "sketches" or heuristic guides for explanation. I shall call "naturalism" any such attempt to apply uniform standards or models of explanation to the social sciences, borrowed from reconstructions of the natural sciences. Here, naturalism is the assumption that the social sciences are, or should be, fundamentally similar to the natural sciences, both in their

subject matter and in their methods. While the many successes of
the natural sciences seem to qualify them as the model of genuine
science, the social sciences do not fit comfortably into the predominant, naturalistic account of explanatory inference. They remain its stumbling block.

The Failure of Hempel's Naturalism: Rational Action

As a glance at almost any treatment of social science methodology
reveals, Carl Hempel's "deductive–nomological" or "covering law"
model represents perhaps the most successful and influential naturalistic approach to the social and human sciences. For Hempel,
explanation and prediction are strictly correlative: that is, all good
explanations are based on a pattern of inference that issues in the
prediction of an event. The event to be explained is taken to be
the conclusion of an argument, which is derived from a set of
premises consisting of at least a description of the initial conditions
and one general law under which the event may be subsumed. All
good explanations, from those of human behavior to the motion
of the planets, are deductions from two different types of statements: an adequate description of the event's initial conditions and
a general law which "covers" the case in question, both of which
are necessary and sufficient conditions for the occurrence of an
explanandum event. Thus, all explanations are fundamentally causal
and, as David Hume argued, all causal statements are simply
implications of empirical general laws. An explanation is causal if,
and only if, these statements conjointly entail the occurrence of the
event under some description. Through this "ideal reconstruction"
of the logic or argumentative structure of explanations, Hempel
hoped that he had indicated "in reasonably precise terms the
logical structure and rationale of various ways in which empirical science answers explanation-seeking why questions."[1]

This general pattern is the same for all empirical sciences, and
Hempel hoped to find it instantiated in good explanations in
empirical sciences such as history and psychology. Hempel's naturalistic generalization to the "human" sciences drew an immediate
critical response from Dray, Mandelbaum, and others.[2] These anti-
naturalist philosophers tried to show that the model was not
appropriate to the domain of human behavior involving meanings
and intentions; few, if any, explanations in the human sciences
approach the requirements of Hempel's model, but they remain

nonetheless perfectly good explanations supported by empirical evidence. Hempel, of course, tried to prove his critics wrong, and he did so by offering a reconstruction of the most common form of explanation in human affairs, one which was particularly important for history, a discipline which Dray claimed was entirely distinct in its methodology from the physical sciences: rational explanation, or the explanation of action in terms of the agent's motivating reasons, namely, beliefs and desires. Hempel tried to reconstruct this type of explanation as a species of causal explanation, showing that it fits the logical form of deductive–nomological inference. In "The Function of General Laws in History," Hempel tries to show that there is no difference in principle between human sciences like history and natural sciences like physics. To the extent that both offer explanations, both appeal to general, predictive laws. Hempel illustrates his argument by appealing to typical explanations of historical events that invoke agents' beliefs and desires. For example, the French Revolution can be explained in terms of the following general law: "A revolution will tend to occur if there is a growing discontent, on the part of a large part of the population, with certain prevailing conditions."[3] This general regularity is assumed in any explanation of any specific revolution, although in each case the extent and specific form of the discontent must be specified. Similarly, in defending Hempel from his critics, Popper appeals to the following general law to explain the unpopularity of the French monarchy in the eighteenth century: "Rulers who ignore their subjects' interests tend to become unpopular."[4] At the same time, Hempel argues against the explanatory value of many law-like hypotheses, such as the claim that geographic or economic conditions "determine" all other aspects of human society. Such generalizations, he argues, have explanatory value only insofar as it can be substantiated by specific laws about specific historical regularities and thus must be made amenable to empirical tests. "The elaboration of such laws with as much precision as possible seems clearly to be the direction in which progress in scientific explanation and understanding can be sought."[5] Such precision can be found in explanations that appeal to general laws about agents' reasons as causes of historical events.

One of the strengths of Hempel's reply, and the key to whatever plausibility it has, is that it is not reductionistic. Indeed, his account of explanation is entirely epistemic and on the level of logical form, having no direct implications for the type of entities required for good explanations. A general law could quantify over behaviors and movements, but it could also quantify over reasons, beliefs and desires, such as in the case that "all agents who want x and believe that y is sufficient to achieve x, do y." Thus, agents who are sufficiently discontent with their political conditions, and believe that a revolution is the best means of changing them, will attempt a revolution. Such laws may form the basis of the most basic "why" question in the domain of human action: why did the agent perform an action? Hempel's naturalism required that his model be general and not limited to a narrow range of cases in the natural sciences, such as the laws of motion in Newtonian physics. It would be a great blow to the program of rational reconstruction if reasons were not causes, if they were not construable as the factors explaining voluntary action. For Hempel, naturalism required neither reductionism nor anti-voluntarism, both of which would mean surrendering the usual explanation of action in history and the social sciences in terms of agents' plans and purposes. If it did, then the unity of science program, epistemically conceived, would fail.

According to Hempel, such explanations of action appeal not only to general laws but also to rationality, construed as a "broadly dispositional trait."[6] What makes rationality an explanatory concept is the presence of such a bundle of dispositions in an agent or group of agents. Rational explanation belongs to that variant of the covering law model known as dispositional explanation, in the same way that "brittleness" is a description of a dispositional trait of glass that explains why it breaks on impact (although both dispositions, rationality and brittleness, must themselves be explicated theoretically). As an explanatory concept, rationality is primarily a higher order disposition, by which agents are ready to act according to specifiable criteria, given their beliefs and desires. For this reason, Hempel separates the explanatory and the evaluative uses of the concept of rationality, its uses as an empirical hypothesis from its use in critical appraisal. As opposed to evaluating whether or not an action is reasonable or appropriate in light of the agent's beliefs and desires, "the hypothesis is to the effect that the action was done for certain reasons, that it can be explained as having been motivated by them."[7] Popper's general law only explains Louis XIV's unpopularity, if Louis is really disliked for violating his subjects' interests. An explanation is adequate only if it can be shown to isolate the *real cause* of the action – that is, that the criteria have been or will be met (such as maxi-min). The normative concept of rationality therefore plays no role in explaining action, except insofar as it provides an explication of what it means to be rational. According to Hempel, we do not even need to consider whether the beliefs or desires are justified, but only that the reasons actually motivated the actor – that is, were the cause of the action. To explain action, the reasons must be the real reasons, according to a descriptively accurate criteria of choice relative to the agent's beliefs and desires (however unjustified they may be relative to other criteria or fuller information). Even if we know the uniquely best thing for an agent to do given certain beliefs and desires, it would not yet be the basis for an adequate explanation: "Any adequate answer to the question why a given event occurred will have to provide information which, if it is accepted as true, would offer good grounds for believing that the event did occur."[8] We cannot assume that the best reason and the real cause of an action are the same, even if the actor is dispositionally rational. Hence, critical–normative concepts of rationality cannot explain actions as well as can descriptions of the agent's actual dispositions.

Adequate rational explanation can then be properly reconstructed according to the following logical structure, which Hempel calls "Schema R." All such explanations have three component parts which, like any explanation, can be arranged in the form of the following argument:

Schema R

(1)   A was in situation of type C.
(2)   A was a rational agent.
(3)   In a situation of type C, any rational agent will do x.

Therefore, A did x.[9]

Hempel's consequentialist theory of action and dispositional concept of rationality expand the schema in the following way:

(1a)   A is able to do x1, x2, and x3, with outcomes O1, O2, and O3.
(1b)   A prefers O1 to O2, O2 to O3.
(1c)   A believes that 1a.
(2)   A is disposed to act according to a specifiable criteria of practical rationality or utility maximization.
(3)   Given 1a, 1b, and 1c, any rational agent in the sense specified by 2 will do x.
Therefore, A did x.

The logical form of this schema is *modus ponens*; the conclusion then follows if all of the premises are true. Statement 1 is a full description of the situation and its range of possibilities, the agent's goals, and her beliefs about the circumstances and consequences of the action. Statement 2 entails a descriptive conception of the general disposition of the agent to be rational, including an explicit statement of the given criteria of practical rationality (a rule for utility maximization) and the disposition to act rationally at the time of the action. Statement 3 involves an "empirical generalization" about how rational agents will act and thus has the character of a general law, causally connecting the beliefs, desires and rationality of the agent to the action. These generalizations, Hempel admits, must be empirical and not analytic; they must make the connection between the disposition and the action not by definition but in the same empirical manner that a disease is connected with its symptoms. Taken as a whole, Schema R is an epistemic analysis of what it would mean for reasons (that is, beliefs and desires, coupled with a disposition to act upon them in a certain rational way) to cause an action, in terms of the logic of any adequate explanation for any field of inquiry.

On a case-by-case basis, such a reconstruction of rational explanation may often successfully capture what is meant by explaining a particular action in terms of a motivating reason or reasons. But one of the main objections raised repeatedly in the massive literature on Hempel's account of rational explanation is that its "laws" are merely analytically true.[10] Given 1 and 2 as I have glossed them, 3 is simply logically necessary and therefore is not in any way an empirical law. Certainly, the "law" which Hempel appeals to in order to explain the French Revolution is more like a definition of a revolution than an explanation of one. Furthermore, there is no evidence for 3 that is not evidence for 1 and 2, and thus the statements lack the independence of empirical causal connections between contingent events. The agent's full preferences can only be established in her choice behavior and not by any independent means.

But even taking 3 at face value as a "law," it still suffers from problems of indeterminacy. This is hardly a new problem, since it was already raised by Aristotle, the first philosopher who attempted to give a rational reconstruction of the explanation of action in logical form, his practical syllogism. "How is it," Aristotle asked in *De Motu*, "that thinking sometimes is followed by action and sometimes not, sometimes by motion and sometimes not?" Aristotle was pointing out the fact that people often do not act upon their beliefs and desires, even given basic dispositions and character traits such as rationality. One could fail to act properly if one is dispositionally irrational or possesses false beliefs. Still, there are numerous instances in which, despite the presence of antecedent conditions like rational dispositions and occurrent reasons for acting, agents do not act at all, as in the case of *akrasia* or weakness of the will. To return to Hempel's "law" about revolutions: there are many long periods of history in which large parts of the population are discontented without the occurrence of a revolution. Yet this failure does not mean that these agents are irrational, but rather that the "law" is false. The problem is that Schema R lacks valid, true general laws that solve such problems and would make the explanation of action adequate, by virtue of subsuming a particular event under a general law. No such laws exist, and even if they did, they could no more assure that the actual motivating reason was the one the law suggests than can the evaluative analysis of the most rational course of action, which Hempel disparages. Hempel's account fails on its own criteria of adequacy. Even if such laws demanded by statement 3 of Hempel's schema existed (and they do not, except as merely logical truths, obvious falsehoods, or statements that have no determinate generality), then it would not supply deductively or inductively adequate grounds for predicting the occurrence of the explanandum event. This is the thrust of Aristotle's own doubts about the theoretical status of the general premises of any rational reconstruction of such explanations, and Hempel does nothing to belie these doubts or to justify a naturalistic logic of the explanation of rational human action.

Hempel's reconstruction of the logic of explanation in general establishes two different criteria of adequacy.

(1) In an adequate explanation, all the premises must be true, or have an empirically assignable truth value or probability. This requirement follows from the logical form of an explanation: a true conclusion can be deduced from a conjunction of premises if all of them are true. On intuitive grounds, the premises supply good reason to believe the conclusion is true if and only if the probability of the premises increases the probability of the conclusion.

(2) An adequate explanation must have at least one premise which is a valid general law.

The explanandum certainly could be deduced from an arbitrary set of premises; but this logical connection is causal only if a general law connects the event to its antecedents.

These two quite strong criteria of adequacy hold for any

rational explanation which, if adequate, can give sufficient reasons to justify the belief that the agent will perform some action. Given requirement 2, there must be a general law about how behaviorally rational agents motivated by such and such a reason and with such and such dispositions tend to act. If agents are rational and know their interests, then their leaders will tend to be unpopular if they violate their subjects' interests. The trouble is that, given requirement 2, requirement 1 cannot be fulfilled, since there are no such true empirical generalizations about how such people tend to act. It is not true that all leaders who violate their subjects' interests are unpopular, as the history of demagoguery shows. Similarly with requirement 1: suppose we establish patterns of voters' behavior for a specific population through statistical data. In this case, we explain the preference in light of the behavior and not vice versa. We have assigned a probability to any particular member of the population voting in a particular way and have therefore fulfilled requirement 1. However, the explanation no longer makes reference to any general laws or to specifiable and identical criteria of rationality. Similarly, if we say that this ruler is unpopular for violating his subjects' interests, we may have only explained *this* particular event. Thus, the dual minimal criteria of adequacy pose a dilemma for Hempel's reconstruction of rational explanation: there seems to be a precise trade-off between truth and generality. If the "law" is true, then it is not general; if it is general, then it is not true, particularly since we cannot be sure that this particular law must figure in an adequate explanation of the action in question. Some revolutions can be explained by the discontent of a large part of the population; other revolutions can be explained by the desires of a small but organized elite. If the law about revolutions and discontent is true, it must be stated in such a way that "revolution" does not appear in it as a general term; if it does, the law is obviously false. On the whole, it is hard to see the difference between the general laws that Hempel criticizes and the ones that he defends: both are equally non-empirical and non-general. At best, the statements of general laws are neither empirically true nor false: they tend to be either analytic statements about the relation between the means and ends of an action, or logical implications of the concept of rationality. In explaining a single action, however, both such logical statements may be inconsistent with the empirically true statements about the agent, such as particular facts about the "real" reason for acting in a given situation. The real reason or cause for a revolution may not have been "discontent" at all, and the violation of people's interests may not make a leader unpopular, as recent American history shows.

The defenders of naturalism have several possible responses to this objection. The first is to say that the sort of general law in question (such as "if A wants some end and A believes that x is a means to that end and A is rational, A will do x") contains many *ceteris paribus* clauses, such as that the agent is physically able to perform the action. Hence, the statement above is at best only an approximation of a general law, or an "explanation sketch," to use Hempel's terms. There is still a question, however, whether such laws could ever be refined enough to make them useful for social scientific inquiry, or even if they were it is still not clear that they would have any determinate predictive value. If they did, the *ceteris paribus* clauses must be finite and specifiable; however, no laws of this type come close to fulfilling this requirement, unless they begin to surrender strict generality by becoming agent- or situation-specific (that is, closer to token, rather than to type, explanations). Some non-intentional (physical or social) causal mechanism must intervene between reasons and action in order to guarantee even low-level predictive success. If that is the case, there is no guarantee that the causal chain linking reasons to the performance of an action is not completely unique to this action or this agent. The dependence of the French monarchy on a popular army may explain their vulnerability to their subjects' disfavour. But we cannot assume such a mechanism always connects rulers to their subjects' interests and favour. Donald Davidson argues that rational explanations are not typically general: they more often provide "evidence for the existence of a causal law covering the case at hand."[11] These highly particular laws cannot be generalized by appealing to the other explanatory premises, such as, for example, a fuller account of the contingent circumstances in which the agent acts. Hempel only gives us very general, second-order dispositional traits of actors who tend to act rationally: that they act consistently according to some criterion of choice given their beliefs and desires. This is not enough to show that the reasons caused the action in the same way that the general law indicates how and that they did. Davidson despairs at this task, since it would mean "finding a way to describe an action that shows the way in which desires and attitudes must cause the action if they are to rationalize the action."[12]

Davidson's conclusion means that *ceteris paribus* clauses offer Hempel and other naturalists no way out of the problem of adequacy. The only remaining option – to construe rational explanation

as a species of statistical explanation – has already been eliminated, since it means that the specific form of rational explanation
is not employed. Here, too, the problem remains, since there is no
way to assign any probability to this type of general law, nor to
do so in a way that would improve their validity. Even as probabilistic laws, it is hard to see how the general law statements in
rational explanations could be improved so as to make them more
reliable, except by making them less general, as, for example, in
explaining the event as the result of single case probabilities.[13] As
much social science research shows, other types of non-covering
law explanations could be so improved. But the results of such
research also shows that gathering statistical data does not generate general causal laws as much as it refines the idealizations and
approximations of various theoretical models. As Nancy Cartwright
has argued, even the simple laws of physics should not be
understood as determinate mechanisms that support general laws,
but rather as idealized models that are shot through with *ceteris
paribus* clauses and hence "fit only highly fictionalized objects."[14]
Such more refined probabilistic explanations and theoretical
approximations are empirically significant, yet neither predictive
nor general in Hempel's sense. Certain types of strategic interactions can be formally represented in various types of "games"; but
these are formal constructs which make certain assumptions about
the rationality of the agents involved and the constraints on the
situation. As opposed to such approaches, the explanations which
use covering laws do not make causal connections between events
that are always, often or even mostly true. Thus, true covering
laws tend also to be non-informative and non-empirical, as much
as any normative theory of rationality. Such laws may be refined
only theoretically: for example, we may assume that all rational
agents are ideal utility maximizers. But this assumption is obviously
false for some rational agents and in some contexts; for those
agents and circumstances of which it is true, the laws about them
are not so much empirically informative as they are models of
what rationality and rational dispositions mean under certain descriptions. Furthermore, such idealized models resemble normative descriptions: to be dispositionally rational is to maximize
utility. In chapter 2, I will regard rational choice theory as just
such an ideal model of how agents will and should act as utility
maximizers.

  Besides this dilemma of generality and adequacy, Hempel's reconstruction fails in another crucial respect, the upshot of which
is to call into question whether or not the other two premises of

the explanation are true, or even qualify as empirical statements. According to Hempel, it is crucial that the account of the situation and of the rational dispositions of the agent be descriptively accurate, in the sense that they are governed by "objective criteria of application."[15] Hempel denies that this means that the concepts can only be behavioristic or refer only to external conditions; their objectivity extends only to the mode of attribution of beliefs and desires as dispositions, analogous to the empirical determination of the symptoms of a disease. In the case of a disease, such attribution is "objective" in the sense that the theorist's point of view is entirely independent of the subjective contents of the beliefs and purposes of the actor: someone has a disease whether they believe it or not.

But the criteria of application of any of these concepts – rationality, beliefs, goals – are not objective. They are agent-relative, as Hempel admits, in that the agent may hold quite different second-order criteria, belief contents, or objects of desire. But more than that, the criteria are underdetermining and overdetermining; they do not fully identify a determinate action, since many different descriptions could all equally apply to the same set of "objective," physical motions. Thus, none ever seems to be definitely established as objectively applicable. Moreover, as Hempel himself admits about beliefs and desires, all of these descriptions are epistemically interdependent insofar as evidence for one requires accepting a particular description of the other.[16] Given the interdependence of ascriptions of beliefs, desires, and rationality, Hempel's requirement of "objective application" fails to obtain. The problem emerges immediately in the first premise of Schema R. Given any action, one could never determinately say that it was rational or irrational to do it. If one fixes the desires motivating the action, all one has to do is add the context of a belief or a purpose: while burning money or intentionally injuring oneself violate criteria of utility maximization, they are rational relative to other practical criteria: both could be intended as a form of protest. Even given a full statement of the agent's beliefs and desires, one could not determinately predict a course of action. The description of the initial conditions of action could never be independent of attributions of beliefs and desires: to say that "A is in a situation of type C" is already to give an interpretation of A's beliefs and desires, to locate the action in a set of practices and in the larger context of the agent's other beliefs and desires. Since such attributions are intentional, we cannot formulate any objective criteria of application for the concepts involved in the ascription of belief: it depends on how practices are described. A move in a game may be a ruthless attempt to win in certain subjective contexts, while in others it may serve the purely pedagogical purpose of teaching a child how to play. If the agent has the latter purpose, certain moves violate criteria of practical rationality that are fulfilled relative to the purpose of winning. Ascriptions of rationality vary according to the subjective purposes of each context and thus are not "objective" in Hempel's sense.

The semantics of intentional terms, even in explanatory contexts, also shows that the criteria of applicability seem irreducibly subjective. Following Davidson, Alexander Rosenberg gives strong semantic grounds for why intentional states cannot be objectively ascribed, since transferring ascriptions from one agent to another may change the truth values of the statements on semantic grounds. "Intentional states are ones in which we cannot substitute synonymous descriptions without risking the chance of changing their truth or falsity."[17] Thus, statements that attribute beliefs are irreducibly interpretive. For this reason, there are further doubts about the logical independence of the premises in a rational explanation. If the statements which attribute beliefs and desires to agents have irreducibly subjective criteria of application, then rational explanations are not like arguments but rather are more like interpretations: they are circular and indeterminate, even while being based on evidence. Hempel cannot find a non-circular and contingent relation between the conclusion and the premises of a rational explanation. Doing so would mean the elimination of a crucial premise in his reconstruction of rational explanation: an accurate description of the intentions of actors as part of the initial conditions of the action. This would entail eliminating intentionality altogether, as in the case of psychophysical laws whose causal structure is primarily physicalistic and not intentionalistic (as when we appeal to neuroprocesses or natural selection). But in that case we are no longer reconstructing rational explanations, but relating reasons to causes, to which they are token identical. Such laws do supply the type of "empirical" relationship which Hempel desires, where the physical state is the disease and the reason is the symptom; in Hempel's own account, however, the relations are non-empirical and interpretive, as they are for any science of social action.

There does seem to be a narrow range of cases where something like Hempel's covering law model results in the explanation of an action. The limits of Hempel's own explanation of action is the same as the ones he finds for decision theory. Such models of decisions do not apply generally to the actions of every agent, but only to "fully conscious rational agents" who are completely informed and whose possible courses of action are rigorously delimited and defined. As Hempel writes about rational decision models, "Consider, for example, a competent engineer who seeks an optimal solution to a problem of design, for which the range of permissible solutions is clearly delimited, the relevant probabilities and utilities are precisely specified, and even the criteria of rationality to be employed (e.g., maximization of expected utilities) is explicitly stated."[18] In this case, some of the problems of Hempelian rational explanation are overcome, since the agent's own beliefs and situation of action permit the assignment of probabilities to various alternative actions and the objective application of concepts like rationality. But short of the fully conscious rational agent acting within constrained and defined circumstances, Hempel's account falls short; even in these cases it is not clear that the explanation accounts for the action for the reasons Hempel thinks it does. Given the general lack of objective criteria of application, it is always possible that covering laws about rationality are as fictitious as any ideal theory; they provide no insight into the causation of actions and decisions in most natural settings, in which beliefs, desires and rational dispositions are all indeterminate and non-general and have no predictive value.

Philosophers have proposed several ways out of the dilemmas of rational explanation. My criticisms here reflect some of them: the attempt to discover objective, psychophysical laws; Davidson's denial of general laws and appeal to singular causal chains; a variety of approaches to models of rational choice and game theory to begin to specify relevant probabilities; and other attempts to give interpretations a place within the explanation of rational action. I shall consider the most fruitful of these approaches for the social sciences in the next chapter. There are many resources for these attempts, since Hempel's reconstruction in no way exhausts the myriad possibilities of already existing styles of explanation of actions using the agent's reasons. Many philosophers, too, have tried out different, non-Humean analyses of the concept "cause." For example, Charles Taylor argues that rational explanation is a sub-species of teleological explanation, with its own general laws which do not merely relate contingent antecedent conditions to some consequent action.[19] Such teleological explanations would not fit Hempel's criteria of adequacy, and it is hard to see how they could be refined into social science. However, there is one social theorist who already anticipated the problems with Hempel's account and yet wanted to retain much of the same analysis of explanatory adequacy, as well as the same conception of reasons as causes: Talcott Parsons, particularly in his *Structure of Social Action.*[20]

In many ways, Parsons anticipates and goes beyond Hempel by squarely facing the dilemmas of explanations which take reasons to be causes. Although he is neither recognized as such in the literature nor by Hempel himself, Parsons was not just the founder of holistic approaches to social theory, in the "structural-functionalism" for which he is so renowned. He also spent much theoretical energy on the problems of micro-explanation of action, trying to balance the demands of voluntaristic social theory and causal explanation. While his attempts ultimately do not succeed, they set the stage for various contemporary attempts to construct social theories based on rational explanation, each having their own logic for explaining action even while accepting the causal indeterminacy of reasons.

Parsons and the Logical Structure of Social Action

The key to unlocking Parsons' theory of social action as an attempt to construe reasons as causes is contained in a remark by Hempel about the situation in which rational action takes place. Hempel admits that even if the available information suggests that there is a course of action which is the best way to achieve a certain goal, the agent may not perform the action as expected. The optimal course of action may violate "certain general constraining principles" which include moral and legal norms, contracts, social conventions, and the rules of a game being played. Thus, the "total objective" of an action must be characterized by "a set E of sentences describing the intended end state, in conjunction with a set N of constraining norms."[21] For Parsons, the force of N is precisely what makes an action a social action, and also why Hempel's account of rationality as means–ends reasoning and action as instrumental cannot exhaust the form of intentional explanation in the social sciences. Such social action is rational and voluntaristic, and yet at the same time takes place within the constraints of institutionalized norms which form the basis of social order. Parsons thought that his complex "voluntaristic theory of action" could become the basis for an account of social action that relates subjective beliefs and desires to facts about social structures, that is, to the social–normative constraints on activity.[22]

Following Durkheim and Weber, Parsons' voluntarism already gives the same emphasis to cultural rules and norms that became current among the Wittgensteinian philosophers who rejected Hempel. Rules, or "norms," further specify the context and situation of action, showing how beliefs and desires actually shape the course and structure of the action itself. While such an appeal to norms does not solve the problem of indeterminacy and inadequacy in the same way as Hempel's engineer example of a "fully conscious rational agent" does, a fuller account of how rules or norms operate in and constrain action begins the task of showing how and in what sense reasons can be the causes of action, once they are understood as part of larger social contexts. According to Parsons, the more we develop the explanatory power of a social *and* voluntaristic theory of action, the less plausible the utilitarian account of action based on the model of the engineer and her probable choices becomes. According to Parsons, Hempel continues the false utilitarian analogy between the rational actor and the scientific investigator, both of which supposedly seek only to know the facts about necessary conditions and the available means of achieving one's ends.[23] Parsons calls this error "rationalism" or "positivism," depending on whether he is talking about the theory or its methodology; both eliminate any constitutive role for the normative elements of action, or the possibility of understanding how norms and normative contexts regulate action in any strong sense.

To correct these positivist and rationalist shortcomings of the utilitarian tradition, Parsons introduces his concept of the "unit act" as a complete analysis of the irreducible components of any explanation of action. Together these components make up what Parsons calls the "action frame of reference" – that is, the set of all the logical presuppositions, or conditions of possibility, of a theory of action. Parsons distinguishes this frame of reference from that of the natural sciences – the "physical frame of reference" – in which we note only that a man jumped, for example, and not why.[24] In permitting the theoretical reconstruction of "the actor's point of view," the action frame of reference is the categorical basis of a science of subjectivity of the non-reductive sort Hempel desired for rational explanations, now including not only a description of social context as an initial condition of action, but also a much more complex description of the normative and cognitive character of the agent's rational motivation. The unit act defines the necessary features of any explanation made within the action frame of reference:

Parsons' Unit Act

(1) the actor or agent of the act
(2) the end, or the future state of affairs that actor seeks to bring about
(3) the situation in which the actor acts, made up of both conditions over which the actor has no control and means of action over which he does
(4) the mode of orientation; that is, the normative and cognitive standards by which the actor relates the end to the current situation.[25]

Thus, the analysis of the action is, as it was for Hempel, relative to the point of view of the actor, yet still general enough to be explanatory. Explanations of rational action thereby attempt to show that actions are motivated by reasons, beliefs and norms which motivate actors not just to conform to external circumstances, but to bring about changes in the world according to their subjective beliefs and desires. Moreover, each of these component parts of the unit act enters into a multidimensional account of the causes of social action.

How does this analysis help resolve problems of rational explanation? Parsons attacks "positivism" not only for overlooking the complexity of factors which figure in the explanation of rational action, but also for its individualism: the individualism of "atomistic theories" of action makes for causal indeterminacy and the essential randomness of ends that agents may pursue on Hempel's account. If individuals simply acted according to their desires and goals, then it is impossible to see how any order would emerge that would influence or constrain those choices of ends. In the cacophony of each agent pursuing her own ends, no order would emerge that would permit the identification of stable desires and beliefs. Hence, it would become impossible to explain why others act as they do. Their actions and ends are random – that is, they do not have an order or common framework that describes them. In effect, Parsons is arguing that it is Hempel's substantive assumptions of utilitarian individualism which undermines the methodological adequacy of his causal theory.

Besides the randomness that is a consequence of individualism, a further aspect of explanatory indeterminacy is the result of abstracting the explanandum event from its context, a complex social–historical environment. Hempel underestimates the abstract character common not only to normative accounts of rationality but also to any theory of action, a methodological problem that becomes unresolvable on individualistic grounds. As Parsons argues against any individualism, "Limiting observation of the concrete phenomena, then, to the properties that have a place in the unit act or other subsystem leads to indeterminacy in the theory when it is applied to complex systems. This indeterminacy, a form of empirical inadequacy, is the fundamental difficulty of atomistic theories."[26] When isolated individual acts are the units of analysis for a theory of action, actors cannot but have essentially random and inexplicable ends, separated analytically from the larger social and cultural processes in which action takes place. Thus, the empirical inadequacy of Hempel's theory is due in part to its individualism, not to its construal of reasons as causes. Until the theory of action sees action as part of a larger system of actions, it cannot discover how reasons cause actions in the sense of motivating them. Individualism thus lacks both the empirical and explanatory assumptions of a social order necessary to make actions explicable.

Parsons argues that individualist assumptions about action are the source of the dilemma of empirical inadequacy and causal indeterminacy. In fact, the dilemma which I have constructed for Hempel is just a form of Parsons' "utilitarian dilemma," which he argues applies to any form of "radical rationalistic positivism." The dilemma facing the utilitarian is, according to Parsons, the following: *either* the actor is independent in choosing his or her end, in which case the ends are random rather than rational; *or*, the actor is not independent, in which case the causes are external rather than voluntary. Parsons formulates the dilemma most clearly in *The Structure of Social Action*:

> Either the active agency of the actor in the choice of ends is an independent function in action and the end element must be random; or the objectionable implication of the randomness of ends is denied; but then their independence disappears and they are assimilated to the objective conditions of the situation, that is to the elements analyzable in terms of non-subjective categories.[27]

Parsons' dilemma is prophetic of individualistic theories' pendulum swings back and forth between the horns of the dilemma: either arbitrary ends which are taken as given "fixed preferences," or the denial of the subjective basis of action in neuroscience or sociobiology. As early as 1939, Parsons suggested that we accept neither horn and come up with a new non-rationalistic, non-positivist theory of action. Otherwise, the problem of "social order" (either of the ends of action or of the coordination of action between actors) can never be resolved short of Hobbes' sovereign and the use of "force and fraud." Both the problems of non-random ends and of collective order can be resolved at the same time by giving a positive role to normative elements in action, where adequate explanations depend on the proper inter-play between conditional and normative elements, external and internal factors. For Parsons, the elimination of either one leads to common theoretical errors in the theory of action: whereas the elimination of the conditional element leads to idealism, the elimination of the normative element leads to positivism.

These normative elements cannot remain external conditions and still explain voluntary action; if they were, they would collapse into external factors, as they have tended to do in the Durkheimian tradition of social theory that follows Durkheim's dictum of "treating social facts like things." In this case, the normative order becomes anti-voluntaristic as well as anti-individualistic, no longer an internal cause or constraint on action. But how can Parsons criticize the randomness of ends and yet avoid Durkheim's prob-lems? Certainly symbols, conventions, and communication all contribute to the appropriation of the social order by individuals. But none of them by themselves is sufficient for a new, non-positivist theory of action. Jeffrey Alexander puts Parsons' basic problem this way: "What mechanism would allow collective forces to achieve an internal position?"[28] Parsons' solution is the concept of internalization, developed after the completion of *The Structure of Social Action*. Following Freud, Parsons argues that individuals introject or internalize social norms and thus adopt the value standards of their society in such a way as to limit their ends and the means which can be employed to achieve them.[29] Internalization solves the problem of how a factor can be individual and social at the same time, as well as Hobbes' problem of the impossibility of order among individuals pursuing their ends randomly. Certainly, some social constraints remain external, or coercive, in the form of sanctions; but what explains non-random and voluntary ends is the internalization of the social value system as part of the "mode of orientation" of the actor.

This theory leads to an important account of social integration; it clarifies the way in which individuals come to have many of the same goals, beliefs and desires by appropriating and participating in the same social order. But Parsons uses this account not only for the collective explanation of social structure but also for the explanation of action by using reasons as causes. Reasons, *qua* internalized social norms, are causes. Thus to succeed in demonstrating that even from the subjective point of view ends are non-random, norms have to be treated as causes. Hempel's "set N" becomes the predominant factor in rational explanation. If this is true, John Heritage's criticism of Parsons seems correct: "Starting from a framework which begins with the subjective point of view of the actor, Parsons had arrived at an entirely external analysis of the norms or values which he treated as constraining and determining conduct."[30] In this way, Parsons hoped to resolve the problem of explanatory adequacy in rational explanations and arrive at fully justified causal statements referring to reasons that motivate actions. Through internalization, Parsons arrived at a causal model of the subjective elements of action which, once articulated, gave him "the objective criteria of application" that Hempel could not discover on a utilitarian basis.

The question for the philosophy of social science is whether this solution is as neat as it seems, and in particular whether it really saves voluntarism, as Parsons believed, or surrenders it to the causal force of the social order, as his critics assert. Eventually, for Parsons, subjective orientations became the "pattern variables" of his full blown structural–functionalist theory. But even in *The Structure of Social Action*, when Parsons rejected what he called "positivism" in favor of what he called "voluntarism," he returned to the same criteria for a good explanation which are required by Hempelian philosophy of science. While repudiating simple empiricism for overlooking the importance of valid theoretical concepts, Parsons also argued for "a methodological core common to all empirical science, no matter what the subject matter."[31] As in any science, the theory of action will construct complex theoretical concepts out of the "analytic elements" of the unit act. In this way, Parsons justified basing his work on an analysis of European social theorists, rather than simple observation or single facts. He argued that all research programs in the sciences should start with the clarification of the basic units of analysis. Unless we merely assume this unifying methodological prescription to be correct, however, the question still remains whether or not the analytic elements identified by the theory really are the same as the subjective factors that actors actually act upon, with their beliefs and desires. Because of this gap, closed by Parsons through an uncritical epistemological realism and an overly determinate account of socialization, one wonders whether Parsons gave an account of rational explanation at all, despite his theoretical advances. His sophisticated theoretical redescription bears little resemblance to the original problem: namely, how agents' beliefs and desires cause their actions. Rather than a "science of subjectivity," Parsons provided an objective sociology of action. His quite proper concern with distancing himself from the dead ends of individualism led his theory away from what actors actually believe about themselves, replacing it with a theoretical reconstruction of the role of values and norms as strong objective constraints on action.

The problem of interpretation that plagued Hempel also returned in Parsons' theory. Certainly, no theory of action needs to privilege the self-knowledge or the self-descriptions of actors in constructing explanations. Further, the "action frame of reference" out of which Parsons draws explanatory factors is nothing if not multidimensional, and his social theory as a whole seeks to combine internal and external, conditional and normative factors.[32] However, the question is whether on Parsons' account "subjective" factors are really subjective at all. The actor's self-understanding need not reflect the real determining or motivating forces at work in the action. These factors are conceived of as more or less opaque to the actor, and it is only in limited cases that the actor's own "theory of action" adequately reflects the truly determinative subjective elements. Thus, although the causal process of the determination of action is voluntaristic, what makes norms or values causes is not dependent on the beliefs and self-understanding of the actor. What makes reasons determining causes is accessible only to external sociological analysis, independent of the actor's point of view. Actors' beliefs and desires are later assigned to the dustbin of "intervening variables."[33] Harold Garfinkel puts the elimination of the actor's point of view from Parsons' explanation in this way: the action frame of reference is like a stage, with a script and scenery, but no actors. This gap led Garfinkel, even while he was still a student of Parsons, to rethink the problem of rational explanation in his "ethnomethodological" approach. As we will see in the next chapter on more recent theories of rational explanation, Garfinkel's alternative makes actors' knowledgeable performance of the action central to its explanation. Already in his correspondence with Parsons, Schütz raised this type of objection to *The Structure of Social Action*.[34]

Besides failing to be really voluntaristic, Parsons' theoretical scheme also does not seem to give any explanatory role to the rationality of actors. If actors are indeed rational, then the reasons that explain their actions must to some degree be known by them. Rational actors not only should be able to give some account of their own reasons and motives for acting, but they also should know about the nature of the norms or rules constraining their actions. One necessary, but not sufficient, condition for rationality is that actors are at times able to act strategically and reflectively within the constraints of such rules or norms. Even if human beings are socialized in such a way as to internalize orientations and constraints, it is also often the case that these orientations are themselves only loosely constraining and do not have enough content to determine actions in a causal sense. Parsons later tried to defend himself from this charge by claiming that individuals do not simply *have* such patterns of value orientation but rather, "in a strict sense, *are*, among other things, a system of such patterns."[35] Like the voluntary character of action, rationality only comes into play within the framework of such orientations.

Rather than saving Parsons' theory, this identification of actors with their pattern of value orientation only makes the fundamental problem of the rationality of action worse. To borrow a phrase from Garfinkel, actors now have become "judgmental dopes" who passively assimilate the rules and roles they are socialized into and merely act out the value orientations of their culture and its institutions. Otherwise, it would be impossible to see how norms could be causal determinants of action, particularly in a way independent of the actor's knowledge and understanding of her own motives. If Parsons' account is correct, then actors cease to be rational agents whose own justifications and accounts can play a role in explanation; rather, norms are the causes of action for social individuals who now are little more than the bearers of institutional norms or systems of pattern variables, token instances of social types like characters in a Japanese Noh play. Thus, by virtue of being causal, such explanations do logically require that the "real reasons" for acting may be independent from the agent's own self-understanding. However, it would seem a minimal desideratum for a reconstruction of the logic of rational explanation that there be some connection between the theoretical description and the agent's own account. Parsons' own concept of rationality is not rich enough to establish this connection, since like Hempel he sees no need to connect the analysis of reasons as causes to the justifications that agents have for believing them. Without this connection, neither rationality nor intelligibility plays an explanatory role other than as conditions much like biological make-up. The failure of either of these factors to have any possible role in causal explanations illustrates why critics can hold that, regardless of theoretical sophistication, any account of reasons as causes remains external to the agent, even on the assumption that agents "internalize" social orientations. If they are to be the material for causal explanation, actors do not internalize them through well-considered, reflective judgments. So socialized, the type of actor for whom such explanations might apply really would be a judgmental dope, acting under the causal, not rational, influence of norms. It is hard to imagine what difference it would make to such agents to have their actions explained by Parsonian social scientists.

In Parsons, then, we have a social theorist who is aware of all the problems of adequacy in causal rational explanations, but who ultimately cannot resolve them. Better than the covering law model, Parsons has clearly construed reasons as causes, and indeed advances a form of analysis that might have causal depth and that might be able to get at the real reason for a particular action. Nonetheless, by remaining external to the point of view of the agent, Parsons' solution does not give subjectivity or rationality any real role in the explanation of action. While overcoming problems of individualism and indeterminacy, Parsons still models reasons, as causes, on external constraints, limiting the choice of ends by his idea of the influence of socialization into a normative social order. In this respect, Parsons' account is no better than the physicalist redescriptions of rational action in terms of psychophysical laws: instead of giving an account of reasons as causes, he simply gives an account of the social causality of norms, as neurophysiology might give an account of the causal effects of neural mechanisms on cognitive processes. This means that Parsons did not succeed in overcoming "positivism" and its reduction of causality to external factors. Parsons resolves problems of indeterminacy and the randomness of ends, but at the price of slipping into a new version of the same old positivism which he so rightly criticized.

Where did Parsons go wrong? It was not for lacking theoretical subtlety, nor for having the wrong explanatory goals. The problem is, I submit, philosophical: Parsons dons the methodological straitjacket of a wrongheaded philosophy of science, which repeats positivism's deeper errors while trying to overcome it. While he explicitly seeks a multidimensional form of explanation, his conceptions of theory, of cause, and of rationality are not multidimensional enough to complete this task. An account of the "subjective factors of action" cannot rely so heavily on a single process or mechanism – in this case, the internalization of social order – nor should a theory determine in advance that an actor's self-understanding or justifications have no explanatory value. In short, any account of the causes of action, whether voluntaristic, behavioristic or utilitarian, will encounter empirical problems entailed by the false generalization of certain methodological prescriptions about explanation. Thus, the problem is that Parsons shares Hempel's philosophical goal: contrary to the post-empiricist acceptance of indeterminacy, he gives a single logic of rational explanation, or of explanation employing the a priori "action frame of reference." No such singular notion of cause and no general standards of explanation or methodology that derive from it are adequate for constructing a complex, multidimensional theory of action. Parsons' notion of internalization is a conceptually clever attempt to reconcile the external perspective of the theorist and the internal perspective of the actor. The lessons to be derived from its shortcomings are post-empiricist ones: not to try to find a new way of making the subjective appear objective, but to abandon the search for a unifying "cause" or "structure" as the goal of the theory of social action. Once this is done, it is possible to replace the theory of social action with multiple theories of a variety of structures that apply to various domains and types of action. Parsons continued his search for a "grand" theory because he accepted the core thesis of naturalism: like Hempel, he thought that the methods of science could be extended non-reductionistically to the subjective sphere by discovering the basic causal mechanism that makes reasons causes. This problem will not be resolved by simply making Parsons' theory more comprehensive or by replacing the model of internalized normative action with a looser, but still singular, general mechanism. In place of a grand theory, the best current social science is messier, pluralistic, and multi-causal; it searches for diverse theoretical means that might provide rigorous explanations of action in rational and subjective terms. In Parsons' terms, the search for a single set of "analytical elements" or a single action frame of reference is misleading; each element itself is multi-dimensional, so that there is no way to assign to its basic theoretical terms a determinate usage or objective criteria of application without significant losses in explanatory adequacy.

All of these theoretical and empirical failures of the Hempelian program should lead us to the conclusion that there is no single method or logic in the social sciences. This is not to say that there is no place for methodological reflection in theory construction, nor that various forms of explanation could not be reconstructed, in light of the analysis of a specific type of factor or a dimension of social action and, in particular, in light of successful explanations that emerge within research programs. This will be the subject matter of the next chapter. In the next section, however, I first want to give some concrete examples of how the failures in the "logic" of naturalistic rational explanation have affected various explanations in empirical social research. I will consider two different examples: first, an example taken from a research program in the sociological explanation of scientific practices that construes reasons as causes, the "strong programme in the philosophy of science." I will then turn, more briefly, to a second set of examples of problems of intentionality and indeterminacy related to the logic of causal explanation, identification, and measurement of significant social actions, in particular in explaining suicide and child abuse.

Two Case Studies in the Failure of Rational Explanation

Attempts to account for reasons as causes have played a significant role in research programs and methodology in many areas of social scientific research. In this section, I will consider examples of certain difficulties in providing causal explanations of various social actions. I will turn first to a research program in the social scientific study of science, the "strong programme," which is based on the idea that the philosophy of science itself has obscured the "real reasons" for theory change in the sciences, namely, the "social interests" governing scientific practice. Instead of attempting to reconstruct theory change according to some ideal "rational–teleological" or logical model of scientific inference, the strong programme attempts to understand science entirely in terms of causal laws concerning the role of "interests" and "forces" that shape the social formation of beliefs.

While the strong programme reflects the post-empiricist turn in the philosophy of natural science since Thomas Kuhn, its own working philosophy of social science and conception of explanation is surprisingly empiricist, in line with Hempel's causal analysis of rational explanation. The leading proponents of the strong programme repeatedly state that the sociology of knowledge in general should give strictly causal explanations of beliefs, which, as David Bloor puts it, are "concerned with the conditions which bring about beliefs or states of knowledge."[36] In a statement about what those conditions might be that is as strong as anything Hempel might demand, Bloor states that such causal laws depend on general laws relating beliefs to conditions which are "necessary and sufficient conditions to determine them."[37] These conditions and laws are primarily, although not exclusively, social, having to do with what the strong programmers call "interests," rather than internalized norms as with Parsons. According to the strong programme, the trouble with past sociologies of knowledge is that they have exempted science from proper analysis by claiming, with Mannheim, that it is interest-free. This claim is false, even for the sociology of knowledge itself, which quite reflexively should also be explained causally. As good naturalists, the strong programmers think that science is the best way to explain both the natural and social sciences and that good science explains things causally. Rather than looking at the methodological writings, here I shall closely examine several empirical studies that are often cited as examples of successful explanations for the programme. Indeed, in response to criticism, Bloor in particular appeals to the "empirical successes" of these same studies in order to silence philosophical critics, who fail "to appreciate the significance and potential of an easily accessible body of literature."[38] Ironically, the success of the causal explanation in the same studies that Bloor cites is so limited as to provide the opposite effect of what Bloor desires: they provide good empirical reasons to reject the programme's causal approach, insofar as they fail not only to explain the necessary and sufficient conditions for scientific beliefs, but even to show clear explanatory connections between natural knowledge and social contexts. Let me first elaborate what type of explanation Barnes and Bloor demand and then show why the studies do not provide anything like it.

As with Hempel's descriptive conception of "rationality," "knowledge" is here understood "naturalistically" in terms of causes, and not evaluatively in terms of good or bad, appropriate or inappropriate reasons. Barnes and Bloor, the strong programme's chief proponents, argue that no such evaluative distinction can be made without begging the question about the explanation of beliefs. All supposedly internal, normative questions really cannot be distinguished from external causal ones, except by appealing to now defunct idealized models of rational reconstruction.[39] Ironically enough, the strong programme finds methodological comfort for its Humean–Hempelian causal explanation in post-empiricist philosophy of science. In the case of the practice of science, causal explanations are required not because of the internalization of norms, but because of what Barnes and Bloor call the "symmetry principle." The symmetry referred to is between rational and irrational belief formation: there is no significant difference between explanations of true and false beliefs. On this account, evaluative titles awarded to beliefs like "rationality" in no way change the basic conditions and causes of their formation. Based on the post-empiricist argument, derived from Duhem and Quine, to the effect that all theories are underdetermined by the evidence and indeed are often empirically equivalent, the strong programmers conclude that the choice between them must be determined on grounds other than rational ones, for reasons other than the appeal to evidence itself. According to Bloor, the symmetry principle requires that rationally justified beliefs must still be explained and that the same processes cause true and false beliefs.[40] Causal explanation is not confined to the aberrant cases of why scientists happen to believe wrong and irrational things: "the same sort of causes generate both classes of beliefs."[41] Taking Kuhn's account of scientific revolutions as their guide, the strong programme claims that whether or not scientists choose to explain away anomalies or to change their theories and adopt a new paradigm is indeterminate when based on epistemic standards alone. The existence of "crucial experiments" that force such revolutions is just a myth of empiricist philosophy of science. More importantly, Kuhn's work in "normal science," the everyday science of problem solving within an accepted paradigm, also shows the social forces at work in the institutions of science, such as authority, professional discipline and socialization; these begin to direct the course of science and are at work even in revolutionary periods, which are no exception to the conditioning of knowledge and beliefs. As Paul Roth has shown,[42] the strong programmers argue for the plausibility of their analysis via a false dilemma: the validity of science is to be explained rationally either in an evaluative sense or in a causal sense. Since rational evaluation is indeterminate in all cases, then the "real reason" that scientific beliefs are adopted must be explained by sociological causes (interests, pressures, and forces) naturalistically described.

It is not my concern here to decide whether or not the strong programme is correct in its quick dismissal of normative philosophy of science. Roth, Turner, Laudan, and others have demonstrated just how problematic this reasoning is, particularly in the attempt to draw such strong conclusions on the basis of the epistemologies of Kuhn and Quine.[43] Rather, what is more important here is their philosophy of social science, or more precisely, their account of their own activity of giving rational explanations through general causal laws. The crucial question is whether the strong programme simply trades epistemic indeterminacy for another kind: the familiar causal indeterminacy of Hempelian rational explanation. Of course, Barnes and Bloor may simply reply that they are only constructing a "program" for the sociology of science. However, if I am correct in my analysis of the dilemmas facing covering law accounts of rational explanation, then it follows that the strong programme is methodologically doomed to failure: its explanations will always be indeterminate and fall short of giving the required necessary and sufficient conditions for belief formation. Social "interests" or "forces" fare no better than "internalized norms" and cannot form the basis of an adequate account of the determining causes for intentional actions in scientific practices, even granting the symmetry principle. The strong programme raises, and then leaves unanswered, a whole series of questions: What are the necessary and sufficient conditions for the formation of a single belief or set of beliefs? Are they always the same? What are the mechanisms of belief formation, and why do the evaluative self-interpretations of scientists have no explanatory value? What is the point of unmasking the real interests in an explanation, if evaluative criteria are insignificant? It is hard to see how the strong programme represents an improvement over Parsons or Hempel, and indeed it has replaced the latter theorists' more subtle models of causality with one employing hydraulic analogies of forces and pressures. Furthermore, the strong programmers have picked out interests as being determining factors without even formulating any general mechanisms, such as processes of socialization or the formation of class identity, which might account for how and when such factors work determinately enough to be explanations.

A look at the case studies done by or inspired by the strong programme illustrates this indeterminacy and lack of specification in the causal mechanism of belief formation. For all their criticisms of Mannheim, their studies do little more than the old sociology of knowledge, usually pointing out vague and unspecific correlations between social events and structures and the process of belief formation in the sciences. At times these correlations are elevated to the status of causal laws, usually ones that are as obviously false as any of the general laws invoked in Hempel's Schema R. For example, Paul Forman, in his essay entitled "Weimar Culture, Causality and Quantum Theory," tries to explain why so many German physicists, including those working in quantum mechanics, repudiated the idea of causality. Following the strong programme's interpretation of theory change, Forman claims that "internal developments" (within physical theory) "were not sufficient conditions" for such a radical change.[44] What external factors or "extrinsic influences" in Weimar culture are sufficient? Forman claims that such an historical explanation would consist not of vague or equivocal expressions like "intellectual climate" but of a "causal analysis, showing the circumstances under which, and the interactions through which, scientific men are swept up by intellectual currents."[45] The question is whether or not Forman's analysis itself is vague and indeterminate, making its causal laws false or making completely unverifiable claims about "social pressures" in a "hostile environment" to science.

A closer look at Forman's essay shows that it primarily consists of rather general intellectual history, a broad account of the anti-rationalist, anti-technological and anti-scientific tendencies of Weimar after the defeat of Germany, finding expression in mysticism, *Lebensphilosophie* and the popularity of Oswald Spengler. But this historical description is supposed to count as evidence for a pervasively "hostile environment" which will exert precisely the sort of pressure to cause the change in scientific theory. This "simple model of circumstances" will issue in the following causal law: basic theory change or "reconstruction" will occur in order to accommodate science to a hostile environment, whenever that influence leads to a loss of prestige. Thus, Forman is claiming that the rejection of causality in quantum theory is the attempt to bring science into conformity with its environment and to recover some of the lost prestige of the practice. Ideological accommodation occurs, therefore, when scientists and their enterprise are experiencing a loss of prestige, and they are compelled by external pressure to take measures to counter that decline. Presumably, such a law and model of its circumstances of application would apply to ideological accommodation of any practice, scientific or otherwise. The loss and then the attempted recovery of prestige is supposed to explain revolutionary theory change, however implausible that might seem. What is so powerful about prestige over other factors? Furthermore, why should scientists continue to hold such beliefs after science's prestige had been recovered?

But is this explanation adequate, or does it fail in the same way that any Hempelian rational explanation does? Is the causal law adequate? Forman admits that "retrenchment" is another possibility, the retreat of the scientist to her own community and its standards and norms. Has the description of the initial conditions of scientific practice eliminated the possibility of retrenchment, a strategy which favors "internal" scientific factors, bolstering rather than reconstructing the theoretical edifice of science? Hostility does not seem to be sufficient here, nor loss of prestige; ideological accommodation as a cognitive process seems a plausible alternative in situations of this type, but nothing in the law or the initial conditions assures that it did cause the action – namely, reconstructing scientific theories. The "symmetry principle" applies not only across true and false beliefs, but also between causal and rational belief formation. Both are equally underdetermined. In the causal case, general laws are inadequate and usually replace the "authority of normal science" with the "dictates of external circumstances." In either case, the explanations of the strong programme work only if we postulate a strong tendency towards conformity in human behavior, and their causal laws tend to follow from this disposition. (Note in particular their conformist account of "normal science.") I disagree with some critics of the strong programme who say that it always fails to deliver on its promise of delineating mechanisms of belief formation. If this case and others are an indication, it does in fact often do so. The trouble is that, like Hempelian laws, these mechanisms are false if general, and not general if true in particular cases.

Other studies do simply fail to specify any such mechanisms, as in Christopher Lawrence's study of early Scottish theories of the physiology of the nervous system.[46] Although like Forman in accumulating detail after detail, Lawrence employs precisely the sort of vague correlation that Forman criticizes, here between formal features of Scottish science and certain features of Scottish social structure, in particular between Scottish society and theoretical analyses of the body in Scottish medicine. The goal of the essay is to supply an explanation of the uniqueness of Scottish physiology in terms of its social context, "the upheaval in Scottish social and economic life in the eighteenth century, and in particular by referring to the social interests and the self-perception of the improving landed class that came to dominate Scottish culture."[47] Lawrence gives us an explanation of physiology as ideology in the classical Marxian sense: as the "cosmology" of the landed class, physiology furthered its social interests and justified its emerging dominant position. But as with Marx's analysis of ideology, the question remains whether the relationships between science and society established in the details of Lawrence's analysis are really causal ones. Couldn't we just as easily say that class society is used as a cognitive model by the physiologists, like the differences in species are used as a model for social relations between clans in some "primitive" societies? Whether or not their model of the nervous system furthers anyone's interests still has to be established empirically rather than by showing the analogies between social and physiological phenomena.

Similarly, Shapin employs the symmetry principle and tries to explain phrenology in terms of similar social interests, this time of the bourgeois and the petty bourgeois in Edinburgh, both of whom benefitted from the emerging modern order and the breakdown of the old hierarchies.[48] Phrenologists as much as physiologists looked to nature to justify the collapse of the old order and the decline of the traditional elites, as their own explicit sociological writings make clear. Apart from "fitting" such a purpose, Shapin provides little in the way of an analysis that supports the claim that such interests caused the widespread belief in phrenology. Despite explaining these beliefs in terms of class interests, no account of the process of hegemony or counter-hegemony is given, nor of the formation of class identities. Since participants' own explanations of their beliefs are rejected, why should these interests explain the beliefs? Why not see phrenology as furthering the interests of the emerging capitalist class, since individual traits are traced back to socially neutral physiological differences like bumps on the skull? In the absence of any theoretical statements about the nature of class interests and the hegemonic process, the identification of these beliefs as caused by any particular set of interests seems utterly arbitrary: phrenology might have been caused as Shapin explains it, but it might not. At best, the explanation that Shapin provides is non-causal, supplementing the intentions of the phrenologists as expressed in their writings with a loose functional account of how these self-described beliefs might have beneficial consequences for the group that holds them.[49] Shapin's account of phrenology may contain true causal statements; but it is not a causal explanation in terms of social interests, and his causal and anthropological idioms of interests and expression do not form a coherent synthesis.

It seems clear that the case studies of the strong programme fail to establish the empirical general laws on the social level that supply the necessary and sufficient conditions of belief formation, or even suggest ways that any could be formed. More often than not, once the distinction of "internal" reasons and "external" causes is dismissed on philosophical grounds, external factors like pressures, forces and interests are assumed to be the only alternative, followed by long lists of such factors. The narrowing of explanatory factors in a theory of interests seems to be simply an unwarranted empirical assumption, as much as Parsons' notion of the internalization of norms is in relation to other, rational or cognitive, factors. But for the strong programme, it is less a matter of seeing science as a normative institution, as Parsons would have done, than of viewing it as a coercive, controlling institution whose mechanisms of belief formation are per force causal: external imposition by force, fraud and authority. Like the sword of Hobbes' Leviathan, the scientific community imposes its authority on the formation of belief in Kuhnian "normal science." But this scientific Leviathan is no more able to solve the problem of the order of beliefs than Hobbes' sovereign, since the scientific community is armed with much less institutional control and violent means for maintaining power. If this assumption were true, the story of science would be full of acts of violent oppression; perhaps it is. However, these acts are more subtle than this account makes them out to be, and can exist even while scientists guide themselves by internal, epistemic standards. In order to supply good social scientific explanations of belief formation, the strong programme needs not only a better account of how beliefs are formed and then socially accepted, but also a much more sophisticated and multidimensional analysis of institutional power and reproduction. Here, again, the lack of an evaluative perspective leaves the strong programme no alternatives. For example, even in the case of interested motivation for the acceptance of a belief, consensus formation might sometimes do the job much better than do involuntary pressures or the subordination to conventions and mechanisms of social control.

Viewed in light of Parsons' analysis of the problems with causal explanations of social action, the strong programme's explanation seems not only non-voluntary but also one-dimensional and positivistic. Barnes states his Hobbesian assumption quite explicitly: "When there is a continuing form of culture there must be a source of cognitive authority and control"; for this reason, he writes, scientists "can always maintain their verbal culture in an unfalsifiable fashion."[50] While this is logically possible, change and innovation seem to be obvious empirical alternatives. Certainly, science is sometimes a Hobbesian institution, and it is informative to view it in the unfamiliar light cast by the political analogy to the sovereign state. But when the philosophical arguments against the idealized models of science derived from the old logic of the "received view" take on the status of empirical assumptions, they become reductionistic methodological fiats, inadequate to fulfill the requirements of explanation. Perhaps the insight of Barnes and Bloor is that Humean causality in the sphere of human action works in explanations only if there is some coercive force holding the correlations of events constant. But short of that, reasons are not causes in this external sense. As with Hobbes' state of nature, the extreme limit case becomes the standard case – in this instance, "normal" science as authoritarian control. The methodological error is to construe causes as being one sort of factor exclusively, here external forces and pressures. By rejecting the internal perspective of practitioners in science as being inadequate for explanations due to the fact that it had been privileged by philosophical rational reconstructions, the strong programme overlooks a source of practical and empirical tests for explanations, a source that it actually uses in its empirical studies: the explanations of reflective actors or participants in practices. I shall return to these internal explanatory strategies in the next chapter as part of the current social scientific alternatives to Hempelian explanations of rational action.

The problems with the interest-based causal explanations of scientific beliefs point to a solution to the problem of causal indeterminacy in rational explanations. Reasons are not connected to actions through anything like general laws, but through various mechanisms which may be both intentional (as is the case for cognitive mechanisms) or non-intentional (as in the case of biological and some macrosociological mechanisms). If a belief is the product of class interests and identity, then it has to be shown how the process that produced those interests and identities also produced the belief. If a belief is produced to maintain the relations of authority in scientific institutions, then it has to be shown how the process of maintaining authority produced that belief, not just that "normal" science is simply a priori an authoritarian institution. It may be the case that many of the statements made in explanations by the strong programme are in fact true. However, causal claims must be distinguished from true causal statements. As Elster puts it, "To cite a cause or a correlation is not enough: the causal mechanisms must be provided, or at least suggested."[51] The social sciences should not, therefore, seek general laws or the necessary and sufficient conditions for intentional events, but instead should isolate tendencies and mechanisms. Here "interests" themselves perform little explanatory work; what is important is relating the processes by which interests and beliefs are formed. Parsons' concept of "internalization," too, seems little more than a place holder for such adequate but non-determinate explanations that refer to a variety of such mechanisms and processes.

Because of their general character, laws fail to deal with problems of indeterminacy; mechanisms, by contrast, do not need to claim generality and thus may be applied to indeterminate phenomena. Elster writes, "When we have identified a mechanism whereby p leads to q, knowledge has progressed because we have added a new item to our repertoire of ways in which things happen."[52] Such mechanisms might include unconscious repression or displacement, which is Freud's account of how a reason can *become* a cause; they might also include processes by which a class comes to dominate others in society, as, for example, in restricting communication or discourse. Merton, too, rejected "total systems" like Parsons' theory of social order and called for "theories of the middle range" with direct explanatory pay-off, such as his own account of latent functions as an unintended consequence of rational action.[53]

There are at least two further problems that result from the externalist perspective of the covering law model and social scientific research which deals with intentional action: first, problems in identifying tokens of the types of action about which general laws are formed; and second, problems related to developing ways of measuring the occurrence of these actions so that they can be quantified over in inductive derivations of general statistical laws. The fact that one social problem has been studied perhaps more than any other since the emergence of social science in the eighteenth century makes it a good candidate for a case study here: suicide. It has been studied by a variety of statistical methods, using different theoretical assumptions. This example is important, since it shows that many of the problems of rational explanation discussed in this chapter hold even if the general laws are probabilistic rather than strictly causal. Nonetheless, the standard problems of adequacy remain: how are the "objective criteria of application" determined such that we can identify an act or situation as a suicide? Even for statistical research, meanings and interpretations enter into the explanation willy-nilly, a difficulty which undermines the methodological assumption that they can be excluded.

As Jack Douglas notes in his insightful study of the social scientific literature on suicide,[54] already in the eighteenth century Voltaire noted the greater frequency of suicide in urban over rural areas. Such regularities could be explained with reference to various reasons for suicide, among which Durkheim posited the most important as being anomie – that is, the lack of the moral repression of individual desires, the lessening of social control, and the lack of integration of individuals into the community. One could imagine trying to formulate a rational explanation according to Hempel's Schema R, where these reasons would be formulated as general laws and the initial conditions would describe the social structure in which they apply. The laws would then be verified,

Durkheim thought, by looking at statistics of suicide rates for various regions and social groups; they are the only possible source of evidence "owing to the complexity of the phenomena and the impossibility of all artificial experiments."[55] Instead of indeterminacy requiring a plurality of possible causes, Durkheim favored a "deeper" explanation, appealing to macro-sociological factors like large-scale changes in social structure, while also considering micro-cultural factors of individual choices as consequences of them.[56] As in Parsonian internalization, the reasons for suicide become causes by embodying what Durkheim called "collective representations" which have causal power. Such representations are discovered through concomitant variation and serve as the underlying reality of all the composite individual causes. As Stephen Turner describes it, the combined effects of politics, religion and the domestic sphere "compose with the current arising from the larger collectivity to produce a total collective influence that compels the given individual to act."[57] Reasons are the meanings given to the action by agents through these collective representations, the shared meanings assigned to action operating in the organizations in which actors take part. Because of this collective efficacy, the reasons that are the causes of suicide are significant for social explanations, connected to but not the same as depth psychological ones. While Durkheim's solution may be ingenuous, it does not solve the problem of causal adequacy; we can never know when the forces of collective representation are at work. As Douglas puts it, "Durkheim did not provide specific enough theoretic and operational definitions of his fundamental forces to establish any adequate systematic criteria for deciding when one force is acting and when it is not."[58] As with Hempel, Parsons, and the strong programme, Durkheim, too, cannot specify the mechanism by which collective representations become the causal force behind reasons. There may be, however, enough resources in Durkheim's theory to construe his account in a different way.

But this is not the only problem with this type of sociological explanation of suicide. There is a fundamental problem in the use of statistics, particularly "official" statistics made up by state bureaucracies. Since the meanings assigned by the actors may not be the same for the collective representations which cause the actions and because the definitions officials have may be different from either one, it is certainly doubtful that they would provide any "deeper," uninterpreted information. Moreover, there have been not only numerous shifts in information-gathering techniques, but also numerous shifts in the meanings assigned to such social terms as suicide. As Ian Hacking has pointed out, "child abuse" is now seen as widespread; yet only a few years ago what is now seen as abuse would have been taken to be only the disciplining of women and children.[59] Does this mean that there is more child abuse now than before, when nothing short of murder and incest counted? In the official statistics today and yesterday, the same things are not measured, since the same acts are assigned to different categories. In the physical sciences, the problem would be the same if one substituted different substances in two thermometers and said they were giving comparable measurements of temperature. But in the case of official statistics, the problem is much worse: there is no independent, objective criteria of application apart from the meanings social actors assign to their action. As Douglas puts it about measuring suicides, "The essentially problematic nature of the social meaning of suicide would lead one to expect that there are always equally valid but different constructions of meaning for the same event, so that there are always equally valid but different measures possible for the same events."[60] Further, as Turner argues, Durkheim dealt with this problem by simply rejecting the agents' interpretations as irrelevant to the explanation: "The participants simply have an erroneous notion of things around them, such as the family; and we must, so to speak, 'bracket' these notions in searching for sociological regularities."[61] Durkheim clearly saw that his commitment to discovering deeper causes and general social laws required abandoning the intentional perspective. As we will see in chapter 4, however, this simply shifts the problem of indeterminacy onto another level.

The same indeterminacy holds for the process of measurement itself, since it is always dependent on an act being taken as a token of a certain type; that is, as being an act in a certain category. This act is itself a reflective social construction whose process of construction can be analyzed and altered. Influential individuals can take control over the process of measurement itself; some individuals, too, may influence measurements through their interest in concealing suicide, as in the case of Catholics who see it as having a negative meaning and the cost of eternal damnation. For all our statistical sophistication today, the 1990 census in the United States routinely changes the sex of one of the partners in a gay couple who respond that they are married. Thus, various individuals may try to exert control over the information-gathering process or the meaning assigned to the information may culturally distort the figures. The question for the philosophy of social science is whether or not it makes sense in this epistemic

situation to speak of the "real" suicide rate, or of the possibility
of the confirmation of an empirical, objective causal hypothesis.
Given that there are no objective criteria of application, could the
data needed to confirm such explanations ever be gathered? Perhaps
only if we abandon the demand that reasons be causes, and search
for confirmation only for entirely external, non-meaningful factors,
could causal models of explanation be employed. This is not to
say that reasons may not be causes, even in a Humean sense (as
in the case of the passions or drives), or that statistics do not
reveal important facts about social structures and identities, but
only that we have no way of collecting the data to determine if
and when they are.

Some methodologists have proposed ways of overcoming this
sort of problem with statistics in the social sciences; they distinguish "quasi-experimental" methods of verification from experimentation in artificial, laboratory settings.[62] Field experimentation
is more appropriate to the human sciences, and it has become the
main basis for empirical verification in many research programs in
social science, including ethnomethodology. Experimental techniques
in the laboratory succeed in resolving problems of causal adequacy
by controlling for the *ceteris paribus* clauses, especially through
techniques like randomization. Field experimentation typical in the
human sciences cannot do this, so that "quasi-experiments require
making explicit the irrelevant causal forces hidden in the *ceteris
paribus* of random assignment."[63] While this is difficult to do,
it is achieved primarily by greatly limiting the scope of various
theoretical terms by setting up operational definitions. While making
observation and measurement possible, such definitions always limit
the scope of the inferences which can be drawn from the results
of a quasi-experiment.

While this does not eliminate all the problems of causal adequacy with regard to rational explanations, it does go some way
toward determining how some such hypotheses supported by specific
mechanisms might be verified. Cook and Campbell's notion of
quasi-experimentation establishes some middle ground, however
limited in scope, between relying on official statistics and strict
verification in laboratory settings. The type of evidence supplied
does not support a Humean analysis of causation, but neither do
Hempel, Parsons, and the strong programme. It is implausible to
demand that all explanations in the social sciences fit this pattern,
particularly rational explanations. The upshot, then, is that perhaps
it is best to pursue an open-ended strategy in the philosophy of
social explanation, analogous to Cook and Campbell's approach

to experimentation. While all the programs for rational explanation suggested so far seem inadequate and unverifiable, this does not mean that we should reject the possibility of applying causality any more than we should reject the importance of measurement in establishing evidence. Reasons may be causes in some sense yet to be explicated, or they may be hypotheses in some non-causal, yet empirically verifiable explanation. It is clear, however, that neither Durkheim nor the strong programme have solved the problem of causal indeterminacy.

Conclusion: A New Post-Empiricist Strategy for Rational Reconstruction

The converging lines of argument of this and the Introduction point in the direction of a non-naturalistic logic of explanation in the social sciences. As we have seen in the Introduction, post-empiricist philosophers of science have emphasized the diversity of patterns of explanation, even in the natural sciences. Indeed, many have come to the conclusion that there is no feature that makes an explanation scientific in the sense that Hempel understood prediction or Popper understood falsifiability. Nor is there any such defining feature of knowledge which makes it scientific other than that it is explanatory. In place of the rational reconstruction of the "old logic" of the sciences, which sought one crucial feature of knowledge or bounded set of such features, or one unifying pattern of explanatory inference, non-skeptical post-empiricist philosophers of social science have turned to history, to examining the actual practice of science. As Mary Hesse has noted, post-empiricism signifies the change from ideal to historical models of explanation. This turn demands that the location of problems in the philosophy of science shift away from those defined internally and legislatively by philosophy to problems as they emerge in the theories and research of scientific practice itself. Hence this historical turn gives a new meaning to the reconstructive task of philosophy and shows the old logic to be an ideal construction and not a reconstruction at all. Once one abandons empiricism, the reconstructive task of the philosophy of a science or a group of sciences is to give an account of the diverse criteria which justify the uses of its various theoretical and methodological concepts, such as "cause," "rule," or "correct interpretation." The philosophy of social science is still not post-empiricist enough, and there are few cases of such historically and normatively guided reconstructions.

This turn to the practice of science suggests a different argumentative strategy. It is Aristotle's anti-Platonic strategy discussed in the Introduction, one which examines the practice of explanation in all the diverse uses of the term "cause." Aristotle's situation in this regard was not unlike that of contemporary philosophy of social science. Faced with a bewildering variety of answers to "why" questions, Aristotle gave a broad account of the limited number of existing, valid explanatory uses of the term "cause," in all of its types. He criticized other philosophers, notably Plato and the pre-Socratics, for arguing that knowledge must be reduced to one type of cause and thus that it must have only one purpose or be of one kind. According to the Aristotelian strategy, any answer to a "why" question – any explanation as such – entails a "cause' in one of the many senses of the term. The social scientist, too, confronts an assortment of explanatory factors. Reasoning backwards, as Aristotle did, the philosopher of social science can find various types of explanation available in social theory; it should then be possible to reconstruct these various valid types of explanation in as explicit a form as possible, stating the logic of the basic concepts used and the general pattern that the explanation typically employs to make these concepts do their explanatory work. Thus, "cause" here would be any necessary factor that can be formulated into a fruitful explanatory pattern. The search for such factors is open-ended, and depends on the available theories in the discipline in question – in this case the social sciences. The goal of the philosophy of social science, then, is to test to see whether or not a reconstructible pattern involving this or that factor exists, and whether its explanatory pattern may involve different types of concepts, such as reasons, institutions, or the macrostructure of social systems. If no such pattern exists, then no verifiable form of explanation can emerge from the concepts or the factor at hand. The debate over functionalist explanations is really a debate over whether such a pattern exists for them, or if the factor so designated – namely, institutions and their mechanisms of reproduction – can become the basis of an explanation. A good reconstruction of the basic statements and pattern of functionalist explanation would show how such explanations work epistemically, how they can be verified, and when they are appropriate.

This same type of reconstruction is suggested by Wesley Salmon in his recent criticism of Hempelian philosophy of science. Salmon argues that Hempel gives an "epistemic" analysis of explanations and causes in terms of laws; as Hempel understands it in *Aspects of Scientific Explanation*, scientific explanation "seeks to provide a systematic understanding of empirical phenomena by showing how they fit into the nomic nexus"[64] – that is, the overall pattern of already known laws. As opposed to Hempel's epistemic approach to reconstruction, Salmon proposes that an "ontic" conception might be superior. "Those philosophers who have adopted the ontic conception of scientific causality have generally regarded the pattern into which events are to be fit as a causal pattern."[65] For Hempel, the pattern is nomic, not causal, and he advises us that Hume has taught us not to look further for hidden causal forces or agencies. Apart from all the implications for the realistic status of scientific knowledge, Salmon's talk of the shift to an ontic level of analysis permits, I think, a diversity in types of causation in various phenomena, indicating different aspects of "the causal structure of the world." While Hume's analysis certainly was a powerful anti-metaphysical tool, it is also an impediment to the philosophy of science in reducing causation to one type or process: regularity of succession. In social science, we are interested in the causal structure of society, institutions, and human action, whose diverse ontic causes cannot be reduced to one variety or captured in one type of why question. Salmon goes on to give a closer analysis of his conception of cause in terms of probability theory, since the structure of the world is best made sense of in this way. "There is a strong presumption in contemporary physics," he writes, "that some basic laws of nature may be irreducibly statistical."[66] Hence, probability relations are a "basic feature of the world" according to the best available theories. For that reason, the philosophy of natural science should be concerned with their reconstruction, in order to make sense of its enterprise of cutting the world at nature's causal–structural joints.

I will not here follow Salmon's lead into probability theory or into ontic analysis. The best available theories of the social world do not suggest it. Rather, I will revise the epistemic strategy and look at what different theories say about the regularities and tendencies at work in societies in order to discover the extent to which each uncovers aspects of their fundamental features. The turn to ontic analysis requires a turn to the best available social theories and what they say about the diverse explanatory features of the social world.

With this end in mind, I shall begin again with the problem of action, one of the basic problems of the social sciences, and concentrate on three well-developed, non-naturalistic social theories and research programs: rational choice theory, ethnomethodology, and the theory of communicative action. I will examine their ontic claims – that is, their claims that the explanatory factors they pick out are fundamental – and see if their explanations of action can be formally reconstructed into an underlying explanatory pattern. I have chosen these theories because they each provide a coherent, non-naturalistic account of their own explanations and also because each one of them now has developed a fairly rich framework for empirical studies, many of which have already implemented and tested their explanatory theories. The various debates between these theories will indicate the range of issues in the non-naturalistic philosophy of social science.

The first question which all these theories must answer is the main question that the Hempelian framework could not answer: Can these various approaches give a coherent and plausible account of intentional social action? Can the theoretical framework and explanatory pattern related to the various ontic factors be reconstructed so as to supply adequate and verifiable explanations of social action? While the theories themselves often make exclusive claims (particularly on the methodological level), here we shall see whether or not the formal reconstruction of explanations of each type can specify necessary but not sufficient conditions for their validity. This pluralistic, multidimensional approach to the explanation of action may find perfectly good explanatory patterns that involve neither probabilistic nor deductive laws. Besides reconstructing the logic of various types of explanation in the social sciences, a post-empiricist theory will also see that the goals and purposes of each explanation are also a crucial part of what is to be made explicit in their reconstruction, where purposes or pragmatics of the theory may vary from explanatory pattern to explanatory pattern. This leads to a fundamental problem in post-empiricist, multidimensional philosophy of social science: how are we to judge the adequacy of alternative, yet sometimes conflicting, forms of explanation of the same events and actions? Such differences can no longer be settled by that neutral arbiter, epistemology, with its appeal to logical form. Hence, the next chapter is not only a study of the problems of recent attempts to explain action in the social sciences, but also is an attempt to resolve questions of adequacy and conflicts within and among them. Neither post-empiricism nor methodological pluralism imply that the philosophical question of adequacy cannot be answered: even under post-empiricist assumptions about knowledge, the crucial reflective question is what makes one explanation better than another. The difference is that now the question can only be answered by first reconstructing the typical explanations of successful research programs.

2

The New Logic of Social Science: Rules, Rationality, and Explanation

Hempel's failure to give a plausible reconstruction of explanations of rational action led philosophers to look to new concepts, particularly rules and rule following, to fill in where causality had failed. Construing reasons as causes left the social sciences trapped in the horns of what Parsons called the "utilitarian dilemma": such explanations are either vacuous or false. Neither Parsons' own explanations nor those of the strong programme escaped this same difficulty. But because reasons cannot be eliminated from social science without tremendous loss in explanatory power, philosophers began to question the appropriateness of Hempel's concept of causality and its naturalistic methodological commitments, both of which were also becoming less and less plausible for a full range of explanations in the natural sciences. But if rational explanations do not refer to general laws, how do they explain? In this chapter I will argue that they do so by fitting actions into various explanatory patterns of research programs that incorporate the indeterminacy of social action into their theories.

Peter Winch's *Idea of a Social Science* represents one of the most influential attempts to establish a "new," non-naturalistic philosophy of social science. Like Parsons, Winch argues that there is not enough structure in the causal explanation of action. As against the primarily behavioristic reception of Wittgenstein in Anglo-American circles up until that point, Winch draws upon a crucial component of Wittgenstein's private language argument to explicate what he calls "the concept of the social": the public character of following a rule. According to Winch, to the extent that human action is social, it is rule-governed and takes place within various "language games." As public and social, actions are meaningful and intelligible to the agents who conduct them and to others who share the same linguistically mediated form of life. In this way, language began to play a substantive and methodological role in a post-positivist conception of social theory and explanation.

This connection of social action to public rules and linguistic meanings did not originate in Winch or Wittgenstein. George Herbert Mead also used games as paradigmatic social activity that discloses what agents must know in order to participate in them (including knowledge of what other agents know), and structuralists found in the features of language a model for social explanation. But Winch's arguments are particularly instructive, precisely in light of their failure to establish strong claims about the centrality of rules in social actions. As Winch elucidates them, rules are not a sufficient basis for social science, because they remain not only indeterminate but unspecifiable. Wittgenstein had already argued in his *Philosophical Investigations*, "No course of action can be determined by a rule, because every course of action can be made out in accord with the rule."[1] If explanations of reasons as causes face the utilitarian dilemma, then explanations which appeal to rules face similar problems of empirical adequacy in the face of their indeterminacy.

Each of the basic research programs discussed in the rest of this chapter tries to resolve problems of the social indeterminacy of causes and rules by giving a much fuller, theoretically embedded account of rational and meaningful action. In the first section of the chapter, I will show how Winch's "idea of a social science" fails to develop any important contrast between rule-governed and causal explanation. Second, I will show how attempts in the social sciences to go beyond rule-governed and norm-guided accounts of action open up the possibility of a new logic of explanation. Rational choice, ethnomethodology and the theory of communicative action all provide greater structure and complexity in their explanations of core cases of social action: each research program can be construed as providing the detailed conditions and patterns of explanation that are needed to fill out Winch's indeterminate reference to rules as the larger context for intelligible social action. After explicating these patterns and their basic features as precisely as possible, I will then return to the explanation of different types of rules that each program can offer. Through the common attempt to develop the explanatory role, if any, that rules may have, we can begin the task of attempting to develop inter-theoretic standards of adequacy that cut across the programs and their explanatory patterns.

Winch's Social Science: Incompatibility and the Indeterminacy of Rules

As is typical in the long tradition of philosophical attacks on the empiricist view of social science, Winch's book tries to establish a radical conclusion: he wants to argue not only that the standard methods of scientific explanation are inappropriate for the domain of the social sciences but that its categories are altogether incompatible with the true aims of social science. Empiricist social science has been based on an epistemological mistake and a conceptual confusion from Mill onwards: the model of natural scientific knowledge as providing the unity of method that conflates the rules with the causes of social action. Hempel is no more than an updated version of Mill's methods of comparison and generalization. Winch argues for the centrality of rules in social life by way of a skeptical argument against causality in the social sciences. In what follows, I conclude that this argument is right in what it criticizes and wrong in its skeptical conclusions. Indeed, Winch's argument is open to skeptical objections on the same Wittgensteinian grounds that he uses to criticize empiricism: like causal descriptions without mechanisms, rules are simply too thin to support all the purposes of social science.

In retrospect, there is a surprising discrepancy between Winch's anti-empiricist conclusions and his logical–conceptual method of analysis. He argues deductively for the incompatibility of social science and causal generalization in light of an analysis of "the concept of the social," from which he also derives his analysis of meaningful behavior. Winch presents this logical and conceptual incompatibility in his Wittgensteinian idiom: "It is not a question of what empirical research may show to be the case, but what it makes sense to say."[2] An analysis of "what we mean by human society" shows that it involves concepts that are "logically incompatible" with any attempt to extend the style of explanation in the natural sciences into this domain. As Winch's critics have pointed out, it is doubtful that conceptual analysis and the diversity of human practices by themselves establish such a strong conclusion. In the end, Winch's social science is really itself ordinary-language philosophy made cross-cultural, the analysis of various people's concepts of their own activities and views of reality.

Winch correctly argues that the view of philosophy that is typical of empiricism, Locke's "underlaborer" view of philosophy as epistemology, presupposed that the methods of inquiry and nature of knowledge were settled and that all that needed to be done was to clear up misleading inferences and the errors of common sense. Such confidence about the qualifications for knowledge has broken down not only in the social sciences but in the natural sciences as well, and Winch was right to challenge the unity of method that empiricism in its various forms assumed. However, Winch expressed his opposition to empiricism by putting the nineteenth century hermeneutic position in new Wittgensteinian dress: because of the unavoidable reliance by social science on rules and meanings instead of causes, the human and natural sciences have entirely incompatible aims and methods.

Winch establishes his "incompatibility thesis" in two separate analyses, one conceptual and the other methodological. The first is an analysis of social action that shows how it must be seen as meaningful, rule-governed behavior. The second is an analysis of what the methodology of the social sciences must be if this concept of social action is correct. Together, both dispute the Weberian thesis that the social sciences can combine both reasons and causes in its methods. I will argue that neither of these analyses establishes such a conclusion and that the Weberian view withstands Winch's criticisms. Winch's failure will be instructive for understanding how recent intentionalist social theories develop successful explanations of meaningful action quite contrary to Winch's conceptual arguments.

According to Winch, the analysis of social action should derive from what Wittgenstein's private language argument establishes about the concept of society. Both the private language argument and the analysis of action are guided by the same epistemological issue: the identity of action. As I argued in the last chapter, identification is a problem for any causal account, since two physically similar movements may be said to be quite different actions, like voting in an election and randomly marking on a page. Further, dissimilar physical actions can still qualify as the same social action, as quite different sounds can be taken to be the same song. Subsuming an action under a rule clarifies such problems of identity: "It is only in terms of a given *rule* that we can attach a specific sense to the words 'the same'"[3] It is by referring to rules that we know that raising one's hand, saying "nay," and punching a computer card are all instances of voting as a type of action. But does this appeal to rules solve the problem? Indeed, if Wittgenstein is right, it just repeats the problem again on a different level.

Winch sees rules as the solution because of their public and social character; it is only by reference to common rules that anyone can grasp what others are doing. Thus, the concept of following a rule implies the anticipations, reactions, and expectations of other people in the social, intersubjective context of action in a "form of life." As the impossibility of a private rule shows, "it is only in a situation in which it makes sense to suppose that somebody else could in principle discover the rule that it can intelligibly be said to follow a rule at all."[4] Although Winch claims that actors use rules "as a matter of course," they must have knowledge of the rules in order to be said to have acquired them. Habit is insufficient to account for the social character of an activity, and for that reason Winch characterizes his view as "intellectualist."[5]

Winch defines what it means to follow a rule in terms of the action itself, not the agent's explicit knowledge: a rule is followed in an action only if it is possible to make a mistake. As Winch puts it, "The test of whether a person's actions are the application of a rule is not whether he can formulate it but whether or not it makes sense to distinguish a right and a wrong way of doing things."[6] The denial of the requirement that the agent be able to formulate the rule permits Winch to make all social action "which is meaningful (therefore all specifically human behavior) ipso facto rule governed."[7] It remains for social science to identify the diverse types of rules, their relations to each other, and their relation to the larger context of the form of life which they constitute.

For Winch, it is this constitutive or "internal" relation between rules and actions that makes the causal model of explanation inappropriate for "specifically human behavior." For a reason to be the cause of an action, it would have to be contingently related to the action that it causes. As the reasons for actions that make them intelligible and identifiable, rules are related to action internally and not contingently and thus cannot be understood as a causal factor. Hence, Winch thinks that he has established the conceptual incompatibility of reasons and causes, laws and rules.

While it is certainly true that causal description alone is too thin to establish the identity of an action, Winch's argument about internal relations fails to establish the incompatibility thesis, or anything else, about social scientific methodology. Even as an analysis of social action, numerous counter-examples are obvious.

Alasdair MacIntyre points out that it is not true that all social actions can be done correctly and incorrectly, and hence they do not all refer even implicitly to rules as constituting part of their description: for example, how do we go for a walk "incorrectly"?[8] Furthermore, sometimes reasons do seem to be causes. Suppose a person discovers that the person to whom she is engaged has committed an infidelity. The belief that this is true, coupled with certain emotions such as jealousy, could be the cause of breaking off the engagement, an action which would not have occurred without the belief. Certainly, this belief would not be a candidate cause without knowledge of the significance of a whole set of marriage and sexual practices, but none of these rules or norms are incompatible with employing a belief as an explanatory term in a causal explanation. If Weber is correct in his version of the compatibility of reasons and causes, then reasons are simply a different type of cause than a Humean constant connection between two contingent events. Because Winch has such a univocal notion of cause, he vastly underestimates the motivating role of reasons, an empirical role which is evident not only in individual cases but also in whole types of actions, like manipulation and deception.

The failure of Winch's claims about incompatibility has clear implications for the methodological conclusions he draws for his version of the distinction between the human and natural sciences. Winch argues that social science not only must deal with the internal perspective of the actor's reasons, but is also itself rule-governed in a double sense: "Whereas in the case of the natural scientist we have only to deal with one set of rules, namely those governing the scientist's investigation itself, here what the sociologist is studying, as well as his study of it, is a human activity" and therefore rule-governed.[9] In the case of the social scientist, the criteria used to understand and evaluate the activity must be internal to the activity itself.

Winch's argument is one in a long line of arguments that use the meaningfulness of actions to demarcate the social and the natural sciences. Even if we grant that the intelligibility of an action can be explicated through rules, it is hard to see why it can only and *exclusively* be understood through rule following. Moreover, Winch is even more restrictive in what counts as a proper account, since social scientists must discover the same rules and criteria that participants employ; even if the social scientist's account is superior, it must use terms and concepts internal to the activities and practices under investigation. Otherwise, it fails to be a "genuine understanding."[10]

Winch uses this methodological exclusion to expand his criticism of naturalistic ideas of causality to any "external" explanation of an activity, such as those of Marxism, functionalism, or psychoanalysis. The concept of "function" is "quasi-causal" and hence outside of the doubly rule-governed activity of the social scientist. But if Winch's attempt to show the incompatibility of reasons and causes is incorrect, then there is little reason for the social scientist to privilege the participants' own descriptions of their activities. Rules themselves may establish second order patterns, whose significance may escape participants as much as the laws of supply and demand escape many buyers and sellers and yet operate in their intentional activities. Rules, too, can have "latent" functions which work through purposes within the agent's grasp. Rules that are supposed to assure free and open access to university education may actually serve to reinforce established patterns of privilege. In order to show how such patterns work, the functionalist does indeed take into account agents' own beliefs, as I will argue in chapter 4. But the concepts describing the functional connection between rules and intentions and their latent consequences need not be restricted to agents' self-descriptions. Winch is correct in arguing that to disregard rules and beliefs can leave the explanation without reference to the shared social situation it is supposed to explain. But Winch leaves out a whole legitimate type of explanation that supersedes the limits of an internal perspective on rules and meanings.

Winch thinks that his methodological argument also establishes strong claims about the nature of society and of social relations. The rule-governed character of action shows that ideas are constitutive of the relations between persons in which they are expressed. Winch draws ontological conclusions from this constitutive character of rules: "If social relations between men exist only in and through ideas, then, since relations between ideas are internal relations, social relations must be a species of internal relations, too."[11] Such idealism leaves the way in which these relations came about mysterious. It simply assumes what needs to be explained – namely, how there is some determinate and explicable connection between rules and the course of everyday activities. The final consequence of Winch's exclusivist methodology is ultimately the denial of the possibility that social theory can analyze how these already existing internal relations have come about.

While Winch certainly shows that the identification of social action raises problems about meaningful social action, his concept of rules is not complex enough to provide the basis for explanation nor to resolve problems of indeterminacy any better than causal theories do. Since rules are reflective and subject to extension and interpretation by agents, it is often hard to say if an action is performed "correctly" or was a "mistake." Rules are certainly not determinate enough to be predictive; they are not followed in the same way by all agents, and many often are not followed at all. As Winch notes, "The rule here does not specify any determinate outcome to the situation, though it does limit the range of possible alternatives."[12] This same indeterminacy, however, undermines Winch's own position: it is often difficult to say when we are applying one rule or another, if a rule is being followed incorrectly or being creatively expanded. Winch's view of intelligibility requires that social practices be a closed set of internal relations. Otherwise, Winch's whole account falls under Wittgenstein's paradox: "Every course of action can be made out in accord with a rule." But the indeterminacy of action makes it more complex than rule-governed behavior: even granted that an action can be described as rule following, that may not be what makes it an action or even what explains it. To use an example from Alasdair MacIntyre: Suppose I make a move in chess, one that follows the rules and may even be the best move on the board at the time. It could still only be a signal to someone in the crowd to begin a robbery. In this case, "conformity to the rules of chess is of course what makes my actions instances of playing chess, but it is not what makes them an action."[13] Viewed in light of the complexity of such typical, nested social phenomena, Winch's attempt to make actions intelligible by reference to rules is no less indeterminate than Hempel's attempt to explain them in terms of general laws. The fact that some social actions follow rules does not require a distinctive or autonomous explanatory approach, nor do the rules themselves even ultimately explain most cases of rule following. As Robert Edgerton points out, there are many different types of rules, rules with exceptions, rules enforced without exceptions, rules about the exceptions to rules. Winch's view belongs to the older conformist models of rule following. As Edgerton describes this conformist "normative theory," "People everywhere not only followed the rules of their societies – but also made these rules a part of themselves and became, almost literally, inseparable from them."[14] But theories challenged this view based upon the indeterminacy of rules – that is, the fact that people often do not follow them, do not incorporate them and frequently use them strategically to further their own interests. Under the new perspective of strategic interactionism, embodied in the works of theorists like Erving Goffman, rules are treated as flexible, negotiable and subject to exceptions. Just like the old approaches, however, the new approaches also fail to capture the diversity of rules and rule following. As Edgerton points out, both theories mislead for similar reasons: "To speak of rules as though they were all alike obscures the place of rules in creating and maintaining social order."[15] If rules are to have any explanatory importance, it must be in some larger context of a theory that explains a whole complex set of interrelationships, namely, the relation between rules and actions, rules and practices, rules and the contingent circumstances of a society, rules and their violation and exceptions, and rules and agents' beliefs and knowledge. Winch's attempt to overcome naturalism ends up in unwarranted scepticism about some of these explanations, and ultimately in the failure to find any logical structure in the explanation of a diverse and indeterminate social phenomenon.

A New Logic of Rational Action:
Three Explanatory Patterns

Even in his account of rule-governed action – and much less in an account of social action as a whole as rule following – Winch stops at the identification of rules and public standards that make actions social and intelligible. There is simply not enough theoretical structure in his appeal to rules to make most social action and contexts intelligible or even to identify the "same" rule. Not only are particular rules open-ended and indeterminate, but the same rules can have entirely different functions: some can permit exceptions and violations more often than others; some conditions and circumstances, such as catastrophes, make rules more strictly enforced and sanctioned. Thus, rules do many things; at the very least, they guide, explain and justify actions. For all his criticism of naturalism, Winch is a good example of how anti-naturalism shares some of the same methodological assumptions: Winch assumes that the logic of "the social" is unitary, that the many instances of following a rule are essentially a matter of conforming to a public practice, even if these practices may vary from culture to culture. As opposed to such an essentialistic human science approach, post-empiricism requires that we abandon the idea that the logic of the social sciences can be discovered by conceptual

analysis of a unitary phenomenon rather than an empirically oriented analysis of multiple types of explanation.

Such a recognition of empirical diversity enriches rather than
impoverishes philosophical analysis. By abandoning the assumptions of the old logic of explanation and squarely facing the
indeterminacy of causes and rules, an empirically oriented approach can get a purchase on a theory of rules that has more
explanatory power. The best way to do this is not to offer an
idealized reconstruction of explanation as such or of rule following as a constitutive feature of social action, but by looking at the
explanatory practices of successful research programs, specifically
ones which employ explanations of rational action: rational choice,
ethnomethodology, and the theory of communicative action. In the
rest of this section I will examine three such research programs
and their explanatory patterns, and sketch the precise features and
conditions of the type of action to which the theory applies. I
recognize that this use of such theories may sometimes violate
their original intention. One of the main problems in using the
theoretical writings of the major figures of each of these programs
is that theorists often try to take over the whole domain of social
action, arguing for exclusive methodological claims that often
overgeneralize the pattern of successful explanations of that type.
After distilling these patterns, I will return to the phenomenon of
rules. In particular, I will address how each theory can treat a
delimited number of phenomena and in explaining them also
overcome the problem of the indeterminacy of rule following.
Their different treatment of rules shall provide the case study for
the chapter and a good instance for inter-theoretical comparison
across research programs.

In reconstructing such patterns, I cannot offer a complete account of the intricacies of the various theories, something others
have already done quite well.[16] My aim is to show how each
approach tries to resolve problems of indeterminacy in adequate
explanations of intentional and social action, problems that are
unresolvable on both naturalist and internalist assumptions alike.
Adequacy cannot be established here by predictive power, although some of the explanations do have predictive consequences,
particularly in rational choice theory. Rather I want to develop
other criteria of adequacy and verification. An explanation is
supported by evidence if all the statements of its well-warranted
pattern can be shown to obtain.

Explanation and Rational Choice Theory

Of the research programs considered in this chapter, rational choice theory most directly continues Hempel's project of a non-reductive empirical social science that explains actions in terms of beliefs and desires or, in the terms of the theory, information and preferences.[17] In this respect, it does what many philosophers such as Winch and Davidson have argued to be impossible. As Alexander Rosenberg notes, rational choice theory is "folk psychology formalized," something Hempel thought his general laws were as well. But rational choice theory does not achieve its formalization by inductively generating laws and hence avoids some of the difficulties that Hempel's account fell prey to. At the same time, its fundamentally causal explanations of purposive action resemble Schema R: it explains actions through the agent's choice of the best means available, given her beliefs and desires, according to some criterion of practical rationality or utility maximization. Rational choice theory is an account of action that explains choice within constraints, namely, those imposed by the choice situation (decision theory) and those imposed by the choices of others (game theory). Two hypothetical examples can illustrate this distinction and the formalism of the theory nicely.

In the first situation, suppose a single agent is trying to decide whether or not to take an umbrella to work. The agent prefers not to get wet, but also prefers not to burden herself unnecessarily. The intentional action of nonetheless taking the umbrella can be explained in terms of the agent's reasons for acting: the desires to avoid getting wet and avoid carrying burdens are construed as preferences over all possible consequences that could result as the joint outcome of the agent's choice (different actions) and the constraining environment (rain). This choice is decision-theoretic, since the environment here is nature, understood as a system of events whose occurrence is the result of probabilistic laws; in a game-theoretic situation, the constraining environment is other agents who are also trying to satisfy their preferences. A matrix like the one below is a convenient device for representing all the elements of such a choice situation. Assume that the probability of rain is 60 percent, that not getting wet and not carrying a burden are equal preferences, and that there are only two options (carrying or not carrying an umbrella).

Possible States of Nature

Choices	Rain ($p = 0.60$)	Not rain ($p = 0.40$)
Take umbrella	(I) not wet, burden	(II) not wet, burden
Not take umbrella	(III) wet, no burden	(IV) not wet, no burden

Possible outcomes: I, II, III, IV

Preferences: IV = 2, I = 1, II = 0, III = −1

Expected utility: Take umbrella strategy $0.6(1) + 0.4(0) = 0.6$

Not take umbrella $0.6(-1) + 0.4(2) = 0.2$

It is rational, then, to take the umbrella, if "rational" here is defined according to the (Bayesian) criteria of maximizing expected utility for decision under risk.

Consider now a decision by two nations, say in Europe just prior to World War I. Both are considering how to respond to the threat of an arms race by the other, a situation in which each prefers not only to be in the position of dominance, but also not to waste resources on senseless weaponry. Neither nation would enter into the arms race if the other also does not. However, under these conditions of not knowing what the other party will do, the nations can only choose strategies, not the mutually optimal outcome of no arms race. The game-theoretical matrix that represents this choice situation shows that the rational strategy will result in a sub-optimal outcome for each nation: each begins the arms race so that the other does not get the advantage. The pairs of choices will be best (B), second best (S), third best (T), and worst (W), each from the point of view of a particular state.

	Not arm	Arm
Not arm	S,S	W,B
Arm	B,W	T,T

The likely outcome is then that both will arm, and each will achieve only the third best outcome by following a strategy that permits the occurrence of best outcome and avoids the worst, the risk of not arming. Thus, the choice of both of them to arm is said to be the "dominant strategy." It is the game's stable equilibrium, despite its sub-optimality for both actors. From the individual player's point of view, arming is the best, utility-maximizing strategy, regardless of what the other nation does. This result does not assume hatred or hostility; they are not altruistic (concerned with the benefits to the others) but "nontuistic," or indifferent. Such motivational assumptions are crucial to the "mixed motive" game represented, which is neither a zero-sum (I win, you lose) nor a cooperative (I win, if you win) game.

Both matrices represent formal elaborations of the theoretical structure of each of these different types of constraint on utility maximizing. This structure gives the theory its formal, quantitative features and explanatory adequacy, even while basing its explanations on subjectively defined conditions like preferences. Its explanations are adequate if, and only if, the constraints formalized in its theories can be shown to apply empirically to the actual choice or action situation. Most rational choice theorists, however, believe that this standard does not in any way restrict the potential scope of the theory, since all such situations may be formalized in some way or other.

For all its emphasis on constraints, rational choice explanations work by assuming that agents are rational in a very specific sense: that they are utility maximizers (although this may mean different things to different theorists). One of the legacies of Winch's view of social science was to raise problems about the generality of norms and standards, including those of rationality. Rational choice theory tries to side-step these issues by appealing to economics, the most formal and quantitatively successful of the social sciences, and specifically to the concept of expected utility as a way to unify a theory of economic behavior. Economic agents can be expected to be utility maximizers who choose that course of action the consequences of which bring the greatest return or best fulfill their preferences (whatever these may be). After much debate about how to measure utility (whether cardinally or ordinally), marginalist economics avoided irresolvable problems of the indeterminacy of interpersonal comparisons by simply measuring utility according to the ranking of "revealed preferences," preferences manifested in the pattern of the agent's choices.[18] Preferences are simply taken as given, and all considerations of their rationality, other than their consistency or "transitivity," are irrelevant to the explanation of action. With these assumptions about preferences and maximization as the defining feature of rationality, utility maximization becomes a broadly applicable explanatory concept. As with Hempel's general laws, the broad flexibility of the theory brings with it a danger of empirical vacuity, since it is always possible to represent utilities experimentally as arbitrary monetary costs and benefits. Unless financial costs and benefits are simply stipulated to be linear with utility, it is not obviously the case that all actors at all times always act to maximize their utility in this sense. This empirical problem raises a basic question of the theory: Is it descriptive or prescriptive, or perhaps somehow both? How does it avoid being unnecessarily prescriptive, as when it brings in economic motivations? The normative status of utility maximization becomes one of the crucial issues of the currently widespread attempts to extend what Herbert Simon calls the "economic model of man" to all the social sciences.

This assumption about maximization is crucial to the theory, since it permits a quantitatively and qualitatively precise specification of how rationality can become a formal property of individual actions. As Jon Elster puts it, the rationality of an intentional action can be specified in terms of "the right relation between the goals and beliefs of the agent."[19] This "right relation" has at least one specific formal property: consistency, or as it is put in relation to actions, maximization. All forms of rationality express some criterion of consistency. The rationality of beliefs consists in their logical consistency with each other, while that of desires is their transitivity: if one prefers A to B, and B to C, then one prefers A to C. Practical rationality is consistency of choice: it is rational to act in such a way as to be consistent with one's preferences and beliefs – that is, in the best or maximizing way to realize one's preferences given one's beliefs. By using these criteria of consistency to restrict the range of rational alternatives in intentional action, these formal features give the theory whatever predictive power it has. This same formal character may bring with it limits on the empirical application of the theory. For example, if an agent operates with several utility functions (and hence maximizes different rankings of preferences, say one at work and the other at home), then consistency has less and less explanatory force. While all forms of rationality are identical with consistency of one sort or another, I will speak of maximization as distinct from other forms of consistency, since it is the crucial assumption of rational choice explanations of action.

The assumption of maximization requires that a rational agent act to achieve the best for herself and thus choose the highest ranking alternative among the set of feasible alternative actions and strategies. Although there are a number of different maximizing rules, from the least risky (maxi-min) to the most risky (maxi-max), each rule is a strategy for choice aimed at the maximum utility for the agent. Powerfully predictive theories in the natural sciences also employ similar assumptions about maximization as well, including Newton's laws of motion as described by differential calculus and Darwin's survival of the fittest understood as maximum reproductive success.[20] All these theories attempt to explain a domain of phenomena by showing how the maximization of a value, like survival rates among offspring, explains everything in a domain. This assumption defines a research strategy: if we know that the behavior of a system tends to maximize the value of some variable and if our measurements of its value in an experiment is at odds with the predictions of the theory, then "we never infer that the system is failing to maximize the variable in question, but assume that our specification of the constraints under which it is operating is incomplete."[21] For example, we might extend decision theory by introducing the theory of games, showing that maximizing choices in this context can be explained in terms of the constraints of the interdependency of choices made by other utility-maximizing agents. Together, consistent maximization is the key element of a minimal theory of rationality, in terms of which the rational choice theorist can try to predict how individuals will behave under certain conditions if they act rationally. Many rational choice theorists add the further assumption that all rational motivation is self-interested, especially in economic contexts, an assumption often justified on methodological grounds, as, for example, by Russell Hardin, who argues that it is "the most useful benchmark to assess the extent and impact of other motivations."[22]

From this series of assumptions emerges a whole set of problems that make up the research program of rational choice theory. One set of problems concerns the knowledge of consequences: the common lack of reliable knowledge about the future has led to research on how decisions are made under uncertainty. There are also fundamental problems related to how cooperation and collective action are possible given the explanatory assumptions of utility maximization and self-interested motivation, which has given rise to research in reiterated games like the prisoners' dilemma and the notion of "selective incentives" as the basis of cooperation. I will return to problems of collective action in chapter 4, since they concern the relation of micro- to macro-levels of explanation. Some theorists have modified the core assumptions of the theory, as Simon did in deriving a theory of sub-optimal choice.[23] Nonetheless, the structure of the theory remains the same, with "bounded rationality" replacing maximization and "satisficing conditions" replacing optimal ones.

For all the formal complexity of its theoretical models, rational choice explanations can be broken down into elements which extend and formalize the basic features of ordinary explanations of intentional action. As a sub-species of intentional explanation, any rational choice explanation must have the minimal elements of intentional explanation as part of its fundamental guiding pattern (statements 1 and 2), which are then completed by a formal–minimal model of rationality (statements 2–4). It is the application of this model that gives the pattern its explanatory power, not any inductive dispositional generalizations as Hempel thought.

Pattern of Rational Choice Explanation[24]

(1) Rational action is characterized by the proper relation between beliefs (B), desires (D), and the action (A) performed. In light of B, A is the best way to achieve D.

(2) Rational actions must be voluntary, insofar as reasons must be real causes and not *post hoc* rationalizations: B and D cause A *qua* reasons and can be connected to the consequences of A.

(3) B and D are internally consistent, and their relation to choice fits the idealizing assumptions of the model of utility maximizing rationality. These conditions make the choice fully rational: the means must be the best available to the agent.

(4) Other conditions depend on the constraining features of the choice situation, including the choices of others, coordinating mechanisms, and other constraints that establish enduring patterns of action which are equilibrium states of a society. Utility maximizing choice must occur within the constraints, such as social mechanisms of cooperation and interdependence, which maintain stable strategic interaction over time.

(5) Given 2, 3, and 4, some course of action must be rationally decidable, as the best among well-defined alternatives.

The specification of these conditions overcomes one of the empirical problems of a formal-maximizing theory: much as Wittgenstein said of rule following, any action can be seen as maximizing some sufficiently arbitrary set of beliefs and desires, much as any adaptation can always be seen as increasing fitness in some respect or another.[25] Rational choice theory, too, must avoid being Panglossian, seeing everything social as the outcome of maximizing–purposive behavior, with no room for causal contingency and environmental effects. If all the statements of this pattern obtain, then the model of rationality is empirically and not merely definitionally applicable to the action.

Once specified in this way, it becomes clear that certain types of action do not fit into the pattern at all. There are actions for which reasons cannot be the cause (and thus statement 2 does not hold), as any insomniac knows. Since not all consequences can be made the goal of an intentional action, the outcomes of these actions are "essentially by-products," including such phenomena as wanting to forget, to fall asleep, or to be spontaneous.[26] In general, the model does not apply whenever any of the conditions does not obtain, as is the case not only for by-products and unintended consequences of actions, but also for irrational behavior, some moral and social norms, addictive behavior and much more (most of which do not fit the rationality conditions of statement 3). Such cases do not refute the theory, but require the social scientist to look carefully at its scope and methodological claims.

The core cases for the theory are economic phenomena in the broadest sense. Consumer behavior shows how the pattern may yield empirical hypotheses with predictive value, such as the way supply and demand relationships predict the movement of actual market prices to the equilibrium price. Neoclassical economics attempts to see such law-like relationships as the aggregate of rational choices made by consumers, all of whom conduct their transactions as utility maximizers. Prices in certain markets function as the sort of constraint that I have in mind for statement 4, and thus serve as a coordinating mechanism: a rise in price will cause a reduction in the amount demanded, so that, for example, a tax increase on gasoline would cut consumption by rational consumers. Such empirical regularities are explained by other sorts of economic analyses as well: John Roemer has shown how Marx's analysis of capitalism fits into the pattern, since the aggregate of all the utility-maximizing behavior of all capitalists results in the failure of the system as a whole to reach any equilibrium state (much like the game of chicken or hyperinflation). By each capitalist seeking to maximize profits, there is a tendency for each to follow strategies such as constant exploitation and technical innovation.

A more problematic case might reveal more about the nature and scope of the pattern and how it guides empirical research. Its application to political phenomena generally and to voting in particular is one such case, a case that challenges claims for the universal scope of the theory. As Elster notes, "Voting does seem to be a case in which the action itself, rather than the outcome it can be expected to produce, is what matters."[27] On utility-maximizing grounds, it is pointless to vote in a large election with a secret ballot. Besides the large number of people in the social interactions that make up an election, one reason that the pattern of rational choice theory does not fit is that the causal condition (statement 3) does not apply. In a large election, it is highly unlikely that any single voter will cast the decisive ballot; therefore, for a rational maximizer to invest any resources, such as time, in voting would be irrational. Some political theorists seem content to condemn all politics to irrationality and see participation as rational only if there are "selective incentives" – that is, rewards specific to the group voting – in the absence of any coordinating mechanisms like the market.[28] But rather than a "market failure" of the political system in coordinating and aggregating choices, these difficulties point to an explanatory failure of the pattern when it is applied beyond the conditions of its validity. Voting is a rational action, but only in a much richer sense that would include self-expressive action along with instrumental action in its domain. Such an account of voting would have to include a treatment of testing and changing preferences in discussion and debate, as might be done in the theory of communicative action.

Such cases could be multiplied, so that the clear presentation of the conditions required to apply the theory can dispute the claim of some theorists, like Gary Becker, that rational choice theory is a complete account of all human behavior.[29] Whether we know it or not, according to Becker, the economic approach to human behavior is unlimited in explanatory scope and power: "All human behavior can be viewed as involving participants who maximize their utility for a stable set of preferences and accumulate an optimal amount of information and other inputs in a variety of markets."[30] Because we compete with others to satisfy these preferences, market-like coordinating mechanisms provide part of the social explanation of how maximizers interact. For example, marriage choices can be explained as utility maximization in a market: "A person decides to marry when the expected utility from marriage exceeds that expected from remaining single or from the additional search for a more compatible mate."[31] This law-like statement has all the marks of a tautology. It is an easy and empirically vacuous trick to redescribe all of the motives that agents may have for marrying in terms of expected utility. Even once the notions of markets and utility are extended in such a way, it still has not yet been shown that utility-maximizing marriage choices actually cause the rate of marriage to be what it is; the theory may only provide a series of accidental correlations between its assumptions about human behavior and statistical patterns of marriage. It should come as no surprise that Becker's theory is, therefore, consistent with all the data, without explaining any of it; there is no independent specification of what the basic terms of his theory are or what the explanatory variable, utility, is supposed to be.[32]

There are also questions about what sort of evidence might confirm or refute the explanation. The fact that actors would not recognize themselves psychologically in these descriptions does not bother Becker, nor does he recognize that rational choice theory does not require the same motivational assumptions as neoclassical economics: "The economic approach does not assume that decision units are necessarily conscious of their efforts to maximize, or can verbalize or otherwise describe in an informative way the reasons for the systematic patterns of their behavior."[33] Certainly, laws of supply and demand do not require that actors choose in light of them. But Becker's remarks show that the generalization of rational choice models of explanation can be done only by abandoning the idea that the theory was supposed to give an account of how reasons cause actions. Instead, the theory searches for unconscious maximizing motives and market mechanisms, making the rationality of actors themselves less and less important as an explanatory condition. Rosenberg is correct in arguing that such overgeneralized economic theories of behavior are more like sociobiology with its maximizing mechanisms than they are like intentional explanations. Generalizing the maximizing assumption in this case means suspending the conditions of voluntary action which make up the core of statement 2 in the pattern.

One result of this criticism of Becker's comprehensive claim is to show that the pattern of rational choice explanation sets out conditions that apply only to a certain range of intentional actions. While any research program can test whether its pattern of explanation can be expanded beyond its core cases, rational choice research itself shows that it is not a "complete theory of all human behavior" and that this imperial aim only entangles the theory in conceptual and empirical difficulties. More methodologically sophisticated proponents of the theory, such as Russell Hardin, argue that the theory simply makes stipulative assumptions about action and that it loses its explanatory power when the individual's calculus is expanded beyond the narrowest cost–benefit motivations. "To attempt a complete decision theory of human behavior would be absurd," Hardin argues, because a complete assessment requires an "extended calculus." Such calculations bring in too many additional variables and unmanageably pack "the context and much of the social history that has brought that context about into one's decision calculus."[34] Despite this modest approach, many argue that the theory's formal and stipulative assumptions have been so often shown not to obtain that some, like Amos Tversky, have adopted a much more modest and empirical approach.[35] Others, like Amartya Sen, have questioned the usefulness of its model of rationality. Purely economic and utility-maximizing agents, acting in some actual historical society, would not be competent actors, but instead would be "rational fools." The reason is, Sen argues, that rational choice theory has "too little structure,"[36] particularly with regard to preference rankings. To overcome this lack of structure, Sen introduces an element entirely lacking from the maximizing, formal concept of rationality: reflexivity, or the capacity to consider the "rankings of preference rankings."[37] Rational agents do not simply choose in light of stable preferences, but can ask the reflexive question: what type of preferences should I have? Such second-order preferences introduce considerations which could not be captured in the explanatory pattern as developed so far. As soon as reflexivity is introduced, so is indeterminacy: what is "best" is not univocal but relative to a variety of different rankings. This reflexivity makes the practical rationality of choice at least in part a matter of judgment about one's preferences themselves and how one ranks them, not just of maximizing one's given preferences. Such a theory would make wider empirical assumptions about the proper relations of reasons to actions. However, it is indeterminate insofar as it cannot pick unique outcomes for a whole domain such as "marriage choices." Hence, the rational choice pattern would have to introduce more explanatory conditions, taken from other theories better suited to deal with the influences of social contexts on choices and the changing and indeterminate character of social actions. Becker's exclusivist theory is no more successful than Winch's exclusivist methodology: because reflexive actors are more knowledgeable than either theory makes them out to be, both simply deny indeterminacy and try to make human beings into rule-following conformists on the one hand and maximizing fools on the other, so as to better approximate the conditions of their explanations. Not so with the next research program.

Ethnomethodology: A Reflexive Approach to Action

Before beginning, I should note an irony: while I am treating ethnomethodology as a pattern like rational choice theory, many ethnomethodologists deny that they give explanations at all.[38] Although ethnomethodologists mean something quite a bit more radical and dubious, this claim could mean that ethnomethodology does not offer "naturalistic" or causal explanations. This view of explanation is not the one that a post-empiricist philosophy of social science employs either, so that many of the more radical claims made for ethnomethodology seem to have lost their force in light of the demise of naturalism and Parsonian sociology. In any case, ethnomethodologists offer close and detailed descriptions, mostly of sequences of interaction. What I would like to show in this section is how a description can be an explanation in a post-empiricist sense, on the condition that it is finely detailed and explicit enough.

Harold Garfinkel began what came to be called ethnomethodology in reaction to the difficulties of Parsons' account of action, and many of his criticisms are similar to the ones analyzed in the last chapter. Parsons' view of norms as causes of social action could account neither for the relation between cognition and action, nor for how order is at least sometimes intelligibly produced by actors themselves. In Garfinkel's terms, the causal approach construes actors as "judgmental dopes" who passively carry out prescribed actions as the bearers of social norms. As opposed to Winch's anti-naturalism, central to Garfinkel's critique of internalization is his rejection of Parsons' notion of determinate and ideal social rules and norms which already exist prior to actions and interactions and define their standard course. In such an analysis of action and internalized norms, Garfinkel argues, causal claims and mechanisms cover over the failure to offer any real explanations: "Hierarchies of need dispositions and common culture as enforced rules of action are favored devices for bringing the problem of necessary inference to term, although at the cost of making out the person in society to be a judgmental dope."[39]

In place of the causal properties of internalized norms, Garfinkel analyzes actions as the product and achievement of knowledgeable and reflexive actors. In everyday practices, actors employ knowledge about the conditions and circumstances in which they act meaningfully and interpret the meaningful actions of others. Hence, contrary to theories that make actors into unreflective fools in order to make what they do fit into a rigid explanatory pattern, Garfinkel proposes that social scientists examine everyday activity as an ongoing practical accomplishment, one that is constituted, produced and maintained by actors themselves in situated circumstances and occasions. Indeed, the guiding hypothesis of Garfinkel's theory of action is that "every feature of an activity's sense, facticity, objectivity, accountability and commonality can be treated as a contingent accomplishment of socially organized practices."[40] This bold claim sets the goal of explaining every feature of an activity as constructed in a contingent situation and hence context-dependent. The meaningful or intelligible character of an action is "radically indexical," to use the linguistic phrase favored by Garfinkel; that is, such features are like demonstratives and pronouns in language use, whose indexicality is now generalized to all activities. On this assumption, the goal of describing an action or an activity is to make it as intelligible as it is to the agents performing it. As opposed to other theories of action, ethnomethodology transforms the indeterminacy of action from a problem to be overcome into a guiding principle of analysis. This leads Garfinkel and other ethnomethodologists to deny that they are giving a theory at all, since there is no such thing as a "context in general" that might be its building block, only many different context-relative features and ways that agents practically manage and order situations.

When it comes to analyzing actual activities in this way, ethnomethodologists do not focus on subjective, reflectively dis-coverable beliefs and desires like rational choice theory does. Rather, Garfinkel describes commonplace actions in terms of their "formal properties," that is, the methods, procedures, and organ-ization of activities that constitute the social situation. These are to be found by closely examining *how* actors do things and what is being done, not actors' avowed intentions and goals. As Garfinkel puts it, "Rational features consist of what members do,"[41] just as social arrangements consist of various methods for accomplishing their organization.[42] Any other approach, Garfinkel asserts, yields results that are "empirically uninteresting."

In light of these claims, Garfinkel proposes a different research practice, one made possible by new technologies like tape recorders and videocameras. Instead of proposing hypotheses and gathering data, Garfinkel proposes a radically descriptive "documentary technique." It consists of the close observation of sequences of interaction and of carefully constructed quasi-experiments, all aimed at revealing the details and textures of sense-making, practical activities. For example, ethnomethodology has examined turn-taking in conversation, that is, how the sequence of talk and expectations it raises shape the next move by a speaker. Garfinkel also con-structed a series of "breaching experiments" whereby experimenters violated rules of games like tic-tac-toe or refused to share the presuppositions behind everyday activities like the reference of simple remarks in conversation. Besides anger and frustration, participants exhibited the myriad methods and procedures by which we all maintain the meaningful order of normal activities: correcting and explaining the mistakes of others, making further assumptions, re-construing the appropriate context, and so on, all of which "make sense" of even a senseless situation.

The main theoretical result of these observations and experiments was that they illuminated the usefulness of the concept of "accountability," processes by which competent members of a setting make their actions intelligible and identifiable to themselves and to others. Garfinkel compares such methods to instructions and recipes. Social science "should treat knowledge and the procedures that societal members use for its assembly, test, management and transmission."[43] Such knowledge and procedures for gender instructions, for example, are discovered in the case study of Agnes, a transsexual who so closely observes the details of the production and maintenance of gender identity that her knowledge is equivalent to that gained by the social scientist in documentary observation.

The reference to actual procedures and methods implies a rejection of "traditional" sociological methodology and its employment of ideal types. A typical argument given by ethnomethodologists is that such idealized models are insufficiently empirical and ignore the specific features of the activity and situation in question. Hence, formal–logical models are of no use in analyzing the "observability of reasoning" in actual occasions and situations, and in this respect ethnomethodological studies of activities in scientific laboratories have challenged idealized models typical of empiricist philosophy of science.[44] At the same time, Garfinkel wants to deny that ethnomethodology privileges the participants' subjective point of view. Using phenomenological terms, its descriptive method "brackets" all such questions of value and rational adequacy. Sacks and Garfinkel call this "ethnomethodological indifference,"[45] by which the observer tries to become an ethnographer of everyday life. Garfinkel asserts that such analyses can disclose features of our practices that have previously been "seen but unnoticed." This proviso does not so much deny as redescribe what is privileged in the agent's point of view: rather than look at norms and values, the ethnomethodologists take at face value the methods and procedures as they "do work" in social settings and are available to reflective social actors. Later I will have occasion to call into question such a claim to "indifference," but it is this non-ironic, detailed and non-corrective notion of description that makes up the core of the basic pattern of ethnomethodological explanation. This pattern can most easily be discerned in one of the better documented types of case studies in ethnomethodology: conversational analysis and its use of documentary techniques. Unlike the pattern of rational choice explanation, here the statements will resemble steps or instructions.

The Explanatory Pattern of Ethnomethodology

(1) Fully describe the action and its context. Actions and interactions must be described in full circumstantial detail. Nothing is left out or deemed irrelevant, and all variations are to be considered.
(2) Establish the framework for accountability. The reflexive framework in which actors make their actions intelligible should be made explicit (as, for example, how speakers account for errors so as to maintain a "reality in common").
(3) Analyze the formal and stable features of the setting. These features show how the situation is produced and organized (as, for example, "adjacency pairs" in sequences of talk).

The first two instructions set forth Garfinkel's version of the symmetry principle – namely, that "both the production of conduct and its interpretation are accountable products of a common set of methods and procedures."[46] The third states the desired result: an identifiable pattern of interaction or set of structural features that makes the action and its context intelligible and is itself part of the framework in which it is produced, a resource upon which actors can draw to produce and account for aspects of the situation.

A simple (perhaps too simple) example of the employment of this pattern can be seen in the greeting–response pair in conversation. We may take it to be the "core case" for this research program. Upon being greeted by someone, some response is expected; the interpretive framework of the actors demands that failure to return a greeting be explained, and a competent speaker is equipped with a whole range of accounts when this occurs. If the initial greeting is not returned, alternate interpretations and courses of action are necessary and the situation is reflexively altered accordingly. This formal structure of social greetings is not simply a rule or norm to which actors passively conform, but a framework for action and interpretation, for accountability.

A richer example of the pattern for a more obvious explanatory purpose is Lawrence Wieder's study of a half-way house for drug offenders.[47] The offenders, Wieder argues, use a "code" to construct an account for their actions. This framework insists on non-cooperation with the professional staff. With this interpretive framework, the offenders effectively resist the goals of the program; even the staff uses the framework to explain actions. In this way, the code is not a set of explicit rules but instead is a loose set of practical maxims that identifies and evaluates certain types of actions and that shapes and maintains the institutional boundaries of the house. Wieder's explanation of the failure of the staff programs in terms of the "code" is a good application of Garfinkel's symmetry principle: it shows how actors both produce and interpret their activities in a framework that structures subsequent interactions.

Even before various wide-ranging empirical studies established the fruitfulness of this pattern, Garfinkel's polemics against other approaches put forward far-reaching claims for the documentary method and the explanatory pattern of context accountability. Garfinkel's criticisms of "traditional" sociology have a ring similar to Winch's exclusivist methodology of rules as a replacement for empiricist causality. Garfinkel's writings and those of other ethnomethodologists are filled with claims such as the following one, which was part of a conclusion drawn from the study of how Agnes maintained "natural" gender identity in interacting with "normals": "We learned from Agnes ... that members' practices alone produce the observable–tellable normal sexuality of persons, entirely and exclusively in actual singular, particular occasions through actual witnessed displays of common talk and conduct."[48] Although it seems quite strong, such a claim made about the results of this study is rather ambiguous. On the one hand, it is clear that gender identity falls within the explanatory pattern of describing contexts and frameworks for intelligible action. Agnes is a knowledgeable actor, manipulating the precise demands of gender roles and expectations in order to produce a feminine identity. On the other hand, Garfinkel is claiming much more than simply that gender is performed by the actor and subject to the accountability of others. Like overly ambitious statements about rule following or utility maximization, this methodological statement resembles a tautology, since "observable–tellable" gender identity could occur nowhere else but in occasions of public display and talk. But Garfinkel argues here and in many other places that his studies show *all* aspects of social order to be a contingent and context-dependent accomplishment: he says that *all* social explanation should be confined to such actual occasions, and gender here is only an instance of a general feature of all social order as such. What Knorr-Cetina calls "methodological situationalism" has now been made into an empirical postulate about the status of the whole social domain, much like Winch's claims about rule-governedness. The contingency and contextuality of phenomena are definitive features, since they are "moment by moment" accomplishments. Institutions and rules have no reality outside of their "actual occasion," so that "every feature of sense, of fact, of method, for every particular case of inquiry without exception, is the managed accomplishment of organized settings of practical action,"[49] from witchcraft to mathematics. Scientific facts, too, have no reality outside of the social networks and setting of those actors who construct them.[50]

What is the force of such claims? Does this verificationist argument in any way exclude the possibility of other accounts that have some empirical reference? To return to Wieder's case study: why can't the interactions between client and staff be seen as moves within a strategic game governed by conflicting preferences and resources? If the latter is possible, then every feature of the facticity of the half-way house setting is not the contingent accomplishment of accountable actions; rather, the institution sets a distribution of resources and interest positions. If the validity of a theory depends on its completely covering all aspects of the phenomena being explained, then both ethnomethodology and rational choice theory do not succeed. However, the problem lies not so much in the structure of the theory as in the self-understanding of theorists like Garfinkel and Becker. In this case, both approaches obtain, but explain different aspects and dimensions of the strategic action going on under the constraints of the half-way house's normative order.

Ethnomethodology fails to be an exclusive and complete research program, particularly since some of the features of a situation may not be dependent on sense-making activities or may be one of their unintended consequences. There is no reason to believe that statement 1 of the pattern could capture all of the interrelationships of actions past and present without further guidance from theories with a larger scope. Even within the context of occasions of interactions, rational choice theory might offer a very different description of the context – not of the "code" as an accounting framework, as statement 2 here demands, but as an equilibrium point in a game. By looking at its explanatory pattern, we can see not only the limits of the contextualism of the ethnomethodological program, but also that its strong methodological claims are hardly warranted by its actual successes in explaining all forms of social order contingently.

The Theory of Communicative Action

Unlike the previous two patterns, Habermas's theory of communicative action is not formulated to be methodologically exclusive or to provide theoretically complete coverage of the whole domain of social action in light of one type of core case. Since Habermas's aim is comprehensiveness, he eschews the sort of legislative methodological restrictions and epistemological assumptions that we found common to Winch, Becker, and Garfinkel. Indeed, Habermas's program does not require any hidden assumptions about the unity of method or any essentialist descriptions of what makes an action "social," the typical gambits of some anti-naturalists. In this respect, Habermas is more of a post-empiricist who takes as his organizing principle the empirical diversity of human actions. Nonetheless, he still holds that the full range of actions can be brought together in a comprehensive theory that supports and extends a basic pattern of explanation. Like the other two research programs, the theory of communicative action emphasizes the central role of rationality in explaining social action. Unlike rational choice theory and like ethnomethodology, the notion of rationality employed here is richer and more practical and at the same time cast in more social and less subjective terms.

Many critics, including Elster and Sen, have noted how narrow and "thin" the standard concept of rationality in much social science is and how its one-sided assumptions about utility maximization reduce the explanatory power and scope of rational choice theory. Based on its minimal requirements of consistency, both bizarre and cruel actions count as "rational." Furthermore, these same requirements are too minimal to explain most collective phenomena, as problems related to social choice and collective action have shown. A broader, "thicker" concept of rationality is needed to explain a wider range of phenomena that do not fit the conditions of the pattern of rational choice theory. Habermas calls this broader concept "communicative rationality," which he defines in relation to knowledge rather than psychological states. Rationality, he argues, does not refer to the truth or possession of knowledge *per se*, but has to do with "how speaking and acting subjects acquire and use knowledge" in actions and utterances.[51] Each type of action has its own rational orientation: for example, strategic actions are oriented to success, while communicative actions are oriented to mutual understanding. Both are part of a theory that elaborates a comprehensive concept of rationality that explains a broad range of social actions, rather than one that extends the specific requirements of one type of action to all others as in the case of game theory's focus on strategic action. This recognition of different forms and dimensions of rationality resolves both theoretical and methodological difficulties which plague the other research programs. Still, Habermas does not expect his complex and multifaceted theory to provide Neurathian closure for sociology.

Habermas's more multidimensional approach also contrasts with the assumptions of ethnomethodology. The latter's unrelenting contextualism leaves little room for idealizing, transsubjective features of rationality and knowledge: ethnomethodology collapses practical knowledge into occasions and settings of its use. Ethnomethodology does admit certain "transsituational features" that make contextual variation possible: not all contexts are unique, as can be seen by conventionally recognizable meanings. These features do not, however, imply context-independence. Habermas, on the contrary, makes central such idealizing, counterstructural features, actions, and practices that cannot be exhausted by descriptions of specific contexts and occasions.[52] Indeed, Habermas regards this sort of knowledge as part of the reflexive character of social action; its idealizing presuppositions permit actors a sufficiently critical distance for them to suspend the boundaries of contexts and situations in second-order reflection. Such reflection on contexts themselves, which makes them accessible and alterable, is part of discursive or communicative rationality, a critical capacity for reflection on interaction much like the second-order dispositions and capacities Sen presupposes in his idea of ranking preference rankings. Just as Sen argues that second-order reflection belies that we are "rational fools," the critical distance afforded by communication about communication permits us not to be "situational dopes." Habermas calls such second-order uses of communicative competence "discourses," in this case "practical discourse" about the principles, norms, and values commonly presupposed in interaction. Similarly, a theoretical discourse employs these same idealizing, reflective presuppositions and suspends the contextual features of action to inquire into the correctness of claims about the truth of our knowledge, including the context-transcendent features of social scientific theorizing and explanations. Habermas's theory of rationality and of rational action has the added reflexive feature of being able to show how social scientific knowledge is the discursive employment and testing of the same sort of capacities that knowledgeable actors have in their everyday activities. A broader theory of such second-order rationality can yield an explanatory pattern of quite wide scope, one that is particularly applicable in formal and institutional settings like science, law, and politics.

This expansion of the idea of rationality requires that it no longer be conceived in terms of the traditional triadic relation between beliefs, desires, and actions that characterized explanations of intentional action in rational choice theory. Habermas's analysis of action is social rather than individualistic; it explains social actions in terms of shared knowledge and understandings. Even explanations of intentional actions must refer to more than

subjective beliefs and desires. Rather, they must also refer to both
the *explicit* reasons which actors give to justify their actions to
others and the implicit presuppositions and abilities that together
make up actors' knowledge. Without reference to both features,
the action remains unintelligible and inexplicable. On the one
hand, the implicit presuppositions and abilities provide the shared
context for the action, which the theorists can analyze and make
explicit. On the other hand, the explicit reasons make sense of this
particular action, its goals, purposes, and justification. In Habermas's
terms, it is necessary to distinguish between (implicit) "lifeworld"
contributions and (explicit) "discursive reasons," between the im-
mense number of shared presuppositions and those brought into
play and thematized in a particular action. His theory of communicative action attempts to discover the structure of such implicit
and reflective knowledge required for the competent performance
of each type of action, each with its own goals, presuppositions,
and reflexive justification. Such an analysis introduces explanatory
possibilities of actors' knowledge that are not available on the
assumption of either fixed preferences or context-specific procedures: it can explain the way in which agents can also transform
their situations or their beliefs and desires. Such transformations
are perhaps the core cases of communicative rationality: shared
understanding can become problematic, and the implicit justifications of a culture can be tested in argumentation in situations of
conflict. Such problems in interaction initiate what Habermas calls
social learning processes, in which the process of acquiring and
using knowledge transforms identities and contexts. The rationality of an action is manifested in cases where its justification becomes explicit, in the capacity of agents to conduct discourses
about its reasons and assumptions which go beyond both preferences
of the agent and demands of the context.

To capture the multiplicity of social actions and their forms of
rationality, Habermas distinguishes four action types, whereby each
type of action is connected to a particular type of knowledge and
to the general features of the type of rationality specific to it. He
analyzes the presuppositions of each type of action by arranging
them in order of increasing complexity: teleological, normative,
dramaturgical, and communicative action. Communicative action
is the most comprehensive and hence the basis of the theory of
action as a whole, since in it actors must employ all the presuppositions of the other types of action in order to engage com-
petently and rationally in the full range of interaction with each
other.

In *The Theory of Communicative Action*, Habermas analyses

these presuppositions in terms of relations between actors and the world; he calls these relations "formal world concepts" which denote the "ontological assumptions" or common reference points for each type of action. Teleological action presupposes only an objective world, into which the actor makes goal-oriented interventions. Normative action presupposes the social world, a set of values and norms to which an actor may appeal in order to make her action legitimate. Dramaturgical action presupposes a subjective world, a world of feelings and desires to which the actor has privileged access. Finally, communicative action requires that the actor coordinate all three in order to reach consensus with other actors about cooperative plans in all dimensions of interaction.

A closer look at this concept of formal worlds reveals that it is misleading to characterize it as "ontological," or even as a referential field in which action takes place. In each case, its analytic function is epistemological, showing the type of knowledge presupposed by actors and the resources available to them to underwrite a form of "objectivity" (or intersubjective validity) for each action type, should the action fail or require justification by other agents. Each formal world refers to a type of knowledge which competent actors can use to correct subjective and cultural errors built into the action situation. Hence, this formal analysis refers to the reflexive possibilities for learning and for rational assessment implicit in the structure of each type of action. For example, self-expression in dramaturgical action may be insincere and untruthful, even though it is the actor alone who knows this directly and others only infer it from subsequent behavior. These possibilities for rational assessment can then become the topic for reflection in various forms of discourse about action, assessments that are not rational merely in reference to revealed preferences or to specific contexts. These modes of assessment are the tools by which competent agents not only understand and evaluate actions, but also explain them as well. They make clear how the reflective capacities of agents can be incorporated into explanations which do not have agents ruled by their own fixed preferences and social settings. Habermas therefore offers a pattern for what Weber called "rational explanation," starting from idealizing assumptions that provide the formal–rational structure of each action type.

Explanatory Pattern for Communicative Action

(1) Actions can be identified according to standard features of an ideal type which is specified in terms of a number of possible basic

orientations (for example, orientations to success, understanding and so on).

(2) The analysis of the ideal type reveals actors' presuppositions, including the action's formal structure and the knowledge required for its competent performance (as developed in the concept of formal worlds).

(3) The formal–typical idealizations of the theory are then tested and used heuristically to analyze action: the actual, empirical case is examined to see the extent to which the action is typical or all of its presuppositions are met (including, for example, whether a particular culture or actor at a certain developmental stage possesses the presupposed cognitive resources).

(4) In light of 1, 2, and 3, the rationality of the action is evaluated in a virtual, reflexive discourse about the reasons offered by actors to justify what they are doing, revealing and testing discrepancies between agents' knowledge and their actual activity, and between agents' self-descriptions and the theorist's explanations.

The basic problem with this program is whether or not its highly formal premises (statements 1 and 2) can be made fruitful in explaining actual social actions (statement 3) and then verified in a public discourse (statement 4). Before evaluating the potential fruitfulness of this pattern, let me give an illustration of the way the statements fit together as a pattern: Habermas's analysis of utterances, or speech as a social action.

For Habermas, utterances are linguistic actions, and each action type involves a different aspect of language use. The medium of language can be used to perform a whole range of actions, where each type of action must be analyzed separately. Habermas can incorporate the insights of rational choice theory by showing how certain utterances use language to achieve certain goals in influencing one's alter (ego), such as "getting someone to form a belief or intention."[53] The insights of ethnomethodology can be incorporated into an analysis of norm-guided action, in which language can be used to build up standardized sequences of action; these same insights are important to dramaturgical action in which the self is presented and constructed with and by others. But neither of these theories are adequate for capturing the reflective aspects of communication, by which agents interpret and justify their actions to achieve mutual understanding. While rational choice theory can only understand language use strategically, ethnomethodology cannot grasp the way in which communication takes place not only within a certain context but can thematize and alter such contexts. Both theories, in effect, ignore what is unique to communicative action and to discourse about communicative actions. Hence, the distinction of action types plays a crucial role in the account of utterances, cutting short any attempt to reduce all language use to one sort of action or another.

The second statement of the pattern developed above requires as complete an analysis as possible of the cognitive presuppositions for competent action of various types. For example, strategic action requires some truthful knowledge, such that agents can bring about a state of affairs in the world. Successful strategic intervention with others presupposes that agents are "cognitively so equipped that for them not only physical objects but also decision-making entities can appear in the world."[54] In norm-guided action, actors presuppose a shared social world with recognizable norms and values that may establish justifiable claims. As speakers in communicative action, agents are able to use the structure of speech acts to reach understanding with others, when they make good on the assumption that other agents can reflectively offer reasons to justify reasons that warrant their actions. Explanations that focus only on teleological and contextual features of action cannot account for such cases.

Once the analysis of ideal types and their formal presuppositions is complete, their actual employment must be tested and the empirical deviations from these models described. Against ethnomethodology, Habermas sees ideal types as part of a broad range of theoretical analyses, useful for uncovering highly general, formal features of social actions common to very many contexts. Rather than being simply formal and hence abstract, the idealizing assumptions of the theory must be continuous with those that competent speakers and actors actually make in concrete social situations; for example, that speakers mean the same thing in nearly identical utterances is not empirically true, but is an idealized assumption that speakers make in order to communicate. Statement 3 in this pattern clearly sees ideal types as a methodological device that reveals formal structure. Each type is only a summary of the result of formal analysis. As opposed to Garfinkel, Habermas sees such idealizations as part of the agent's own reflexive ability to engage in rational actions and to judge the actions of others. Once such an ideal and formal analysis is complete, the next empirical task "consists in reversing step by step the strong idealizations" by which the theory of action was constructed.[55] For example, if an agreement is formed in an actual public discourse, it must be arrived at in a coercion-free manner if it is to be rational: everyone must have an equal chance to express needs, make claims, and raise objections.[56] If scientists who doubt the current theory are unable to publish and express their views publicly, it is doubtful that any agreement arrived at under such conditions is rational, or establishes the truth of the theory, except accidentally. If these ideal conditions are not met and yet are presupposed by the social activity of public discourse, the theorist can "reverse" these idealizations until we arrive at something like the actual situation of discourse in a particular society. This process reveals structural features of the institutions that make agreements formed in them open to normative objections; it also explains why the limits on communication in scientific institutions might help to maintain current beliefs. Similarly, the communication in political institutions may not be oriented to reaching understanding but may only maintain relations of power and domination that subvert their goals and violate the idealizing presuppositions of real discourse on practical decisions, including symmetry between speakers and reciprocity in chances to speak.

Statement 4 serves not only for the verification of the theory, but also establishes the explanatory link between action and knowledge. This knowledge is not merely contextual or implicit knowledge, as in the case of ethnomethodology. Rather, its core hypothesis is that reflexive social actors engage in certain activities because they find certain reasons to be compelling and legitimate grounds for acting. For example, obeying a king's commands requires the actor's recognition that a certain reason (monarchical authority) and discourse (usually theological) is legitimate and convincing. This recognition is a condition of participation in certain institutions and is part of the integrative effect of the institutional framework for action. As actors learn and begin to test such reasons when presented with certain social problems and crises, a whole type of reason can be devalued and thus no longer serves to motivate rational agreement. Preferences, values, procedures, and contexts can all be modified by reflective and knowledgeable agents. At this point, large-scale changes in institutions can be brought about by actors. Such discourse "generalizes, abstracts, and stretches the presuppositions of context-bound communicative action."[57] Within a given institution in the same continuous culture, participants may be motivated by the legitimating reasons produced in a discourse at one historical juncture and not so motivated at another. Such innovations are simply unintelligible on contextualist assumptions. Habermas holds that such "devaluative effects" can be made the basis for a theory of social learning and evolution on a developmental model for collectivities much like Piaget and Kohlberg's model for individuals.

Such learning processes make actors themselves not only able to identify what reasons motivate themselves and others, but also to evaluate and change them, even as they form a shared context for social action.

By making the evaluative and discursive aspects of reflexive competence theoretically explicit, Habermas's theory of communicative action has critical implications built into its explanatory pattern. Habermas can contrast standard and deviant forms of communication, just as rational choice theory can show certain beliefs to be deviant and irrational. Besides his theory of social evolution which traces learning processes from one type of reason to another, on a more formal level Habermas elaborates a theory of distorted communication to discuss such deviant cases as self-deception and agreements formed under the influence of power and domination. I will develop this normative theory further in chapter 5. Here I want to show how it employs each of the basic statements of the pattern. First, the ideal type of communicative action permits an explanation of why some cases of communication succeed and others do not, as in the case where strategic components undermine conditions of success for mutual understanding. Second, such deviant cases can be shown to violate formal presuppositions of communicative action, often without the actor's awareness. When so violated, agreements reached in attempting to achieve mutual understanding can be called into question by agents who doubt their validity. Third, neither such actions nor such agreements can be justified in discourses about reasons and typically occur in contexts with strong barriers to such reflection.

Such idealizations are said to present an insufficiently flexible characterization of rational agency: ideal actors all do the same thing. In this explanatory pattern, however, there are a number of different levels of indeterminacy. First, as with many cognitively oriented theories, it employs a basic distinction between competence and performance. As Chomsky's concept of linguistic competence shows, the competence of speakers and actors does not uniquely determine the correct action or utterance; competence permits a wide range of variability. Second, the reflexive relation between action and discourse is itself indeterminate, insofar as agents can call into question cultural schemata and the acceptability of given norms. Third, the pattern treats action as potentially transformative, whether cognitively in learning processes or practically in changing the situation itself – that is, its social conditions and its presuppositions. In this respect, it treats actions as indeterminate and transformable in ways that are not accounted for within the other explanatory patterns.

What distinguishes Habermas's method of theory construction from that of the other two research programs is that it attempts to be comprehensive rather than exclusive. The exclusivist theories of the other programs operate at different levels: rational choice tries to cover all rational action by the substantive hypothesis that it is always utility maximizing; ethnomethodology does so through the methodological postulate of a "situationalism" that is justified by a naive form of verificationism. Habermas's program is both multidimensional and comprehensive, organizing the different rational features of diverse types of action into a unified pattern. His theory fulfills the requirement of a post-empiricist reconstruction of explanations of rational action. Such a theory achieves rigor without sacrificing the multiplicity of explanatory factors or the reflexive indeterminacy of rational action. This same comprehensiveness also permits one to make theoretical connections between rational action on the one hand and collective structures (such as institutions) and historical processes (such as social change) on the other, both of which seem excluded from view in the other programs. The problem of such a theory is to develop the empirical strength of these connections and not to deny, like Winch, their possibility in advance.

In order to judge the adequacy of various patterns, the best strategy is to analyze their differing explanations of a common phenomena. Perhaps the best such case study is the analysis of rules and what it means for an action to "follow a rule."

Testing Patterns of Explaining Rational Action: Rules

If these patterns have explanatory power, then Winch's claim that meaningful action is "*ipso facto* rule-governed" is clearly false. On close examination, few areas of social life are actually governed by explicit rules, the kind of rules that make games and sacred rituals what they are: special, well-defined interactions. Furthermore, there is such a variety of different instances of action and language use that may be called rule-governed in a looser sense that it is unlikely that all of them can be made to fit a single concept. David Lewis is correct in arguing that the idea of a rule is "a messy cluster concept" with many different senses.[58] Baker and Hacker go further, finding not just a cluster but instead a jumble that does not seem useful in explaining social activity.[59] As I have argued against Winch, rules do not determine social action, and agents do not very often conform to them without exception. It is equally true that almost all societies have some rules, such as taboos, that are not open to exceptions and negotiation and that apply to everyone in all situations, as Edgerton points out; yet, even these rules cannot determine all contingencies.[60] Once this complexity and diversity of rules and rule following is recognized, rules can be explanatory factors that fit into one of the patterns developed in the previous section. But do rules have a role in these explanations, or do these patterns explain rules themselves?

If the argument of both this chapter and the last is correct, then the diverse phenomena designated as rule following fit into a variety of different explanations. If reasons are not determining, then neither are rules when they function as reasons. The different types of rules test the limits of the different patterns and the claims of the various research programs.

In the explanatory pattern of rational choice theory, explicit rules must be explained as intentional, that is, in terms of the goals or purposes the agent pursues in following a rule. Rule-like patterns of behavior might also be the unintended effects of individual utility-maximizing behavior; in that case, they need not be recognized as explicit "rules." Moreover, rule following must be rational in a utility-maximizing sense and hence caused by consistent beliefs and desires. According to the Hobbesian variant of the social contract tradition, the only category of rules that can fulfill these desiderata are what David Lewis calls conventions: intentional agreements and regularities of behavior which express a common preference and coordinate actions according to expected outcomes. The typical case of such a convention is driving on the left or right side of the road. Either rule will do, so long as we can expect that it will be followed in the future. No one will be better off by acting contrary to what others are doing: because everyone wants to get where they are going safely, one or the other rule will be an equilibrium state for rational actors. Conventions are explained in rational choice theory as "coordination equilibria," a regular pattern of behavior that satisfies the interests and preferences of each actor. They may function with or without explicit agreement, although each actor expects that others will behave in a certain way for a convention to exist. Thus, conventions are the solutions to certain coordination games in everyday life. Lewis quotes Hume's example of two rowers in a boat who fall into a smooth rhythm and develop the expectation that the other will keep to it. In light of the interests of each known to both, the actions of each come to "have a reference to the other, and are performed on the supposition that something is to be performed upon the other part."[61] Hobbes thought that even self-interested, "vainglorious," and asocial creatures like ourselves could arrive at stable conventions in the state of nature. But these unenforced "laws of nature" are eventually insufficient and rational creatures begin to construct stronger rules: they will bargain away lawless liberty for peace, commodious living, and artificially con-structed social order. They will be enforced by a sovereign, who sanctions those who violate these stronger rules out of self-interest.

Lewis's defining condition for the existence of a convention may be used to specify when the rational choice model may explain rule-following. Conventions exist if people conform to them be-cause they believe that others will. Lewis sets out the specific conditions for conventions in terms of preferences and beliefs:

> A regularity R in the behavior of members of a population P when they are agents in a recurrent situation S is a convention if and only if it is true that, and it is common knowledge that, in any instance of S among members of P: (1) everyone conforms to R; (2) everyone expects everyone else to conform to R; (3) everyone prefers to conform to R on the condition that others do, since S is a coordi-nation problem and uniform conformity to R is a coordination equilibrium in S.[62]

Lewis does not mean conformity in any law-like sense, since it is the beliefs and preferences of the agents which cause conformity to R, not the convention itself. Conventions also permit a range of actions within certain constraints; no convention determines every detail of behavior or simply eliminates all alternatives. This de-scription fits all of the conditions for applying the explanatory pattern of rational choice theory; it does seem to explain the persistence of some of the conventional aspects of social life. Indeed, the more arbitrary and unenforced the convention, the better suited to this type of explanation it is. Certain coordination problems are solved by some explicit agreement or widely recog-nized expectation, no matter what it is, so long as it is regularly observed and a common preference exists to resolve the problem.

However, as rational choice theorists recognize, not all rules are solutions to coordination problems and not all social situations approximate S, the solution to a coordination game. Some rational choice theorists attempt to generalize the notion that rules emerge out of different choice situations. Following some rules requires the commitment of time and resources: while driving on one side of the road or the other might go on even in the absence of sanctions, speed limits are followed only if they are enforced. One can better fulfill one's preferences by being a "free rider": so long as the rule is generally followed by others, an actor receives all the benefits with none of the costs. Sanctions and incentives are one solution, but they, too, are costly, and require that others sanction not only those that do not conform but also those that do not sanction, increasing costs even more.[63] Hardin and Axelrod have argued that repeated decisions or "iterated plays" within the prisoners' dilemma situation show the long-term rationality of cooperating.[64] While this result is formally true, it may not accurately describe most social situations in which strategic and self-interested agents interact. If each agent is sufficiently self-interested, repeated plays may not occur and the game as a whole breaks down. The possibility of such repetition needs to be explained on grounds other than those supplied by coordination equilibria or by maximizing choice. Even sanctioned rules would not be carried out unless agents had independent, non-self-interested and impersonal reasons for enforcing them (since enforcing is not necessarily utility maximizing). Social norms to which strong obligations and sanctions are attached would be difficult to explain on maximizing assumptions, except perhaps as irrational or quaint. But a reflective agent who considers alternative rankings for his or her preferences might be able to make judgments about the justice or legitimacy of such norms for each and for all and observe them despite the costs.

This difficulty can be illustrated by the inadequacies of various attempts to explain rules or norms other than conventions in terms of maximizing behavior. For all the weaknesses of Parsons' own positive account of norms and social order, he is correct that the Hobbesian solution to these difficulties, the sanctions of "force and fraud," cannot create a social order stable enough for even conventional rule following. Such stability is a consequence of rule following and is not caused by agents maximizing their own utility, even as an unintended consequence. Once an order stable enough to permit repeated interaction is in place, then it can become clear that following rules in the long run may be utility maximizing for all agents (including themselves). This consequence of rules entails that utility maximization does not explain their emergence; it comes into play only if stability can be assumed in interactions between utility maximizing agents. Even a coercive sovereign cannot create a stable order, since then it is difficult to explain how such a person or institution comes to possess so many resources among utility maximizers. Thus, the other types of norms cannot be explained by agents' preferences or practical rationality; however, once a system of norms already exists, some behavior within it can be explained in these terms. At the same time, some regularities that appear to be coordination equilibria can be explained better as the result of force rather than rationality. The Irish do not speak English in order to solve their own co-ordination problems, but as the result of military force and cultural domination that created a coordination problem for the English. In this case, the convention serves as a coordination mechanism for the dominant group's purposes and fails on Lewis's criteria (3) to meet everyone's preferences; for that reason, although it functions as a convention and is not often enforced, it does need sanctions by institutions like schools and courts.

In *The Emergence of Norms*, Ullmann-Margalit tries to explain various types of norms other than conventions ("coordination norms") in terms of the rational choice model of explanation. These include "prisoners' dilemma norms" and "norms of partiality," each denoting the type of recurrent choice situation out of which different norms are generated. The problem posed by "p-d structured situations" is "that of protecting an unstable yet jointly beneficial state of affairs from deteriorating, so to speak, into a stable yet jointly destructive one,"[65] perhaps a truce in the arms-race situation discussed above. Such rules are norms of cooperation within the framework of utility maximizing rationality. But the beneficial results of cooperation are a consequence of repeated and stable interaction, and not its cause; they do not explain the stability. Indeed, the longer the interaction and the greater the benefits of it, the more likely cooperation is to "deteriorate" on the utility-maximizing grounds, as when one nation knows it possesses superior resources for a potential arms race. Further assumptions about agents' rationality or about already existing institutions are necessary if the initial "p-d situation" is itself comprehensible on the theory's own terms. Similar objections can be raised against Ullmann-Margalit's treatment of "norms of partiality." They are generated out of a "status quo of inequality," in which the disfavorably placed have a rational interest in improving their position and the favored in keeping it the way it is. Norms of partiality serve to maintain the status quo and hence to "promote the interests of the party favored by the inequality."[66] On rational grounds, it is difficult to establish why it is that the disfavored party would conform to such norms. Indeed, in this case, the situation is unstable, if the less well off have practical rationality; the adherence to such norms can best be explained in terms of cognitive dissonance and other forms of irrationality, as Elster has done in his rational choice extension of the theory of ideology. Such norms cannot be explained if everyone in the choice situation is a utility-maximizing, rational agent. Once again, however, utility maximization has not explained the causes of either type of norm, anymore than it really explained the marriage choices in Becker's analysis. On the whole, rational choice explanations of rules and norms are adequate only with respect to conventions that are intentionally caused and explicitly recognized as such. The explanations of other rules or norms as the unintended consequence of utility-maximizing behavior often must assume the stable institutional order it seeks to explain.

Ethnomethodology starts from quite a different analysis of rules: no matter how detailed a rule is, ethnomethodologists argue, it is never determinate enough to be a "systematic regularity" of the sort Lewis claims for conventions. Like Wittgenstein, ethnomethodologists are fond of pointing out the many variations of following what seems to be the "same" rule. Rules do not simply regulate behavior, as Lewis would have it, but provide interpretive frameworks in which meaningful behavior takes place. They do not "merely regulate action in 'preexisting' circumstances; they are constitutive of the sense of the circumstances, of 'what the circumstances are' in the first place."[67] Ethnomethodologists argue that the predefined situation S and regularity R of Lewis's account are fictions. Rules are not "conformed to" but instead elaborated upon, interpreted, and transformed; we can indeed change the rules and reconstitute the situation of which we are a part. Rules represent frameworks in which skillful actors negotiate and maintain their common understandings. Rules are never fully explicit or algorithmically applicable; they are full of "et cetera clauses," of room for *ad hoc* modification by knowledgeable subjects who make choices that others can hold them accountable for, since they are the result of practical reasoning in concrete situations. On this view, neither conformity to conventions nor preferences explains how people act with reference to social rules; passive conformity and standardized expectations cannot explain how competent actors deal with the diversity and contingencies of social situations.[68]

Such constitutive rules are not the hypothetical imperatives of rational choice but instead are frameworks in which actors account for what they and others do. The analysis of this framework is the job of statement 2 of the explanatory pattern of ethnomethodology, in which rules are seen as an ongoing, openended accomplishment. We can hold others accountable for departures from a rule, and do so even if the actor is not aware of violating it. If I do not return a greeting, my action is interpreted as fitting within the indeterminate pattern of reasons and mistakes that typically accompany this situation: I am angry, distracted, etc.[69] These et cetera clauses to the rules are not like the *ceteris paribus* clauses of causal indeterminacy. Rather, they are never filled in and can never be completed, but only reflexively applied and elaborated. Because of the reflexive character of rules, Garfinkel argues that the rational properties of social activities cannot "be assessed, recognized or categorized, described by using a rule or standard obtained outside actual settings within which such properties are recognized, used, produced, and talked about by the setting's members."[70] The framework used for accountability is itself produced by members' performances, and this theoretical postulate becomes the justification for Garfinkel's verificationism, in this instance applied to rules.

Habermas shares with ethnomethodology an interpretive concept of rules without buying into such methodological restrictions. By comparison, Garfinkel's concept of rules is not complex or multi-faceted enough; it is too inclusive and often generalizes particular cases over all types of rules. In the sentence quoted in the paragraph above, Garfinkel puts all manner of rules on the same footing. In the theory of communicative action, different types of rules and actors' relations to them need to be distinguished. Habermas tries to capture both the contextual and idealizing features of rules and rule-guided action. Indeed, reflective agents themselves may be able to distinguish between norms on the one hand and values on the other. Both can be implicit presuppositions in communicative action, as agents come to an agreement about how to coordinate their actions in light of them; both can also be explicit points of reference in a discourse when asked for a justification of an action and hence can figure as reasons for action. Thus, values and norms have both contextual and idealizing features. Where they differ as rules is in their epistemic character and social function. "Cultural values embodied and fused in the totalities of life forms and life histories permeate the fabric of the communicative practice of everyday life through which the individual's life is shaped and his identity secured."[71] Because of their function in preserving identity, values are called into question by crises of various sorts, a distancing experience that is "of another sort than the distance of a norm-testing participant in discourse from the facticity of existing institutions."[72] The function of norms is to legitimize particular institutions and to solve problems of interpersonal conflict. They, too, can be merely implicit in the ongoing course of interaction; however, norms become explicit when actors take a critical distance from this ongoing social life and publicly reflect upon and justify their beliefs and interests from the point of view of claims and expectations that others may have. This type of discursive activity is not situationally specific and contextually limited; indeed, the very capacity to distinguish norms from values, justice from the good life, requires a certain capacity of the agent to abstract herself from her culture and life history. At this level of competence, actors can not only elaborate a practice, as Garfinkel argues, but also change it. Both norms and values entail reasons for action and are conditions for the possibility of sharing a practice; the capacity for reflection means not only that agents are aware of such rules, but that they can demand justifications of them and modify them. Hence, ethnomethodology's methodological assumption that every explanatory feature is indexical limits its theoretical account of the reflexive character of action. Habermas's account of these different types of rules is similar in its open-ended character, but equips actors with a wider range of discursive and cognitive abilities to make judgments about the rules themselves and whether they ought to be accepted based on compelling reasons. Just as rules can stop proscribing actions, they can also cease to provide the framework for accountability, if the very type of accountability is called into question as illegitimate, unjust, or unfair.

For Habermas, typical social actions like voting and promising are guided by norms, which both explain and justify them. When I make a promise, I enter into an interpersonal relationship based on certain norms, which can be formulated as legitimate expectations. Competent agents know not only how to make promises, but also to judge their legitimacy; when these expectations are challenged or contested, agents have to enter into a discourse and reflect upon promising and the nature of the relationship established by such a communicative act. In the promises made in a setting like a marriage ceremony, such communication does not so much regulate the partners' future actions as define and constitute their relationship and expectations within a recognized institution. In some cases, however, rules do have a regulative function, although not in the sense of requiring precise uniformity in behavior. Such rules regulate behavior through the recognition of their validity, and with such a shared recognition actors form "generalized expectations" that others will act accordingly,[73] as in the case of one person, one vote; those who act otherwise and stuff the ballot boxes do so for strategic reasons that cannot be publicly avowed or shared within the institution of voting. The validity of such public expectations can be questioned and can lose their rationally motivating force for actors who have undergone certain experiences and have acquired certain types of knowledge. To function as reasons, rules must be cognitively acceptable relative to individual and collective forms of knowledge. In this case, the challenge to rules may be a challenge to the institution that is the larger context of its justification.

In this way, the theory of communicative action provides the framework for developing a comprehensive account of rules as explanatory factors within different action types. For strategic action, rules function to open the social space for maneuvering, delimit permissible alternatives, and serve as a resource that enables actors to achieve their ends. In dramaturgical action, they present a means of social expression, whether it be in conventional gestures or in their purposive violation. For norm-guided action, rules are generalized expectations that regulate actions according to the common recognition of their validity. In communicative action, they are open-ended and subject to interpretation and elaboration by the actors themselves, insofar as they are resources for achieving understanding. Second-order rules may emerge in discourses, including rules about public discussion and debate. Such rules function as non-local regulative ideals in the Kantian sense. They are neither conventional nor interpretive but part of the cognitive ability to judge and assess reasons publicly. Habermas argues that certain of these reflexive rules are universal and necessary, in that action of a certain type is inconceivable without them. Such a rule is, he argues, "so general that it cannot be replaced without a functional equivalent."[74] Certain structures and formal features of an action may be universal; these rule-like presuppositions may be made theoretically explicit in the standard cases of the theory. The violation of these presuppositions would then play a further explanatory role in explaining why some actions fail, or are deviant cases like "distorted communication." Such universal rules and structures are the general basis for the assessment of the rationality of an action.

In each research program, rules are used to explain the public, rational character of social life. Successful intentionalist explanations of rules as conventions show the conditions under which certain problems of social life can be solved: coordination games and their equilibria. Ethnomethodology shows how mutual understanding can be maintained in open-ended practical reasoning, where rules refer to frameworks of accountability. Each research program becomes problematic when it tries to extend its basic analysis of rules and norms to other types of phenomena; in doing so, they lose certain features of the rationality of rules. On the one hand, the overemphasis on intentionality in rational choice explanation entails the loss of the social context as an explanatory factor. On the other hand, the overemphasis on the contexts or settings in ethnomethodology obscures the role that regulative ideals and idealizing suppositions play in rule-governed social action and therefore impoverishes its notion of practical rationality. While these ideals presupposed in different types of action may no longer be legislative like Kant's categories, they do still regulate conduct and its interpretation, showing how certain ideal expectations govern many of our activities that are open to discursive reflection. Without this stronger and broader notion of rationality, it is hard to see how rules and norms are obligatory for knowledgeable agents, other than that they reflect our preferences or permit intelligible interaction to proceed. In his communicative ethics, Habermas wants to ground obligations cognitively in the minimal presuppositions of communicative action and discourse; communicative action entails the "unavoidable presupposition" of accepting the burden and constraint of justifying our actions publicly and reflexively. This obligation is "implicitly recognized" by competent actors as an idealizing assumption of engaging in communicative action.[75] Like Durkheim and Mead before him, Habermas wants to explain the obligatory character of norms as transcending individual self-interest; like Mead, Habermas sees public rationality as a potential achievement of communication – that is, the reflexive capacity to enter into a "universe of discourse" which "transcends any specific order."[76] The question which this view of moral obligation raises is, of course, the extent to which such a reflexive capacity is able to transcend interpretive and social contexts and initiate innovative learning at the cultural–structural level. I will address this question in the next chapter when I examine the character of interpretation in the social sciences.

A public conception of reason with strong normative and universal claims could be developed in cooperation with the social sciences through the concept of rules. However, it depends on a number of distinctions that Habermas tries to develop: namely, between *de facto* and ideal legitimacy, and between regulative and conventional rules. Such a universal and regulative concept of reason must be shown not only to be normative but also explanatory for discursive practices like science and morality. Among the phenomena to be explained by such a public, reflexive concept of reason and learning are the social sciences themselves, as an attempt to make theoretically explicit the contingent and non-contingent features of knowledgeable and competent actions. Social science is perhaps the best instance of the use of these abilities, since it is a discourse about the social conditions for the employment of practical and theoretical reason. Public reason in all its forms always has recourse to rules and to institutions in which unforeseen conflicts over their nature and meaning will be adjudicated and thereby become the occasion for social learning. In this regulative sense, science and law are rule-governed, formal institutions for learning and resolving the conflicts and problems that are a historical feature of social practices.

3

Interpretation and Indeterminacy

Winch's turn to rules was supposed to solve problems with narrowly causal explanations of social action. Simple intentional actions, he argued, make sense only if they are fit into a larger pattern of actions, that is, into the recognized rules of a shared form of life. But these rules, too, fit together into the larger patterns of cultural traditions and social relations, which themselves must be explained by a broad range of social and historical factors. While placing actions and rules in ever larger contexts enriches explanations of them, it also raises new problems of indeterminacy: in what of many possible contexts does the action belong? Which one best explains it? How do the actors themselves describe these contexts and patterns? It is precisely the attempt to conceptualize this larger context that led directly to renewed debates about the role of interpretation in the social sciences. In offering interpretations, social scientists usually fit an intentional action into larger sequences of actions and cultural contexts of significance. One of the fundamental questions of this chapter concerns how the new social theories can incorporate interpretations into their explanations and give some, if any, consideration to how actors make what they are doing intelligible to others.

As I argued in the last chapter, rules are only one aspect of the social contexts in which actions become identifiable. To adapt MacIntyre's example once again: the permissible move made within the constitutive rules of chess may be intelligible only in light of purposes embodied in some larger context (say, as a signal). The move may not be the utility-maximizing move in the context of the game and its rules, yet it is rational relative to this purpose and in this set of agreements. In this case, the "intelligibility of the action" – that is, how it fits into a larger pattern and sequence of actions – can be clarified only by referring to situations and purposes outside of the practice of the game itself. It is neither conformity to the rules of chess nor maximization relative to the current position of the game that makes it the action that it is. Still, the question of which one of many such larger contexts best makes sense of the action is now a question of interpretation: which of the various features of the action makes it intelligible to those performing it? How can we decide in any particular case, if those same features may have a different significance in a different context? Such multiplicity and indeterminacy demands that actions be constantly interpreted and reinterpreted as they unfold. Observers and participants alike constantly "make sense" with the multiple features of the contexts that they produce, find themselves in, and reshape.

Besides such multiple possibilities of indeterminate contexts and features, another reason that interpretation is necessary is the reflexivity of social action. Reflexivity permits thick, as opposed to thin, description.[1] We pass a group of people in a car, and someone raises her hand. Is it a greeting, a signal to stop, or a gesture in conversation? The gesture can be described "thinly" as the physical movement of her hand; the "thick" description of that movement as a signal to stop requires much more. Or, to use Gilbert Ryle's example: a twitch and a wink have the same "thin" description as a contraction of a muscle in the face. A wink in a public place acquires multiple possibilities of "thick" description or interpretation, depending on age, norms like sexual mores, and the type of locale in which the gesture takes place. As any traveller knows, gestures are intentional acts fraught with significance and are equivocal and easily misunderstood. This same indeterminacy multiplies when the social scientist also turns her attention to interpreting the gestures and expressions of members of alien cultures. In this case, the interpreter has to establish what these multiple possibilities are and hence "thickly" describe the action. As this example shows, certain social sciences like ethnography and history are constantly faced with problems of indeterminacy in dealing with culturally and historically distant peoples.

As happened after Winch's turn to rules, the realization that we are interpreting whenever we describe actions has led many to reject empirical and causal approaches entirely and announce that the social sciences have taken an "interpretive turn."[2] Indeed, post-empiricism finds interpretation even in the natural sciences, which are social and interpretive practices like any other.[3] But just as with the expansion of claims about rules, such extensive interpretive claims have met with skepticism, particularly about whether interpretations establish anything like rigorous knowledge. Many advocates of the interpretive turn embrace such skeptical consequences as part of the criticism of false claims to "objectivity" in the social and natural sciences. In this chapter, I will examine the source of such claims in the analysis of interpretation itself: in its indeterminacy and circularity, in what many have called the "hermeneutic circle." I will argue that the hermeneutic circle does not justify skepticism about the justification of social scientific knowledge. As a case study in this chapter, I will consider current debates between "post-modern" and "interpretive" approaches to cultural anthropology and, in particular, that between James Clifford and Clifford Geertz. My second case study comes from recent sociology of science, where "ethnographers" of science like Woolgar argue for skepticism about objective knowledge based on a view of the limits of interpretation similar to that of Clifford. Finally, Habermas's theory of social evolution provides a good example of interpretations that employ strong criteria of rationality.

First, I will return to the patterns of explanation developed in the last chapter and show that none of them escape problems of interpretive indeterminacy and circularity. However, this unavoidability of interpretation is not always reflected in the theories themselves. Two of the research programs, rational choice theory and ethnomethodology, try unsuccessfully and unnecessarily to escape the hermeneutic circle. It is again a sign of the comprehensiveness of the theory of communicative action that it can incorporate interpretive circularity without losing explanatory power. The other programs could do the same, although not without some modifications to the scope of their explanatory claims.

Interpretation and Explanation:
Trying to Escape the Hermeneutic Circle

The necessity of "thick" descriptions of action and the failures of various "thin" explanatory strategies has important and serious epistemological consequences for the social sciences. These consequences are important to establishing the necessary relationships between methodologies of explanation and interpretation. They are also serious consequences, since they lead to an end to certain theoretical pretensions that are part of social scientific practice since Comte and Neurath. In undermining these pretensions, interpretive indeterminacy runs the danger of deflating all knowledge claims in the social sciences, so much so that two of the research programs find it better simply to avoid the problem altogether. However, two arguments show that this avoidance strategy is self-defeating: first, it is not possible on the very assumptions made by each program; and, second, it is not necessary if interpretive indeterminacy is no cause for skepticism in the first place. In fact, attempts to avoid problems of interpretation in both rational choice theory and ethnomethodology lead to the loss of empirical content. The cure is far worse than the disease.

Interpretive indeterminacy is different from the forms of indeterminacy discussed so far: the circular and perspectival aspects of interpretation are not extraneous features but part of its conditions of possibility. As Gadamer notes, the circle was originally applied to the parts–whole relation in interpretations: the interpretation of each of the parts depends on the interpretation of the whole, and vice versa; this dependency implies that all interpretations are partial and never complete.[4] Incompleteness, however, does not exhaust hermeneutic circularity. Its partiality is further heightened by another condition of possibility of interpretation: that it takes place against a "background" of unspecifiable assumptions and presuppositions, a network of beliefs and practices not always fully available to the agent. John Searle has illustrated what the background as a condition entails by attempting to show the impossibility of explicating all that a single sentence presupposes.[5] Alternatively, Charles Taylor argues that to identify an act as an action of a particular type, such as voting or negotiating, is not possible if one only describes the behavior. Negotiation is not merely exchanging offers, but presupposes a whole set of beliefs (such as autonomy and the potential independence of human beings from each other), other practices (such as contracts), and a whole range of actions (bargaining, making offers, concluding the negotiation, and so on). Such interpretive assumptions do not apply to the background practices of other societies in which conflict resolution is based on consensus as the highest value, as in a traditional village in medieval Japan: "Our whole notion of negotiation is bound up, for instance, with the distinct identity of the parties, with the willed nature of the relation; it is a very contractual notion."[6] In order to understand one move in a negotiation it is necessary to understand the whole practice, as well as a whole network of other beliefs and practices. Interpreting conflict resolution in medieval Japan requires slow ethnographic and historic description of this social background, which is never conclusive and always revisable.

Taylor argues that such background conditions exclude the possibility of appealing to "brute facts" or to "the given" in the human sciences: they would result only in a thin description of actions, stripped of their contexts and significance for actors themselves. Whereas brute facts are univocal descriptions of physical states, thick description is inherently circular: it is already an interpretation of interpretations, of the self-interpretation which knowledgeable social actors already make about their own actions. Whether this further circularity is essentially different from the first is a matter of some dispute. For Taylor and like-minded philosophers and social scientists, it marks the continuing essential difference between the human and natural sciences: unlike other objects, human beings are "self-interpreting animals."[7] For others, it is not so much a categorical distinction between the object domains of the various sciences as it is a methodological assumption about considering agents' interpretations as available, though not decisive, evidence.[8] For the social sciences, we need only to construe this requirement of circularity minimally, as a distinction between thick and thin description: to refer to a belief as a reason for acting requires that we know what it is like to act upon it as a reason and thus to interpret it as one. For the hermeneutic tradition, the natural sciences and their "thin" descriptions need only first-order interpretations, not interpretations of interpretations. While this requirement for describing action may not distinguish the human from the natural sciences once and for all, it does distinguish interpretive approaches from other forms of explanation: they are, in Anthony Giddens' phrase, "doubly hermeneutic," including both interpretations and interpretations of interpretations.[9] Perhaps it is better to say that the social sciences are "multiply hermeneutic," including at best a variety of interpretations from participants' and theoreticians' perspectives.[10]

There is still one more level of interpretive circularity, one with consequences that are perhaps the most compelling reasons to avoid interpretation altogether: the problem of justification. Once inside the hermeneutic circle, it seems that all that we can appeal to in order to justify interpretations is other interpretations; there is no metalanguage outside of it in which neutral justification is possible. As Taylor puts it, "What we are trying to establish is a certain reading of a text or expression, and what we appeal to as our grounds for this reading can only be other readings."[11] While Taylor goes on to draw what I believe is an erroneous conclusion that interpretation is a matter for practical wisdom or *phronesis* rather than intersubjective verification, he is nonetheless correct that interpretive circularity applies at the level of justification as well. Interpretations are not fully objective nor are questions of their validity settled by any theoretical procedure.

These deep problems with interpretive circularity most directly affect those social sciences whose task traditionally has been the understanding of meanings, such as cultural anthropology. One thread of post-empiricist philosophy of social science goes so far as to deny the traditional understanding of these disciplines as guided by an interest in uncovering the "true" or "correct" meaning of a text or a practice. According to these critics, the very attempt implies that there is a "fact of the matter" to be discovered which would settle disputes between various competing interpretations, much as the "meaning of the text" supposedly settles the issue between two different translations. Quine's thesis of the indeterminacy of translation suggests that meanings are not entities about which there are such facts.[12] Such lack of determinacy about meanings suggests that it is best just to ignore them, since what matters is what people do, not what they think they are doing. The Wittgensteinian therapy of "meaning is use" may be too strong for the social sciences, although it rightly suggests that social scientists abandon the search into the philosophy of language for guidance. Rather than being a question about "meaning realism" or the status of meanings as entities, a better way to ask the question is the following: do existing explanatory patterns lose anything by avoiding reference to meanings, to agents' self-interpretations? The answer is most certainly "yes," especially if one examines the sort of lengths that theories must go to in order to avoid the difficulties of interpreting meanings in explaining actions.

The "hermeneutic avoidance strategy" of rational choice theory evolved out of internal theoretical problems which are connected to interpersonal comparisons. Rather than tackle interpretive problems about what utility means for each agent and how to compare such disparate descriptions, rational choice theory simply appeals to "revealed preferences," to what the agents' choice behavior reveals about how they weigh various preferences relative to each other. Economic theory ran into difficulties in measuring the utility maximized in choices which do not consistently reflect increasing quantity or quality. Consumer choices did not maximize the unit amount or the ordinal ranking of commodities. Such measures do not prove stable over time and in differently framed choice situations. In the absence of any measure, utility is simply made a matter like taste: *gustibus non disputandum est.*[13] Once the search for intrinsic characterizations of utility is abandoned, the theorist assigns preferences according to actual behavior and choices, such that each consistent pattern permits the construction of a "preference map" for an individual or group. Such maps, however, do not explain intentional behavior as rational. As Rosenberg puts it, "With revealed preference, we surrender the age-old economic aim of explaining individual choice by assuming people are rational."[14] Thus, giving up the interpretive problems of older economic theories means substituting a black box for an explanatory theory of rationality.

Avoiding interpretation not only requires giving up on rationality, but it also weakens the scope and power of decision theory. It now tells us nothing about beliefs and desires (preference orderings) independent of the behavior itself; hence, explanations based on revealed preferences have little predictive power, limited as they are to generalizations over variables in the domain of already observed behavior.[15] This lack of independence makes revealed preference explanations circular in their own way, since preferences now appear in both the explanans and the explanandum. Avoiding one circularity has only led to another, since there is no independent specification of the variable of the explanatory statements basic to the pattern of rational choice explanations. Such a specification requires an interpretation of the agents' choices.

What is more, the limitation to revealed preferences undermines the normative implications of many of the statements of the pattern. If questions about the identity of beliefs and desires or about criteria of utility maximization are settled in this way, the theory can never really claim to show that any consistent pattern of choice is irrational so long as the behavior is specified to be maximizing relative to certain given preferences or tastes. The lack of any normative idea of rationality raises further explanatory problems that can be exhibited in an example taken from MacIntyre's criticism of Davidson's similar notion of rational explanation. If an action is explained by reference to ranked revealed preferences, these preferences may make any action rational without regard to context and intelligibility. This explanation is too impoverished to warrant the name "rational choice." Consider another of MacIntyre's illuminating examples:

I am being shown by my fellow scientists the first and so far the only specimens of a new hybrid fruit developed because of its possible ease of cultivation and food value for people in some particularly barren and starvation-prone part of the world. I snatch them from the hands of the scientist who is preparing to analyze them and gobble them down. When asked, "Why on earth did you do that?" I reply, "I just felt hungry. I like fruit." It is important to note that this answer renders my behavior more rather than less unintelligible than it was before.[16]

In the context of scientific practice, eating a specimen for these reasons is unintelligible, even if strong preferences are present. Yet, without some interpretive analysis of the context, such an action must be deemed rational relative to the given revealed preferences of a hungry man who likes fruit. This absurd consequence can be avoided only by accepting hermeneutic circularity, by considering more than endogenous preferences for explaining rational *and* intelligible action. It requires considering both the contextual and rational features of the action, here the context of scientific institutions and roles and the rationality of satisfying immediate impulses in that setting.

Just such interpretation is required to identify the intentions that cause an action, which in MacIntyre's example would be quite difficult for the scientists present. All the intentional terms in each statement in the pattern can be applied to an action only through thick description, usually presupposed in the explanations themselves. The identification of desires, the distinction between rational and irrational dispositions, and the proper use of the concept of maximization (the issue in MacIntyre's example) all require interpretation and make the explanatory success of rational choice theory, *qua* a species of intentional explanation without behavioristic reductionism, dependent on the prior correctness of the thick descriptions contained in its basic statements.

Similar problems can be found in ethnomethodology. Its behaviorist reduction of the interpretive aspects of intentional explanation is more methodologically than theoretically motivated. With its emphasis on reflexive agency in constructing social situations, such a reduction seems impossible on theoretical grounds alone. But some ethnomethodologists try to avoid interpreting meanings by claiming that "meaning is use," in much the same way that rational choice theorists resort to "revealed preferences" in order to avoid interpreting desires. According to ethnomethodology's anti-hermeneutic methodology, the significance of an action is only the work it does in a certain context. While a theoretical commitment to seeing how actors produce and construct social settings is a crucial assumption of the pattern, nothing about the success of ethnomethodological explanations depends on its verificationist methodology. The two forms of reductionism are mirror opposites: whereas rational choice theory leaves out social context, the avoidance strategy for ethnomethodology is to explain everything in terms of contingent features of the context or setting. The setting explains the outraged reactions of the violated expectations of the scientists in MacIntyre's example.

Rather than agents' preferences, ethnomethodology suggests treating rationality itself as "revealed," as a "phenomenon" to be described and studied as it is produced by "settings' members." To see "practical rationality" at work, Garfinkel suggests that the social scientist "bracket" all considerations of norms like intelligibility, adequacy, and consistency and take up an attitude of pure description necessary for his documentary technique. Garfinkel puts the theorist on a par with the members of the setting to be described: his "policy" is that the rational properties of actions must not be described using standards obtained "outside actual settings within which such properties are recognized, used, produced and talked about by settings' members."[17] Actions must be understood as "indexical," shown to refer to nothing outside the setting itself through fine-grain descriptions of what "members" are doing. While such a perspective may yield insights that its distance affords, it does not escape the hermeneutic circle simply by saying that its "pure" descriptions establish a "symmetry" between theorists' and members' categories: members' descriptions are themselves already subject to hermeneutic problems. The problems of describing "phenomena" are no less great. Theoretical descriptions are always subject to problems of selectivity, perspective, parts–whole circularity, incompleteness, and unspecified assumptions. Without dealing with these problems, the ethnomethodologist cannot claim that her descriptions are accurate, since members never undertake to describe their practical activity in the full detail that the ethnomethodologist does. Even if we grant a "symmetry" between theorist and participant, there is no necessary identity between the two. The theorist's account is at the very least more explicit: it may require reformulations that are less ambiguous, or have missing features, or exhibit any other characteristic of a problematic interpretation.

Ethnomethodology may be seen as a reflective and practical

analysis of interpretation itself, discovering the ways in which interpretation goes on in mundane settings and everyday occurrences, like taking turns in conversation. Aspects of our activities help specify features of the context that are relevant for interpretations. For example, when utterances are "adjacent," speakers assume relevance, an assumption that provides "a framework in which speakers can rely on the *positioning* of what they say to contribute to the *sense* of what they say as an action."[18] But this framework is itself understood and interpreted; adjacency expectations can be purposefully violated and used, as much as the rules of chess can be used for signals, in which case other capacities and contexts for understanding are required. No amount of documentary detail can replace standard hermeneutic understanding of the contexts and contents of utterances, which ethnomethodologists simply assume in order to extend our idea of interpretation to practical activities. Hence, while ethnomethodologists want to avoid interpretation, they end up simply assuming it; while they claim to replace hermeneutics, they simply enrich it. The failure of ethnomethodology to deal with its own interpretive problems leaves it with odd methodological prescriptions that restrict the same theorists who want to develop an anti-prescriptive theory of a highly reflexive and knowledgeable agent.

At least on the assumptions of the explanatory patterns of the research programs of intentionalist social theory, there is no way out of the hermeneutic circle. What I want to argue next is that this is no cause for skepticism about explanatory rigor in the social sciences, just as I argued in chapter 1 that the absence of general laws does not eliminate the discovery of causal regularities. For this purpose, I will consider certain skeptical arguments about the possibility of scientific knowledge based on evidence that appeals to interpretive circularity and limits. This skepticism is based on a one-sided analysis of one particular sort of interpretation, what I call "holistic–contextual interpretation," that entirely ignores "rational–comparative interpretation." While they have different purposes in various explanations, both forms of interpretation are still governed by epistemic norms of correctness. This contrast will permit me to raise a further problem of interpretive circularity: the problem of its limits, as exhibited by the ethnocentrism of most social science which is now old enough that we can take historical distance from it. Can we conclude that there are inherent limits on social scientific knowledge from the mere fact that they depend on interpretations? This problem can best be developed in two case studies: first, the debate between James Clifford and Clifford Geertz about interpretive ethnography (which will also shed light on Woolgar's post-modern "ethnography" of science); and, second, the use of a theory of social evolution in Habermas's comparative–rational approach to interpretation across cultural boundaries. The difficulty of dealing with ethnocentrism and other limiting and distorting factors raises pointed problems about the moral and epistemological constraints on interpretive knowledge in the social sciences. Now that social science cannot escape the hermeneutic predicament, it must be shown that the consequences of it are not skepticism or despair about achieving critical–practical knowledge.

Interpretation and Social Scientific Skepticism

According to the analysis presented by Charles Taylor in his seminal article, "Interpretation and the Sciences of Man," three conditions must be met for something to be an "object of inter-pretation": (1) the object (a text or text-analogue) must have sense (and hence be describable in categories of coherence or its opposite); (2) this sense must be distinguishable from its expression, which must be capable of bearing more than one sense (like the gesture described above); and (3) there is a subject that produces it and for whom these meanings are identifiable (interpreting a rock for-mation makes it meaningful, but for us as subjects). Armed with this analysis, Taylor defends a unique method for the social sci-ences against the intrusions of the natural sciences. He makes the distinction in order to formulate the specific goals and purposes of the "human sciences": interpretations make sense of texts or text analogues by finding a coherent meaning out of all the possibilities of the vehicle of expression. "A successful interpretation is one which makes clear the meaning originally present in a confused, fragmentary and cloudy form."[19] However, the problem with this criterion of success should be obvious: how can we make sense of the idea of "the meaning originally present" if investigators cannot avoid the hermeneutic circle? As Taylor proceeds, it is clear that coherence is only a provisional criterion, making way for an appeal to "unformalizable insight." In some cases of conflicting interpretations, differences cannot be settled by appealling to further evidence, but rather by what Taylor calls "deeper insight": when evidence fails, "each side can make appeal to a deeper insight than that of the other."[20] Matters are made worse in cross-cultural encounters, in which such appeals seem irresolvable given that their assumptions are quite different from our own. Anthropologists show that things may not be as they seem to us, as when Clifford Geertz tries to show that cockfights are not so much games as commentaries on status. When faced with competing claims, many now doubt that there is only one way to settle interpretive disputes rationally or that there is any criterion to decide success or even comparative superiority. From followers of Quine to deconstruction, many doubt that "correct interpretation" is even the proper goal at all.

Such skepticism is supported by some version of the thesis commonly called "universal hermeneutics"; it is captured well in Stanley Fish's colloquial slogan that "interpretation is the only game in town" or Hans-Georg Gadamer's more formal assertion that "all understanding is interpretation."[21] Since no cognitive activity can privilege a particular content as "given" or "self-verifying" apart from the whole of all other contents and activities, it follows that all such activities are interpretive and that any belief or practice can be understood only in light of all other beliefs and practices. Hence, contextualist skepticism is a two step thesis: first, that interpretation is universal; and second, that it takes place only against the background of all of our beliefs and practices and hence its presuppositions cannot be fully specified. Together these two theses imply that no interpretation can be singled out as uniquely correct, since the assertion that it is so would itself be an interpretation. Thus, holism is but one way of expressing the famous "hermeneutic circle." Everything is interpretation, and interpretation is itself indeterminate, perspectival, and circular.

My contention is that holists are correct in arguing that indeterminacy and circularity are epistemologically inevitable aspects of interpretation. But from these warranted assumptions many holists, whom I shall call "strong holists," draw the unwarranted skeptical conclusion that interpretations do not constitute knowledge based on evidence.[22] For example, the perspectival character of interpretation leads to the most common form of skepticism about interpretation: since we can interpret things only from "our" point of view, interpretation is inevitably ethnocentric. It is impossible to understand others as they understand themselves: we understand them only according to "our own lights."[23] I will discuss this argument in detail later in the chapter; for now, I will show that it illustrates a common notion of the limits on interpretation, here of the worst sort.

Various arguments have been given to support this type of skeptical conclusion, including considerations of the theory of meaning for natural languages. However, as Gadamer and others have done, I will present a reading of such arguments as being transcendental in form, that is, as dealing with the conditions for the possibility of interpretation. While some contextualists may dispute this reading, I want to show that the analogy illuminates fundamental problems in the argument – in particular, its unwarranted skepticism. Indeed, the skeptical conclusion usually drawn from holism is, I will argue, established through something like a transcendental argument from holistic limits on acts of interpretation, limits which would disallow any epistemic clarification of "correct" interpretations or "true" meanings. It is precisely this transcendental limit argument that I want to challenge, while invoking neither determinate meanings (and hence avoiding semantic objections) nor a non-circular process of interpretation (and hence recognizing what is true about holism).

In what follows, I will focus primarily on the more extreme skeptical inferences drawn from the holistic nature of interpretation, since they reveal the structure of the inference that can be found in much more modest and weaker forms as well. Against the interpretive skeptics, I will argue that there is evidence within the "hermeneutic circle" to underwrite fallibilistic claims to public knowledge for interpretation that are intersubjectively valid and capable of public adjudication. I will call such skeptics "strong holists" in order to contrast them with "weak holists" who accept their holistic premises but not their contextualist and skeptical conclusions.

It is important to challenge this implicitly transcendental argument because it is as widespread as it is unacknowledged; it is commonly found in hermeneutic, empiricist, and post-modern philosophers and social scientists alike. Strong holists come in two common varieties. On the one hand, there are strong holists *per se*. Among those who turn universal hermeneutics into an explicitly skeptical position are Derridean literary theorists, "anthropologists of science" like Latour and Woolgar, and Clifford and post-modern ethnographers. Members of this group make their skeptical purposes quite clear. In his analysis of science as an interpretive and practical activity, Woolgar argues that the impossibility of objective, representational knowledge of facts shows that "science itself is not scientific."[24] Deconstructionists argue that because "there is nothing outside the text" to warrant claims to true meanings or the manifest content of texts, interpreters can only proliferate alternative readings.[25] In the social sciences, self-proclaimed "post-modernists" challenge interpretive ethnography on epistemological grounds, pointing out the various textual ruses anthropologists use to establish "ethnographic authority."[26] On the other hand, the second variety of strong holists do not make anything like such sweeping pronouncements of skepticism about knowledge as such. Instead, they draw specific skeptical inferences based on holism in order to cast doubt upon the possibility of various particular theories or to criticize specific knowledge claims. Such specific skeptical claims based on holism include Taylor's assertion that prediction in the human sciences is "radically impossible";[27] Dreyfus's arguments against theories of artificial intelligence, decision theory, and formal theories of rule following;[28] and Gadamer's criticism of the Marxist theory of ideology.[29] Because both groups draw the same faulty inference from the same premises, the specific conclusions of the more modest second group of strong holists are no more warranted than the more general skepticism of the first group.

This brief but easily amplified list of various recent claims in philosophy of science, literary theory and anthropology show both how common global and specific arguments for skepticism are and how often they are based on arguments about the role of interpretation in knowledge. Often this interpretive skepticism sometimes serves quite good purposes, as when it rids ethnography of residual Romantic exoticism and colonialism or disabuses the philosophy and sociology of science of an overly idealized picture of actual scientific practice. But this critical work can be better done by other means, and a proper analysis of how interpretation works in these various fields supports, rather than undermines, public claims to correctness which guide moral and epistemic practices. In the next section, my arguments will be primarily negative: I will only show that the skepticism about interpretive knowledge is not warranted by proper inferences from the main premises of holism, which I shall simply accept as true. I will argue positively that interpretation has a variety of types that fulfill a number of purposes, including holist–contextual interpretation and comparative–rational interpretation, each with different epistemic presuppositions.

The Transcendental Argument for Holism: Limits or Constraints

The most widespread skeptical argument about interpretation and the limits of knowledge employs two main premises; while each one could form the basis for a separate argument for holism, they are usually united as the twin supports of an overall, anti-epistemological, skeptical position. Both premises can be read as presenting fundamental conditions for the possibility of interpretation: its circularity and hence its necessary reference to other interpretations; and its assumption of an unanalyzable background, the presupposition of an indefinite set of other beliefs and practices. If these two premises hold as conditions for any interpretation, then it is easy (so strong holists think) to construct an argument for contextualism – that is, for the skeptical conclusions that there are no uniquely correct interpretations and that the validity of interpretations are limited to their context. After discussing the premises on which these views are based, I will argue against the conclusions of the "strong holists,"[30] in order to show the superiority of a non-skeptical argument from the same premises favored by "weak holists."[31] Strong holism is skeptical about whether the scope of claims made in interpretations qualify them as knowledge; weak holism uses these same premises to establish a transcendental analysis of interpretation and its own public warrants for correctness.

The Transcendental Argument for Strong Holism

(1) Interpretation is circular, indeterminate, and perspectival (thesis of the "hermeneutic circle").
(2) Interpretation occurs only against a "background," a network of unspecifiable beliefs and practices (thesis of the "background").
(3) The background is a condition for the possibility of interpretation which limits its epistemic possibilities of correctness (thesis of transcendental limits).
(4) All cognitive activities take place against a background and are interpretive and hence circular, indeterminate, and perspectival (thesis of the universality of interpretation). *Therefore*, the conditions of interpretation are such that no "true" or "correct" interpretations are possible (interpretive skepticism).

In my analysis of this argument, I will defend premises 1 and 2. Properly interpreted, they form the core of a more defensible "weak holism." Premises 3 and 4 do not follow from them, and hence the inference to interpretive skepticism is unwarranted.

The thesis of the "hermeneutic circle" (premise 1) has formed the core of almost every holistic theory of interpretation since Schleiermacher, both in terms of the relation of parts to wholes in interpretation and as a denial of the possibility of a separate metalanguage to discuss interpretations. (Because interpretation is circular, every treatment of an interpretation is itself an interpretation.)[32] If correct, it also means that interpretations cannot be independent of the standpoint of the interpreter, in that interpreters are embedded in their situation and hence their understanding remains partial and incomplete. The language of the interpreter is not some metalanguage outside the circle, but a fallible and partial understanding within it.

The thesis of the "background" (premise 2) is also a statement of the practical and conditioned character of interpretations: any attempt to explicate the intention or meaning of an action or utterance requires the assumption of an indefinite number of other beliefs and purposes, as Searle tries to show by attempting to specify all the presuppositions of a single, simple sentence.[33] Far from being contingent facts, these indeterminate and holistic constraints are part of what makes communication possible, since we may understand the assertions of the true beliefs of others by reference to publicly shared beliefs.[34] But in its most radical form, the background thesis makes all actions, theories and expressions context-dependent. Taken together, circularity and reference to a background exclude the possibility of reducing interpretations to semantic explication or some other procedure for fixing determinate meanings without reference to holistic constraints.

These two premises alone are insufficient to warrant skepticism about interpretation. It is a commonplace in hermeneutics that circularity need not be vicious. As Gadamer argues, it can be an ever enriching process of relating parts and whole, with an "anticipation of completeness." Similarly, Heidegger argues that "positive possibilities for knowing" emerge in the hermeneutic circle when we overcome our "fancies and popular conceptions" and work through "these fore-structures in terms of the things themselves."[35] But skeptical problems begin when this circularity applies reflexively to the standards of correctness themselves: what is "completeness" but itself something to be interpreted? What are "things in themselves," and how do we gain access to them as evidence against which we modify the preconceptions that make up the background to our interpretive acts? Even if such norms of "completeness" or of the evidence of "things themselves" exist, circularity at least makes it indeterminate how they should be applied in any given case: "correct" interpretations are not produced by some standardized method, algorithm, or semantic theory. Even so, circularity still might only support fallibilism, not skepticism, in that interpretations are put forward in a public process and subject to constant revision. It is the addition of the third and fourth premises that transforms the holistic conditions into finitistic limits on the capacity of interpretations to support knowledge claims. After examining the conceptual and empirical cogency of these next two premises, I will test the validity of the inference as a whole.

Quite apart from closely examining the argument as a transcendental fallacy, a good case can be made that both skeptical premises (3 and 4) fall prey to conceptual confusions, particularly with regard to the thesis of interpretive universality (premise 4). This thesis makes an overly quick identification of all forms of indeterminacy with interpretation. As the arguments of the last two chapters show, there are any number of other, distinct forms of indeterminacy. First, observational indeterminacy may result from the unavoidable involvement of the observer in certain social and physical processes, or from contingent facts about them. Second, there is causal indeterminacy, as in the case of identifying whether or not a particular intention "really" brought about an action; this problem emerges in giving a causal account of the "real" reason for an action that might not be known to the agent, as in the case of mechanisms such as psychic repression or ideological distortion. Third, indeterminacy in following a rule, insofar as a rule does not strictly determine what particular actions are required in following it; as any game like chess shows, the variety of possible moves may have more to do with differences in skill and strategy than with how the rules are interpreted. Since none of these forms of indeterminacy can be identified with hermeneutic circularity, on closer examination "the reign of universal hermeneutics" is often mere decree and stipulation. From a methodological perspective, "universal hermeneutics" also suffers from the problems of all reductionistic and overextended programs: in order to fit all the variety of human cognition and action into its interpretive framework, its categories must become more and more vague and less and less informative.

But even when conceptual distinctions among different forms of indeterminacy are made, interpretive circularity might still undermine the truth claims made in interpretations, especially if the presupposed background supplies a finite limit on validity or correctness (premise 3). If this premise is also true, the universality thesis would then make these limits general and hence would warrant skepticism about the valid application of any epistemic norms to interpretations: as always against a background, they might be inevitably subject to ethnocentrism and other reflectively inaccessible limitations. For this reason, the limit thesis as an interpretation of background constraints does all the work in this skeptical argument and is therefore the real defining premise of a strong holist position. Such a limit thesis can be found not only in Clifford and Woolgar, but also in Taylor's claim that interpretations rely on "unformalizable" insight rather than public evidence.

Such contextualism is, I believe, open to two different objections, one weaker and empirical and the other stricter and logical. I will make the first objection quickly to cast doubt on the empirical plausibility of such limits. Suppose that they are operative: what would the cognitive capacities of actual interpreters have to be like if they were so limited? Second, I shall turn to the core of my criticism of strong holism, its interpretation of background constraints. How must the background conditions function in interpretation if they act as determinate limits? The argument about limits involves a fallacy of "amphiboly" (confusions of the empirical and the transcendental concepts, as well as determinate and reflective judgments) in the use of the background as a condition of possibility of interpretation.

My first objection is that the limit thesis is empirically implausible: it implies that the involvements in the shared practices and beliefs that make up any particular "background" or culture are so strong that we cannot take any distance from them. Strong holists argue that the reference to a background means that our involvements in our shared language establish "a way of living and grasping the world that has us";[36] they are, in other words, interpretive orientations that cannot be brought under our reflective control all at once and that we incorporate by being socialized into a set of interpretive practices and acquiring its context-specific, pre-thematic skills.

It is certainly empirically correct that socialization involves acquiring a number of prereflective orientations to the world, and that as a whole they are not reflectively accessible all at once. But it is unlikely that our involvement in them, both individually and as a whole, is always so strong or immediate that they act as determinate limits; nor does their prereflective immediacy preclude the possibility of thematizing them reflectively, of freeing them from their local context, and thus of revising any one of them. Not only is it possible to thematize and change such orientations, but being conditioned by social constraints in no way precludes the possibility of valid knowledge emerging within them, any more than the organic constraints on the human eye's ability to see color implies limits about what we may know about the spectrum, or, similarly, the fact that we see within a horizon limits the knowledge gained by visual perception. More modest strong holists might reply that some beliefs or skills can be brought under reflective control, but not all. If that is true, the strong holist has lost the argument. None of our practical involvements sanction skepticism about any specific knowledge claim since it may be one that has already been taken out of its practical context and submitted to public scrutiny, as in the sciences, or to explicit formal interpretation, as in the law. Indeed, in many complex societies there is already a social division of labor in formally testing and validating our pre-thematic orientations in different institutional settings, from Talmudic discussion to legal review. In general, this thesis transforms what can only be an empirical question into one of principle. Not all involvements and backgrounds are the same. While the holist is correct in pointing out that the interpreter is never a Cartesian ego, various forms of socialization into practices permit greater or lesser degrees of autonomy and prereflective involvement. "Backgrounds" are always empirically specific, and nothing apart from some very formal properties (like their holistic character) can be settled a priori. Certainly, on the basis of the existence of specific backgrounds for specific practices, it cannot be established that scientific knowledge acquired in them is "local" or "contingent,"[37] unless there are independent reasons for thinking so. A more empirical strategy is needed here to avoid empty conceptual claims. Feminist analyses of science show just how such empirical limits operate in community-wide gender biases that are a matter of social fact.

The same is true of the supposed unavoidability of "prejudice" in interpretation.[38] While the appeal to some unexamined assumptions is a formal requirement of interpretation, it remains an empirical question the degree to which the prejudices of a specific interpreter on the background of a specific culture distort his or her interpretations. As the ethnomethodologists put it, being socialized into a culture or background does not turn us into "judgmental dopes" who passively and unreflectively assimilate roles, norms, and skills.[39] The necessity of the background establishes nothing about the status of any particular belief or skill, any particular interpretation, or any particular practice. Despite these remarks about socialization and reflection, however, this empirical objection does not yet show definitively that there are no such limits on interpretation, especially if "everything is interpretation." By eliminating all empirical differences, we are left, as Hegel put it, in a skeptical night where all cows are grey.

The more fundamental challenge to strong holism is its error in transcendental logic. It is certainly true that something like a "background" makes up the public conditions for the possibility of interpretation; it is also true that we cannot detach ourselves completely from our involvements or leap out of our skins. While some deeply interested interpretations are for that reason limited, these conditions are no cause for a general skepticism about epistemic and critical reflection on interpretation. They warrant skepticism only when various conditions of possibility are confused in its transcendental argument: the main problem with strong holism is that it confuses constraints with limits, or, more precisely, enabling conditions with limiting conditions.

The strong holists' inference works only by ignoring the many differences between these two types of conditions. Whereas limiting conditions are determinate and fixed, enabling conditions are variable and alterable. Certainly, all conditions act as constraints on that which they condition. However, the variability of enabling conditions makes them formal: any number of different beliefs and skills can function as a background. A limiting condition is specific and material in character: it is *this* belief or *this* set of skills within which the actor operates whether they know it or not. Enabling conditions also have quite different epistemic properties: they are reflectively accessible and alterable. Most importantly, each type of condition has different functional properties and hence works differently. As opposed to limiting conditions, enabling conditions are open-ended and permit different degrees of knowledge; as determinate, limiting conditions permit only those specific things within its field. Different aspects and levels of the ability to speak a language illustrate this contrast. While it is a formal property of my linguistic ability that I can speak some language, it is a material property of my linguistic competence that I specifically speak English. This material condition is not necessarily limiting, since I can always learn another language. Now compare two speakers of a foreign language, one using a phrase book and the other fluent. The phrase book speaker's expressions and interpretations have determinate limits (the number of sentences in the book), while the fluent speaker's do not: she can form and understand an indeterminate number of sentences, constrained only by what native speakers find acceptable and by the contingent occasions of language use.

In order to untangle this confusion further and to show why it leads to skepticism, an analogy to transcendental argumentation is helpful. This analogy shows that the thesis of the background, or of context dependence, does not justify epistemological skepticism about correct interpretations any more than Kant's thesis that concepts require sensation is meant to limit the objectivity of knowledge: Kant's formal conditions on cognition and the holistic conditions on interpretation are both epistemologically neutral in exactly the same way. Contextualists deny purely formal and hence universal conditions that enable interpretation, putting in their place particular material and ontological conditions that limit interpretations: formal constraints are replaced by the possession of the prereflective stances and background knowledge necessary to participate in a particular culture or one of its practices. In order to engage in scientific practices, for example, we must have acquired an unspecifiable but still finite set of presuppositions and orientations appropriate to the science of our age. The reflective and prereflective aspects of the background function quite differently in this example. While the acquisition of specific orientations makes it possible for our statements and activities to be recognized as "scientific," it has nothing to do with whether or not they are well warranted. Such ontological conditions by themselves only make it possible for a claim to be part of meaningful scientific practice; it does not guarantee its truth or objectivity. With regard to any particular content, whether it be a statement, theory, or text, the transcendental presuppositions of interpretation do not determine the extent of the capacity to know or judge what something means, nor do they determine how we reflectively judge the adequacy of such an account.

With regard to the content of judgments, Kant makes a similar point in his analysis of the subjective conditions for the possibility of experience. Kant saw that these conditions have two sides: they are enabling conditions with regard to objective knowledge of phenomena, and limiting conditions only with regard to knowledge of noumena, or things-in-themselves. Despite the constraints on human knowing such as the unity of consciousness or the space–time character of intuitions, knowledge claims are not merely subjective. While the formal conditions for the possibility of knowing make it impossible to know all the determinations of an object, this conditioned character does not imply that what we do know does not have objective status.[40] The anti-skeptical requirements for interpretation are much more minimal: they need not be objective, but only capable of being intersubjectively warranted and publicly adjudicated. Because what makes a set of assumptions and stances a background is the fact that it is shared, the conditions of interpretation also make possible a process of testing governed by epistemic norms of publicity and employing the same skills that made the interpretations themselves possible in the first place.[41]

Such confusions of formal and empirical concepts are the skeptical counterpoint to the metaphysical error that Kant calls "the amphiboly of concepts of reflection."[42] Whereas Kant saw metaphysicians like Leibniz as making illicit inferences from formal concepts to empirical truths, skeptical strong holists infer determinate and empirical limits on knowledge from the enabling conditions of interpretation. The confusion begins in the universality thesis, since the holist loses sight of the fact that holism is itself a formal theory resulting from transcendental reflection on the general conditions of interpretation and not an interpretation itself. If holistic concepts like the background are formal, reflective, and interpretive, the premises of the holistic argument violate its own anti-theoretical account of interpretation as always contingent and contest dependent.

Once the formal and reflective character of transcendental concepts like the background is clarified, it should also be clear that the background describes an enabling and not a limiting condition of interpretation. This is precisely the way that Searle uses the concept: the background refers to a whole set of non-representational presuppositions that enable intentionality. As he puts it, the background is not any particular set of beliefs or practices but a set of presupposed practices and stances that "provide the enabling conditions for the operation of intentional states."[43] Thus, the second amphiboly of strong holism is the confusion of enabling conditions with limiting conditions that is equivalent in Kantian terms to confusing the enabling conditions for the objectivity of sensibility with the limiting conditions of transcendental notions like the noumena. Or, to return to our example: speaking a particular language is an enabling condition of communication. It is not a fixed limit on our capacity to communicate with others, since it may be expanded to incorporate new contexts and possibilities of understanding, as well as novel, never heard or uttered sentences. Thus, like speaking a particular language, interpreting within a certain background is best understood as presenting a set of flexible constraints, rather than strict limits, on activities of interpretation and understanding. Certainly, even limiting conditions have two sides as well: they may enable a certain type of performance: the traveller can read the determinate list of sentences in the phrase book and order her meal. This capacity does not require much reflective access to the structure of the activity of speaking this particular language. Such knowledge is indeed local and contingent. In order to interpret the sciences, for example, as "locally, materially and socially situated skills and practices," these limits are seen as instrumentally and socially enabling the things science does. If these conditions are seen as limiting ones, then it follows that these local limits enable only a non-universal theoretical knowledge that is "indexical" and "contingent," a description that seems difficult to understand without resorting to some form of skepticism.[44] As opposed to the material limiting conditions on skills and power, the social enabling conditions of science do not necessarily say anything at all about the epistemic status of theories: they could be universal and transcend the context that produced them. That they do limit knowledge has to be established independently from the mere fact that they are socially conditioned. Thus, the skeptical argument from enabling, rather than disabling, conditions that are also determinate limits also fails to establish the necessity of its skeptical conclusions.

Restating the Argument:
The Case for a Non-Skeptical Holism

The failure to establish the skeptical conclusion of strong holism suggests that a revised version of the same transcendental argument could establish a non-skeptical conclusion. The theses of the hermeneutic circle and of the background were accepted as part of a transcendental analysis of the conditions for the possibility of interpretation, and it remains only to recast the offending premises into enabling transcendental conditions of possibility for fallible and revisable claims to interpretive correctness. Here the analogy to good transcendental argumentation serves us well again. While Kant defended the objectivity of knowledge within formal enabling conditions, he did not provide a transcendental justification that supported the overly strong claims of a metaphysical realism. So, too, with interpretation: weak holism will have to modify overly strong criteria of correctness, as in the case of a semantic realist notion of fixing "true meanings." However, such conditions enable interpreters to engage in publicly shared epistemic practices like the social sciences, in which revisable, well-warranted interpretive claims may be put forward and criticized. Here interpreters are guided by epistemic considerations of evidence to warrant their specific claims, in the same way that scientists revise their theories in light of new experiences. Thus, hermeneutic circularity and indeterminacy point in the direction of fallibilism, not skepticism.

Transcendental Argument for Weak Holism

(1) Interpretation is circular, indeterminate, and perspectival (thesis of the hermeneutic circle).

(2) Its circularity may be defined by the necessity of a "background," a set of shared and accessible conditions of possibility (the background as a reflective–transcendental concept).

(3) As a formal condition of possibility, the background acts as an enabling condition and not a limiting condition (given the distinction between "enabling" and "limiting" conditions).

(4) The conditions of interpretation are neutral with regard to the warrants of knowledge claims, including claims about interpretations (the denial of hermeneutic universality). *Therefore*, interpretations can produce revisable, public knowledge based on evidence.

This weak holistic argument tries to show that there is no reason for skepticism in properly understood interpretive circularity. Rather, it argues not only that this circularity is non-vicious, but also that it is based on enabling conditions analyzed as shared background constraints. Like other public and constrained epistemic activities, such as Rawlsian reflection, the constraints are not strong enough to act as a fixed limit or to make it impossible to decide normatively between interpretations on the basis of evidence. Indeed, such evaluation will always be comparative, fallibilistic, and revisable in that yet a better interpretation could come along, encompassing the strengths and overcoming the weaknesses of previous interpretations.[45] Strong holism cannot really make sense of a process of evaluating interpretations comparatively, for a number of reasons. First, it excludes a priori the weighing of public evidence to settle interpretive disputes and conflicts. Second, it makes any such process of reflection and evaluation limited by its contingent background. Its version of the background thesis entails that few conflicts are manageable except within the limits of more or less identical implicit assumptions. If my criticisms of the assumptions of this argument are correct, such unreflective consensus is not necessary for adjudicating interpretive claims. Background constraints on reflective evaluation only eliminate the possibility of uniquely true interpretations; they imply nothing determinate about how better or worse interpretations can be established. Questions involving the comparison of conflicting interpretations emerge on the basis of shared understandings, no matter how minimal, and can be answered by closely examining the reflective practices in which interpretive claims are publicly warranted and adjudicated.

As opposed to strong holism's non-reflective account of the background, weak holism incorporates a dimension of interpretation that makes it a potentially evaluative and critical act. As in Neurath's boat, interpreters may modify their assumptions and thematize their constraints, although not all at once. Holistic constraints and circularity do not limit in advance what the critical assessment and evaluation of interpretations can achieve in changing whole interpretive patterns that may be deeply imbedded in a culture. For example, in evaluating the strengths of two interpretations, different parts of a scene or text can be shown to be problematic on the pattern suggested by one interpretation and less problematic and fragmentary on the pattern suggested by another. Thus, interpretation is better understood as including critical appropriation, a process that, while circular and fallibilistic, is also governed by epistemic norms like coherence and correctness. This is not to say that some epistemic value like coherence may not be overemphasized in some interpretations; but when it is, that very exaggeration can be shown by public adjudication in light of opposing claims and supporting evidence.

The Limits of Interpretation: Interpretive and Post-Modern Ethnography

What does the "weaker" version of the transcendental argument establish about interpretive social science? The significance of this debate about holism and the limits of interpretation can be seen by examining the presuppositions of the debate about the possibility of ethnography: the exchange between Clifford Geertz, a defender of a style of enthnography based on the model of the interpretation of texts, and James Clifford, the post-modern, political critic of twentieth century ethnographic discourse. Before Clifford's criticisms can be understood, it is necessary to examine the type of interpretation used by an enthnographer like Geertz. Since Geertz does not offer a systematic theory, this can best be done by a close look at a particular example, one that is arguably an exemplar of hermeneutic social science: Geertz's detailed interpretive analysis of the betting at a Balinese cockfight as a social text.[46] This same analysis is also read by proponents of the interpretive turn as an example of a successful interpretation, while it is the object of repeated, if not virulent, criticisms by "post-modernists" who challenge the "ethnographic authority" of the interpreter.

Geertz begins his interpretation with a brief meditation on the difficulties of showing up as a stranger in a small village, especially a Balinese village. On the one hand, critics like Clifford see these anecdotes as an attempt to establish the authority of "being there," especially through Geertz's dramatic narrative of being caught up in a police raid on one of the first illegal cockfights that he attends. For Geertz, on the other hand, it is clearly an attempt to establish the problems of cross-cultural distance, which far from setting up his authority presents him with a series of problems to solve. The main problem is that the cockfight is not *really* (for the Balinese) what it *seems* (to us): a sporting event, a game, with irrationally heavy betting of several months' salary. In Taylor's terms, Geertz is textually and rhetorically creating the conditions for analyzing the cockfight as an object of interpretation: as having a sense for subjects (the Balinese) whose vehicle of expression (bets, fights between animals) and symbolic context (Balinese myths) might have a different sense for other subjects (Western anthropologists). The solution to the problem of distance is contained in Geertz's main interpretive claim, which is made in the beginning of the essay and then supported by the evidence of the rest. Geertz distinguishes between what appears to be going on to us and what is going on for the Balinese; this sense need not be their own explicit self-interpretation, but is provided by putting the fight in the whole context of Balinese cultural practices and symbols. "For it is only apparently cocks that are fighting. Actually it is men."[47]

To support this claim, Geertz engages in holistic and contextual interpretation, placing the odd features of the cockfight within the background of Balinese culture as a whole, its network of traditional beliefs, religious practices, and social relations. To use the hermeneutic term favored by Geertz: contextual interpretation discloses the "common world" in which the practice of betting on cockfights has a place and makes sense to its participants, like the common world that makes sense of Western bargaining in Taylor's example. It is important to note that disclosing this world may require the self-interpretation of participants, but it may go beyond them and find coherence and relationships that they may not assent to immediately. Geertz reports very little that the Balinese themselves say about the cockfights and denies that a Balinese must agree with his interpretation, a main point of contention with his post-modern critics.

Geertz presents his contextual interpretation in ever-widening, concentric circles, each time redescribing the world in which the practice makes sense for its subjects. He begins with his perplexity about the betting structure, the great differences among the size and odds of the various bets. The "center bet" between the two owners is usually at even odds and of enormous size relative to monthly income. It is the economic irrationality of such bets that is Geertz's main interpretive question, using Bentham's term "deep play" to denote its disutility. Geertz argues that utilitarian or rational choice explanations could not account for the main features of the fight as examples of maximizing utility. Rather, it is precisely because of the size of the bet that the fight takes on symbolic and dramatic significance. If the cock represents the owner himself, the fight is "deep" because it is more about symbolic status and honor than economic gain and utility. It is an "art form" and a "social commentary" that renders the Balinese experience of social hierarchy and status comprehensible in terms of acts and objects whose "meaning can be more powerfully articulated and more exactly perceived."[48] The fight's "encompassing structure" links it to the wider context of Balinese social structure and symbols.

Because many take Geertz's essay to have exemplary status, it is challenged as representing all that post-modern anthropologists find wrong in the discourse and rhetoric of post-war ethnography.[49] Much of the criticisms focus on Geertz's style and "rhetoric," such as his shifting use of pronouns from "I" to "they," or his use of the term "the Balinese" to denote a mythic, unified subject. As some critics of post-modernist ethnography have shown, much of this highly self-reflective focus on style contributes little to substantial criticism of Geertz's social science.[50] Nonetheless, despite their misplaced emphasis on style, post-modern critics have rightly challenged the falsifying aspects of much traditional and interpretive enthography: its exoticism and fixation on the odd, its tendency to see cultures as overly unified and coherent wholes, its hidden projections and fantasies. More importantly, post-modernism has reflectively located anthropology as a practice in the context of colonialism and the globalization of Western culture. Laborious contextual interpretation does not solve the problem of ethnocentrism, to be found in the "very Western way" that Geertz understands the cockfight as an art form.[51] It is for Geertz and not for the Balinese that this interpretation makes sense, and Geertz is accused of failing to explicate the sense of the practice for those participating in it. Clifford sees contextual interpretation as falsifying: "the ethnographer transforms the research situation's ambiguity and diversity into an integrated portrait."[52] In this way, holistic interpretation necessarily occludes the dialogical and political context out of which ethnographic interpretation itself emerges.

In their criticisms of Geertz, Clifford and the post-modernists are raising fundamental epistemological difficulties for cross-cultural interpretation. More than that, their emphasis on dialogue brings up the decisive problem of this interpretive context, however much they have displaced their critical insights into mere matters of style (as if it were an aesthetic issue like a dispute over realistic representation). Dialogue shows the fundamental, ineluctable moral and political dimensions of responsibility that are part of every act of interpreting the utterances and actions of others, especially the culturally distant Other. In claiming to interpret what others are saying or doing, we take on a moral responsibility to them, not to debase them or subject them to the violence and abuse of misinterpretation and misunderstanding. Correct interpretation of others is thus a practical–moral imperative, not because it is based on "insight," as Taylor argues, but because of the responsibility we accept in claiming to represent the views of others that is present in both morality and the social sciences. The post-modern search for a "dialogical ethnography" is best understood in these moral and political terms, as attempting to formulate a type of interpretation that respects the integrity and the autonomy of those whom we interpret.

But this relation of theory and practice is so far unrealized in post-modern ethnographic writings; instead, post-modernism has been content with the posture of radical skepticism akin to what I have called strong holism. Geertz's response to his critics is quite in the spirit of a non-skeptical, weak holism: while he grants the discursive and moral constraints on ethnographic interpretation, he finds in them only "the end to certain pretensions" rather than a cause for skepticism. In *Works and Lives*, also a self-reflective work that interprets the history of ethnographic writing, Geertz writes, "The moral asymmetries across which ethnography works and the discursive complexity within which it works make any attempt to portray it as anything more than the representation of one sort of life in the categories of another impossible to defend."[53] To argue that we can understand others as they understand themselves in such an asymmetrical context is hermeneutically naive. The problem is that Clifford's appeal to dialogue also cannot escape the predicament that they find Geertz in, and their difference with Geertz is either a transcendental illusion or a matter of aesthetics.

The debate between post-modern and interpretive anthropology turns out to be yet another debate about the hermeneutic circle and how to escape it. By preempting skepticism, Geertz does not suggest that there is some kind of cross-cultural unity or transparency. The problem stands: how does one responsibly and accurately portray other forms of life within one's hermeneutic circle? As correctly and responsibly as possible, subject to constant revision based on free and open dialogue with participants and with other interpreters. When faced with such constraints, ethnography as an interpretive science should not (with Clifford) produce "multiple interpretations" but rather (with Geertz) produce better, morally and epistemologically justified ones. The flight into "the proliferation of multiple interpretations" is as much a moral as it is an epistemological dodge of the deeper issues of interpreting across cross-cultural boundaries. Such problems only reappear in the form of uncommitted and irresponsible multiplicity. Dilthey argued that the theory of interpretation should help us to avoid "the constant irruption of Romantic whim and skeptical subjectivity" in the human sciences.[54] Post-modernism simply trades the first for the second. Weak holists like Geertz instead continually reflect upon the ways in which interpretations are justified within their constraints, as claims to know something about what others are doing and saying, not as claims to jump into their skins.

The basic thrust and usefulness of this argument against Clifford's interpretive skepticism can be illustrated by briefly examining the use of a similar argument in Steve Woolgar's challenge to "the ideology of representation" and standard sociology of science.[55] Here as before, holistic assumptions about interpretation lead to an unwarranted skepticism about scientific knowledge claims, the "scientific status of science." At least in the social sciences, concerned as they are with social conditions of knowing, strong holism and interpretive skepticism is alive and well. It comprises a common philosophical mistake that undermines the purposes of many contemporary analyses of social contexts of knowledge and interpretation.

As its title suggests, Woolgar's *Science: The Very Idea* is a skeptical work, offering a "reflexive ethnography of the practice of representation."[56] The critical purpose of this ethnography and its detailed descriptions of what scientists actually do is to cast doubt upon the idealized picture of science as objective knowledge of an independent world of facts. Woolgar's skeptical strategy is to show that if science is a social practice like any other, then "objective, representational knowledge is not possible." The mythologies of representation are justified by what Woolgar calls a false objectivist epistemology. Its main contention is that science is able to "capture some feature independent of the activity itself."[57] For example, objectivism asserts that the inscriptions on a meter are said to register "voltage," a feature of the world independent of the scientific activity of measuring and not produced by it. The contrary, non-objectivistic account of this scientific activity is "constructivist": voltage is defined by the background context of the practices and instruments that produce it, and truth claims about it are confined to the social networks that produce and reproduce the beliefs in them. In order to establish these strong claims, Woolgar repeatedly argues against "objectivism" and for "constructivism" by employing a version of the usual two step holistic argument from the indeterminate, indexical, and context-dependent character of science as interpretive practice to determinate and contextual limits on the knowledge so gained. Apart from the first premise, Woolgar's argument should now seem familiar:

(1) Science is a social practice.
(2) As a practice, science always takes place within the assumptions of a larger context and social network (the thesis of the background).
(3) As social and contextually bound, science and scientific facts are as perspectival and indeterminate as any other interpretation (the thesis of interpretive circularity). *Therefore*, science cannot attain objective, representational knowledge.

Leaving empirical questions aside, the conclusion simply does not follow from premises 2 and 3. Woolgar simply never considers that both premises could just as well be indeterminate enabling conditions for scientific knowledge. To return to my analogy: there is no reason to suppose that the inscriptions of the experiment that measure voltage are like the sentences in the phrase book, since the experimenter's knowledge is not as limited as the phrase book speaker's. Thus, the skeptical conclusions about the possibility of warranting representational knowledge through public evidence do not follow, nor do the conclusions that the objects of knowledge are "constructed" or have truth value "only" in certain social networks, or that theories are like indexical utterances. What does follow from a weak holistic interpretation of premises 2 and 3 is only a reflexive awareness of the socially constrained character of scientific knowing as an interpretive practice, constraints which may or may not enable particular publicly warranted and context-independent truth claims.

Woolgar draws an explicit comparison between his conclusions about the social study of science and Clifford's reflexive ethnography of Western anthropology. Just as Woolgar wants to show that the "very idea of science" is radically impossible in order to attack the "authority of science," he interprets Clifford as demonstrating that in light of interpretive limits the very idea of achieving an "adequate understanding" across cultures "involves a relatively uncritical reliance upon conventional forms of representation."[58] The comparison is more telling than Woolgar imagines. Both Woolgar and Clifford are led to skepticism through false inferences from well-warranted reflexive criticisms of naive knowledge claims, properly showing that they are not independent of interpretive and social constraints. Both misunderstand the enabling conditions, for the possibility of knowing scientific objects or, more importantly, for achieving dialogical knowledge of other peoples from within some hermeneutic circle.

In any case, Woolgar and Clifford are correct that contextual interpretation in the social sciences is not a matter of direct representation. If we do "understand one form of life only in the categories of another," or if ethnography gives "our understanding of other people's symbol systems,"[59] then contextual interpretation only takes us so far. It is the attempt to reconstitute in "our" terms "their" world. It is governed by norms of public evidence and moral responsibility. But it does not do the comparative work that interpretation also requires to test for adequacy within a hermeneutic circle. Thus, it seems that another sort of interpretation must be present in the social sciences, one I shall call "rational interpretation" that deals with comparative contexts. In a later essay, Charles Taylor recognized the need to supplement his own view of interpretation as explicating the world of a text with a more directly comparative approach in cross-cultural situations. I will argue that Taylor's version of rational comparison is inadequate, but that better versions are available in Habermas and Davidson, heirs to Weber's approach to the problem of *Verstehen* with all its difficulties.

Cross-Cultural Comparison and Rational Interpretation

In his essays "Understanding and Ethnocentricity" and "Rationality," Taylor tries to avoid the relativistic consequences of holism. In his earlier essays, he argues for a coherence criterion for evaluating interpretations of other cultures; in these later essays, he develops a more critical and comparative approach, which is based on evaluative criteria.[60] But instead of trying to find some neutral method with which to compare other forms of life, Taylor insists that comparison requires "a language of perspicuous contrast." This language creates a common space of comparison that avoids the impossible dilemma of understanding across cultures: either to accept incorrigibility and privilege others' self-understanding, or to be ethnocentric and privilege one's own understandings. Such a language of contrast is neither "ours" nor "theirs," but the "fusion of horizons," a constructed common ground that is not any specific natural language. Further, the contrast language is "perspicuous" only if it permits mutual understanding and criticisms of both forms of life. "This would be a language in which we could formulate both their way of life and ours as alternative possibilities in relation to some human constants. . . . Such a language of contrast might show their language of understanding to be distorted or inadequate in some respects or it might show ours to be so, or it might show both."[61] While this description of mutual understanding points in the proper direction, it does not solve the problem. It relies heavily on metaphysical assumptions that there are indeed uninterpreted "human constants." Taylor gives some interesting cases of contrasts that employ this concept, such as comparing the benefits of technical control versus the integrative effects of symbolic understandings of nature. However, he does not give us any clear criteria for making such judgments, since it will always turn out that any culture can be said to be better than any other in some respect. Nor does he clearly show why such cases are really "perspicuous" or reflect a "common language." In place of such strong metaphysical and essentialist notions, a weak transcendental analysis might yield more interesting results, which give clearer criteria of success while not excluding the possibility of failure.

Such an analysis has already been formulated by Donald Davidson and Jürgen Habermas, whose solutions are remarkably similar for all the differences in their philosophical outlooks. Put in terms of the philosophy of social science, both develop forms of rational interpretation with clear implications for the problem of comparison. I will argue that Habermas's transcendental argument is more effective than Davidson's in establishing the conditions for the possibility of comparative criticism; Davidson's attempt to dismiss problems of relativity works too well, since it obliterates rather than resolves differences between "us" and "them" and gives us no clue about what to do when we as social scientists find them.

The recognition of differences requires a second, comparative form of interpretation that I will call "rational interpretation."

Weber formulated his concept of rational interpretation as part of a theory of purposive social action. The interpretation of these purposes need not be defined by the subjective point of view of the actor, but can also be assessed by the social scientist from an "objective" standpoint. However, as Habermas notes in discussing Weber's concept of interpretation, such a standpoint is really that of the social scientific interpreters themselves if they were to perform the same action. "Rational interpretations," Habermas notes, "are undertaken in a performative attitude, since the interpreter presupposes a basis for judgment that is shared by all parties, including the actors."[62] Weber argues that in the case of purposive actions such judgments can be made, since these judgments are related to the value attitudes of the actors (they are *wertbezogen*), but do not presuppose the validity of these norms or values themselves (in explicit value judgments or *Werturteile*).[63] If the distinction works at all, there is no reason to limit it to purposive action, so long as similar forms of "objectivity" could be established for other types of rationality.

The linchpin of Weber's argument for objective comparisons in the interpretive framework is that there is "a basis of judgment" shared by all parties. To establish this basis, some transcendental argument is necessary, and Davidson and Habermas both think a form of weak holism can supply it.

Davidson's argument is quick and easy. He argues that the assumption that an agent is rational is required for any action to be intelligible to us. Rather than subsuming an action under a general law, explanations of rational actions "make others intelligible only to the extent that we can recognize something like our own reasoning powers at work."[64] This presupposition is the basis for a strong version of the principle of charity in interpreting actions as rational and utterances as in large part true "by our own lights."[65] To show that it cannot be that others' beliefs are largely false is to give a negative transcendental argument against the "very idea of a conceptual scheme."[66] Weber's common basis for rational interpretation is found in the principle of charity as a holistic condition for the possibility of understanding any language at all; interpretation is possible at all only on the background of shared and largely *true* beliefs. Hence, the conditions of interpretation are connected to the theory of truth by demonstrating the incoherence of the opposite view: the implication by conceptual relativism that there are belief systems that we can understand that are largely false.

Davidson nicely summarizes his transcendental argument at the beginning of another essay: "In order to communicate, most of our beliefs must be true."[67] Conceptual relativism of the usual varieties, particularly those associated with skeptical varieties of post-empiricism (such as Kuhn's paradigm shifts and Quine's ontological relativity) presupposes an incoherent, "final dogma of empiricism": the idea of uninterpreted experience that is uncontaminated by interpretation. Davidson's argument shows that massive error is simply unintelligible and hence that there is always a basis for rational interpretation. He makes a similar argument with regard to actions as well as utterances, so that here, too, there is a basis for interpretation not confined to the subjective point of view of the agent. As interpreters, we may use our own "norms" as a reliable basis for explaining actions, just as our own truths are a reliable basis for interpreting utterances. As Davidson puts it, the point of interpreting and explaining intentional action is that "in explaining actions we are identifying the phenomena to be explained and the phenomena that do the explaining as directly answering to our norms."[68] An integrated theory of action and speech finds a basis for explanation in two different aspects of rationality – namely, shared norms and truths; such standards of rationality apply to all forms of intelligible behavior.

Habermas, too, makes a similar argument for the same Weberian purpose when he defends what he calls "the disquieting thesis" that all understanding is evaluative and accepts all its "shocking" methodological consequences.[69] Habermas's view of rational interpretation is ultimately more Weberian than Davidson's principle of charity, which connects rationality and interpretation in so holistic a way as to make differences that can be meaningfully compared impossible: in order to avoid problems of indeterminacy, Davidson places everyone in the same hermeneutic circle. The "language of perspicuous contrast" is all inclusive, so that there is only the normal problem of dealing with particular errors. While anti-skeptical, Davidson paints with the same holistic grey.

Davidson might reply as he does to a hypothetical objection in "The Very Idea of a Conceptual Scheme": the criticism of the idea of relative conceptual schemes does not mean that we all share the same one.[70] Nonetheless, Davidson eliminates any place for contextual criticism, since all puzzles about differences dissolve into bad translations and pseudoproblems.[71] The problem is that this argument works only for semantic differences about "meanings," not for other problems of unintelligibility of actions and practices. Making sense of the Balinese cockfight is not simply a matter of interpreting their beliefs, desires and norms of rationality. Apart from Davidson's powerful arguments about the role of truth in making sense of beliefs, it is questionable whether this same argument holds using our "norms" in the same way for interpreting actions; at least no argument has been made that general agreement about norms of action is a necessary condition of communication on a par with truth. Determining just what the Greeks thought about the gods and their commands does not resemble Davidsonian interpretation. Rather, it takes a lot of contextual interpretation of the sort that Paul Veyne supplies in his detailed analysis of the various modalities of their beliefs and its relation to their actions.[72] Understanding these complex relationships is not possible by imposing our beliefs and norms on the Greeks, but only by comparisons related to specific differences, like those that Veyne shows about the Greek concept of reality and their willingness to act upon things that they did not recognize as "real" in the same way as tables and chairs.

Like Davidson's, Habermas's theory of meaning also connects evaluation and understanding, the conditions of truth with those of communication. To understand an utterance is to understand its truth conditions in a more generalized sense of its "acceptability conditions," what it would mean to accept it as rationally justified or intersubjectively binding. This connection between interpretation and evaluation is not simply an implication of a theory of utterance meaning. Rather, it is implied by Habermas's weak holism, by the fact that the interpreter is always in some hermeneutic circle. Habermas concludes from this perspectival character that interpretation is always engaged, always in the "performative attitude" of the first person participant rather than the third person theoretical observer. If this is the case, there is no avoiding comparison for all forms of rational evaluation, from truth to norms to aesthetic judgments. In this way, Habermas hopes to turn the tables on the hermeneutic skeptic: because of our engaged and situated character, because we are inevitably participants in a background of practices, we must always evaluate in order to understand and relate "their" beliefs and norms to "ours."

Habermas's main point is to see that the conditioned character of interpretation makes it a form of practical knowledge, knowledge that must be gained within the constraints of the participant's perspective. Since she is dependent on the interpretive standpoint to achieve any evidence, the social scientist is always a participant, if only a virtual one. Habermas squarely faces the dilemmas this involvement poses: like ethnomethodology, Habermas argues that the social scientist has no access to special evidence and starts entirely on a par with the lay participant in a lifeworld. The social scientist must "already belong in a certain way" to the lifeworld whose elements he wishes to describe. "In order to describe them, he must understand them; in order to understand them, he must be able in principle to participate in their production; and participation presupposes that one belongs."[73] Rational interpretation offers a weak holistic solution to this problem which ultimately distinguishes the knowledge of the social scientist from the participant as a matter of degree and not of kind.

Habermas sees disputes about interpretation not just as a matter of imposition (Davidson's assumption of identity), but as a matter of taking stock of differences (evaluating reasons). In this way, the interpreter must compare her reasons to theirs in the performative attitude; that is, she must take a position *vis-à-vis* their validity. Interpretation therefore requires not only identifying what the reasons are (in contextual interpretation) but also understanding why they are valid or invalid as justifying reasons or "validity claims." Habermas puts this comparative element of social scientific interpretation in the strongest possible terms: "An interpreter cannot, therefore, interpret expressions connected through criticizable validity claims with a potential of reasons (and thus represent knowledge) without taking a position on them."[74] In this way, the relativistic consequences of the hermeneutic circle are blunted, while the possibility of specific and recognizable differences is preserved.

Just what it means for the social scientist to "take a position" has a lot to do with the plausibility of the main thesis; namely, the intrinsic relation between understanding a reason and evaluating its correctness or validity. On the one hand, Habermas indicates that we should take his thesis as having the broadest possible scope: all types of interpretation are necessarily evaluative. To interpret something is already to evaluate it. So boldly stated, this broad claim seems clearly false, as contextual interpretation of the sort performed by ethnography indicates. In the example borrowed from MacIntyre above, the evaluation of the rationality of the strange action of eating the single specimen of fruit depended on understanding the context of the action in order to identify what it actually is. To understand it as strange requires that the scientific context is not the same as a grocery store. Hence, the scope of Habermas's claim should be modified: interpretation requires evaluation to the extent that what is at stake in the interpretation is a "validity claim," a claim that the action is justifiable relative to some form of shared knowledge. Interpreters bring their own cognitive resources and well-justified knowledge claims to bear on the claims of others. The use of subjective preference of "liking fruit" and resulting means–ends inference does not justify eating the specimen. If understanding an action or expression requires taking some such justification into account, then its interpretation requires the employment of the interpreter's knowledge *qua* participant; not to do so is to set the interpretation adrift in some "view from nowhere." But this does not mean that *all* interpretation is evaluation, since the interpreter may not be in a position to identify the expressions of others as recognizably justified at all. The strong claim of identity between interpretation and evaluation therefore cannot be correct, although on this weaker interpretation there is a potential for rational criticism built into all forms of interpretation.

This more restricted scope for explicit evaluation actually reflects Habermas's own practice of rational interpretation. Justifiable comparisons can be made only if the presence of certain "learning processes" establish commonalities across cultural boundaries, commonalities in particular between the past of one culture and the present condition of another. These commonalities based on learning can be identified by more general suppositions that make communication possible, what Habermas calls "suppositions of commonality" between interpreter and participant. They qualify the interpreter as a "virtual participant," one who can participate in "their" way of life by establishing a dialogue with them from "our" point of view. The commonalities that make this possible need not be constants of human nature. While these minimal suppositions are able to establish communication enough for minimal understanding (and thus are quite like the principle of charity), differences can be established when learning processes have taken place. Such differences become clear when the reasons given for an action fail to be convincing to the interpreter as virtual participant.

If contextual interpretation identifies an action or a practice and its accepted form of justification, rational interpretation requires making judgments about the reasons given for such actions or practices. Its scope does not include judgments about forms of life as a whole, but judgments made frequently in the history of a society. MacIntyre makes similar claims in his criticism of Winch's relativism about Azande witches and divination. The reasons for such practices can be evaluated because of a certain historical "commonality" between European and Azande cultures. In early modernity, the existence and effects of witches were also at issue, as

much as they are now in Africa as a consequence of moderniza-
tion and cultural disintegration. Rational interpretation of this
practice is possible precisely because the reasons for rejecting witches
in Europe bear upon Azande claims about their practices.[75] The
"disenchantment of the world," as Weber described it, brings
about a basic change in how we evaluate certain types of reasons,
which in turn has changed symbolic and cultural structures. Trial
by ordeal has ceased to be recognized as a legal public procedure
because the reasons for it are no longer recognized as valid or
decisive, much as scientists no longer accept the reasons for
phlogiston theory.

By giving a full account of rational interpretation as the evaluation of a validity claim, Habermas can resolve the problems that
Taylor's idea of a language of perspicuous contrast leaves unresolved
and Davidson's principle of charity does not illuminate. Habermas
has systematized his conception of social learning in a theory of
social evolution, which he hopes provides a theoretical backing for
comparative claims in "species-wide" patterns of development
modelled on the cognitive–developmental theories of Piaget and
Kohlberg. But even the evaluation of a whole type of reason (say,
one derived from mythic narratives) must still be the subject of a
rational interpretation; this developmental logic does not justify
claims to superiority like some external standard or hierarchy. In
each case, the theory merely organizes a series of arguments in a
developmental fashion, and can be recapitulated internally. Specific
learning processes and specific reasons must always be identified
even apart from this theory, as MacIntyre does in discussing various
beliefs about witches. Belief A could be said to be superior to
belief B only if this is a devaluative learning process that can be
internally recapitulated, so that stage A beliefs are superseded by
stage B beliefs. This general theory of learning and comparison
only generalizes the results of rational interpretation and provides
a good case study of the problems of rational as opposed to
contextual interpretation: even though a rational interpreter may
always find the others' reasons more convincing than her own,
ethnocentrism is the greater methodological difficulty, as the history of the rationalist tradition in European social science shows.

The Theory of Social Evolution as Case Study:
Eurocentrism as a Problem for Rational Interpretation

Since the Enlightenment, and particularly in the work of Condorcet,
the social sciences have attempted to establish a strong relationship between learning and social change, between the cumulative

growth of knowledge and moral progress. If what is later is better, then the approval of modernity could be underwritten by a teleological and progressive philosophy of history. Today such views are greeted with skepticism, especially the "post-modern suspicion of all grand metanarratives," as Lyotard puts it. Such reconstructions of our past now seem obviously Whiggish and empirically dubious, given the unabated European taste for atrocity. But such suspicions too broadly cast lead to doubts about the very possibility of rational interpretation, even one that takes the hermeneutic circle seriously, just as Clifford's suspicions of representation lead to problems for contextual interpretation. In the case of comparative judgments of superiority, skepticism is hardly confined to postmodernism alone.

Habermas's theory of social evolution as a species-wide learning process is an attempt to provide a theoretical and methodological answer to the problems of rationality and relativism. Like Weber's account of the role of the West in the rationalization of culture, Habermas's theory of social learning gives universal significance to cultural trends that involve the development of certain competences necessary for acquiring and using knowledge – that is, for a rational form of culture. These developments can be "rationally reconstructed" as learning processes analogous to Piaget's theory of universal and necessary stages in the sequence of cognitive development. Habermas is particularly interested in moral development, since, as we have seen, changes in what counts as moral justification are the "pacemakers of social evolution."[76] This theory, therefore, generalizes MacIntyre's criticisms of Winch in that certain universally significant transformations establish the criteria for evaluation in cross-cultural settings. Just as on the individual level of cognitive development from one stage to the next, in social learning certain reasons and interpretations become devalued: "With the transition to a new stage, the interpretations of the superseded stage are, no matter what their content, *categorically devalued*."[77] In this way, a whole type of reason is no longer convincing to the interpreter, and when that reason is encountered again in another culture, the learning process gives the interpreter the means to evaluate it negatively on formal grounds, in terms of what type of reason it is: the way it is offered as a justification is criticized, not what it is supposed to justify. One of Habermas's best developed examples is the devaluation of myths as legitimating reasons.[78] Mythic narratives rely on the cognitive confusions of the subjective, natural, and social worlds, all of which are fused together in the events of the myth's narrative.

Once these worlds are distinguished cognitively, myths lose their force as justifying reasons for institutions. The modern world view, which makes these distinctions, can be used as the basis for a negative comparative evaluation; undoing them is the only way that we can understand the world view of certain social actors.

Because of its level of generality, it is hard to verify such claims in the usual indicative sense. Not all societies have undergone these same learning processes, so the claims made here are extremely formal. Certainly, alternative pathways of development must be possible, although their existence cannot be verified given the thousands of years over which such developments occur. But as a methodological solution to the problem of rational interpretation, Habermas wants to make comparative judgments an empirical question, the answers to which depend on theories that organize the best available evidence. The theory of social evolution does not avoid the problems of rational interpretation, but explicitly takes an internal perspective; it makes "our" beliefs the basis for the framework of the theory, which then tests this assumption empirically. This is what Habermas has in mind when he writes, "In claiming universal validity – with, however, many qualifications – for *our* concept of rationality, without therefore adhering to a completely untenable belief in progress, we are taking on a sizable burden of proof."[79] Certainly part of the proof, at least, is empirical if any specific comparison is to be supported; at the same time, Habermas is also pointing out the unavoidable presuppositions of rational interpretation from within the "performative attitude" that the theory of social evolution also shares.

If this is the case, the scope of successful rational interpretation is clearly limited to cases where disputes about interpretation can be resolved by giving good reasons pro and con: it is confined to formal cognitive structures and reason-giving epistemic activities. Many evaluative questions may not be equivocal: there might be many different versions of "civilized humanity," to use Weber's term, each rationally interpreting each other's practices and knowledge. Not only might there be many different valid justifications and developmental pathways, many questions of value are "posed as contextual and can be answered only within the horizon of a particular form of life."[80] If this admission is accepted, such questions of value, identity, or the good life might only be indirectly accessible to rational interpretation. Nonetheless, such evaluative questions are norm-related, to adapt Weber's term for the value-relatedness of means–ends value judgments. Questions about the justification of norms and institutions may still bear upon such questions of value and the good life: rejecting certain norms as unjust may require new values, identities, and institutions, as occurred historically in the secularization of European culture.[81]

Even with this pluralism, Habermas seeks an approach to rational interpretation that is universal enough to regard "this multiplicity of forms of life as limited to *cultural contents*, and it asserts that every culture must share certain *formal properties* of the modern understanding of the world," if it is to be rational and self-reflexive. These refer not to the content of European beliefs, but to "a few necessary structural properties."[82] One such formal property is the ability to distinguish what is merely accepted culturally from what is actually valid. If two forms of life are on the same formal level, then there is no basis for claims of superiority. In this case, we go back to contextual and dialogical types of interpretation; we may enter into a common discourse about our differences. Post-modernists have rightly pointed out that other cultures are more capable of entering into such a dialogue than European social science has cared to admit.

This admission does not lead to the conclusion that each culture follows the call of its own "gods and demons." This decisionistic impasse occurs in Weber only because he restricted his universalist assumptions to instrumental action and logical consistency; Habermas believes the same structure of rational interpretation can be extended to a cognitivist and universalist treatment of the justification of moral and aesthetic norms. Even so, Habermas stops short of *Werturteile* about the content of practices, while providing a systematic way for rational interpretation to avoid the dilemmas of incorrigibility and ethnocentrism. The theory of social evolution carries with it the latter problem, given its avowedly Eurocentric starting point. However, by reflecting on this constraint and on the conditions of interpretation within it, Habermas can avoid the problem of imposition and misunderstanding, all the while keeping intact the clear and unavoidable differences between social scientists and participants, available only from a first person and hence fallibilistic perspective.

Conclusion: The Purposes of Interpretation in the Social Sciences

One of the main results of this analysis of interpretation is that there appears to be a variety of types of interpretation, each with its own governing constraints and norms. While contextual interpretation forms the basis of the "interpretive turn" in the social sciences, rational interpretation performs methodological functions that contextual interpretation cannot fulfill. Each can correct the other: while contextual interpretation places actions and utterances in larger wholes to make them intelligible, rational criticism focuses on the unresolved differences between the interpreter's and the actor's points of view and carefully compares and evaluates them. For both, correctness is a regulative ideal, although not an actual achievement of any interpretive claim. Weak holism is still holism enough to see interpretation as a fallible process guided by norms of accuracy, coherence, and comprehensiveness, where each points to different types of public evidence within the hermeneutic circle. Habermas's insistence on the evaluative component of interpretation reflects a commitment to specifying what makes one interpretation better than another in the social sciences.

The problem of interpretive validity is made more difficult by the presence of diverse types of interpretation in the social sciences, each with its own purposes and theoretical contexts. Philosophical theories are replete with global claims about interpretation, including the works of the philosophers that I have called weak holists. Philosophers make claims such as Dreyfus's claim that "all interpretation is a skill," or Gadamer's claim that it is "the fusion of horizons," or Davidson's claim that "all understanding of the speech of another involves radical translation," or Habermas's claim that "all interpretation is evaluation." All of these statements ignore the multiplicity of interpretive contexts and tasks. Even if we speak of various disciplines, we are still not specific enough. Neither "social science" nor "literary criticism," for that matter, provides a unified enough context to justify generalizing about any definite set of purposes for all interpretations: they can settle historical disputes, make something strange become more familiar, something familiar become more strange, produce consensus, or problematize the consensus already present. Various competing interpretations often serve opposite purposes and therefore must be more complex and diverse in their structure than most analyses admit.

Different social sciences employ interpretation for different ends and vary in the priority assigned to different types of interpretation. While sociology has tended to give methodological priority to rational interpretation in its search for explanations, in this century ethnography has sought to increase our understanding of diversity and aid the imagination in conceiving human alternatives

through contextual interpretation. Even Richard Rorty, a philosopher who counsels "frank ethnocentrism" as an alternative to
relativism, sees a role for contextual interpretation in the more
ethnographically oriented discipline of the history of philosophy:
"There is nothing wrong with self-consciously letting our philosophical view dictate terms in which to describe the dead. But
there are reasons for also describing them in terms other than our
own."[83] Once this is admitted, it is Rorty's description of these
purposes that is objectionable: placing the dead in their "benighted
times," understanding their "outdated language," and other Whiggish purposes "for which it is useful to know how people talked
who did not know as much as we do."[84] We understand others in
"their own terms" to show how they know less than we do, on
the model of the way historians of science understand the past.

There is nothing about the holistic character of contextual interpretation or even the evaluative character of rational interpretation
that forces this ethnocentric predicament upon us in the social
sciences. There are purposes other than condescension to the past
and to other cultures that interpretation in the social sciences may
serve. These are the "uses of diversity" which include, in Geertz's
apt phrase, overcoming "the comforts of merely being ourselves"
as well as finding alternative possibilities for living.[85] Against Bernard
Williams, I do not think that these alternatives are confined to
appreciating only what represents a "live option" for us; rather,
understanding alternatives is cognitively necessary in order to expand
the horizons of our own discourses and our capacities for mutual
understanding and responsibility. Gadamer's requirement that interpreters be willing to learn from the text interpreted is correct,
but not so much as an epistemological generalization about interpretation as an elaboration of one of its basic moral purposes.
Besides the epistemic goal of correctness, the best ethnography has
had this non-relativistic and highly moral purpose of increasing
the capacity for dialogue with others, a purpose not inconsistent
with Habermas's description of the reflective character of social
knowledge in modernity. The proliferation of multiple interpretations makes sense in this context as part of the cognitive ability to
see things from many perspectives and to break down authoritative, habitual, and restricted ways of thinking and reading.[86]

According to the weak holistic analysis of this chapter, there is
a variety of types of interpretation in the social sciences, fulfilling
a variety of different valid purposes: explanatory, critical, aesthetic, and moral. Even with this diversity, interpretation has its own
exigencies and demands, reflected in its normative epistemology.

This epistemology concerns the ways in which interpretations can be justified within holistic constraints, constraints that are neither relativistic nor ethnocentric limits.

Because of its holistic character, the interpretive turn in the social sciences has tended to be totalizing, to be thought to cover all of social inquiry. Interpretations are required in so many critical and explanatory contexts in the social sciences that it seemed to exhaust their methods. Yet, traditional social theory from Durkheim to Parsons has not been oriented to interpretation but to collective forms of explanation, often independent of actors' beliefs and intentions. For some research programs, the newer intentionalist approaches to social action have meant abandoning the traditional forms of explanation, as in the criticism of older concepts of social structure by ethnomethodologists and the criticism of functional explanation by rational choice theorists. However, other theorists have attempted to reformulate, rather than abandon, concepts of function and structure by linking them more closely to explanations of social action. This "micro–macro link" presents the possibility of resolving one of the endless controversies of the "old" logic of social science: the fruitless debate between methodological collectivism and methodological individualism.

4

The Macro–Micro Relation

The analyses of various types of explanation and interpretation in the last two chapters show that problems of indeterminacy arise in many different contexts and at many different levels. To settle such problems and justify their claims, both explanations and interpretations that appeal to meanings, intentions, and rules ultimately refer to larger contexts of action. For example, the existence of exceptions shows that following a rule is often what needs to be explained. Why are some rules followed more frequently than others? Furthermore, understanding an action as intelligible or rational requires placing it in a larger context of practices and norms. What context best illuminates an action, and how do we compare across various contexts? Both of these types of indeterminacy suggest a fundamental problem for social theory: how do explanations systematically relate actions to these larger contexts and settings? How do such contexts influence and constrain actions, and how do actions produce and reproduce these contexts? These questions raise age-old philosophical problems concerning the relation of the individual to society, of parts to the whole. In the current usage of social theory, it is common to distinguish between two different levels of analysis: between "macro" and "micro" levels of explanation, or between micro-level explanations of *agency* (typically agents' purposes, beliefs, and rationality) and macro-level explanations of the *structures* within which these actions take place (such as social structures, institutions, and norms).

Such distinctions are not confined to the social sciences. In biology, some version of the distinction between micro- and macro-levels is fundamental to explanation in evolutionary theory. While the basic processes of change occur on the genetic level (the genotype), such changes emerge as properties related to the adaptive capacities of the organism, its structure, and its behavior (the phenotype). Hypotheses about the various mechanisms that connect these two levels have flourished in the history of biology. Before the "neo-Darwinian synthesis," evolutionary theory operated without any good account of the micro-level genetic processes of evolutionary change, nor any real account of how macro-characteristics (like behavior and other adaptive traits) were connected to any micro-processes except through Darwin's differential survival rates of organisms. Nonetheless, good natural–historical accounts of adaptation and survival could be developed on these Darwinian grounds in the absence of any good micro-theory and any synthetic theory of their linkage. Even armed with the micro-theory of genetics, the macro-level accounts of natural history are not necessarily much improved. They remain fundamentally historical forms of explanation that trace observable sequences in the fossil record, not deductions from general laws at the micro-level. As Lewontin puts it, "To the present moment no one has succeeded in measuring with any accuracy the net fitness of genotypes for any locus in any species in any environment in nature."[1] While examples from other sciences exist, including metallurgy and thermodynamics,[2] evolutionary theory provides a good methodological lesson for the often fruitless debates about reductionism, including debates about the reducibility or irreducibility of collective social phenomena. In the absence of causal completeness and determinacy, there seems to be little reason to think that the explanation of the complex phenomena of the evolutionary change of species needs to be reduced to the laws governing the constituent parts of organisms.[3]

The connection of these debates to biological explanation is stronger still, in light of the historical use of analogies to the biological sciences by early proponents of collectivism in social theory. Durkheim saw societies as highly organized entities much like organisms, in which each part served some function for the good of the whole. In light of his commitment to a distinct level of "social facts" above and beyond "psychological facts" about individuals or aggregates of individuals, Durkheim explained suicide rates, for example, in terms of the lack of social integration and the failures of various institutions in modern society. In his *Rules of Sociological Method*, Durkheim argues that the autonomy of social facts and the interrelated character of the social whole establishes an anti-reductive methodology in the social sciences: "Whenever a social phenomenon is directly explained by a psychological phenomenon we may be sure that the explanation is false."[4] There are also those philosophers from Hobbes to Popper who give equally strong methodological prescriptions requiring reference to individuals in explanations and reduction as the proper goal of inquiry. As Hobbes puts it, "It is necessary to know the things compounded before we can know the compound,"[5] and societies are composed of individuals. Many different approaches are individualist in this sense, from Mill's empiricist idea that sociology is based on psychological laws to various interpretive approaches that demand that social science understand things from the agent's point of view. For Durkheim, these views all repeat Hobbes's mistaken injunction to treat individuals like "mushrooms sprung suddenly from the earth"; their attempt to explain everything at the level of constituent parts reduces society and social organization to "only artificial and more or less arbitrary combinations."[6]

Certainly, "methodological individualism" is often a corrective to the metaphysical excesses and reifications of some holistic social theories, including orthodox Marxism and Parsonian structural functionalism. It is also a reaction against the poverty of some holistic explanations, particularly ones linked to the idea of objective teleologies governing large-scale social and historical change, such as theories of inevitable progress. Instead of giving purposes to collective social units like "Europe" or the "East," methodological individualists argue that persons and persons alone can have intentional properties. Thus, on this view, all social theories must have "micro-foundations"; that is, their explanations must ultimately be reducible to, or entail, explanations of individual behavior. In a recent statement of this view that is close to the views of Popper and Watkins, the main proponents of individualism in debates in the 1950s, Jon Elster defines methodological individualism as "the doctrine that all social phenomena – their structure and their change – are in principle explicable in ways that only involve individuals – their properties, their goals, their beliefs and their actions."[7] Yet, Elster immediately qualifies this bold prescription with the admission that individuals also have "relational properties" that have explanatory value. This admission raises doubts about whether the debate is not so much methodological as metaphysical. As early as *The Structure of Science*, Nagel brought the debate about individualist objections to functionalism to a close by showing why they are not exclusive alternatives and how questions of the adequacy of explanations involving functions and teleologies can be resolved empirically.[8] It is questionable whether anything empirical is really at stake in this new round of debate as well, once we admit Elster's "relational properties" or Danto's "social individuals."[9] Further, a priori claims about the completeness of either type of theory lead nowhere: while individualists can claim that all "social" phenomena are merely aggregation effects, holists can argue that individualism itself can be explained by the breakdown of traditional collective structures and the emergence of modern social and economic institutions.[10]

Much of the debate seems to revolve around false antinomies or overly prescriptive views of the philosophy of science, both unrelated to social scientific practice. In this chapter, I will first show why all in principle arguments for or against holism or individualism fail: they are either bad metaphysics or bad methodology. Indeed, apart from the usual few holdouts, a new consensus is emerging in the social sciences. The basic question has changed, and it is time philosophers caught up. The proper theoretical and methodological question is not how to reduce one to the other but how they are linked and interconnected: theoretical debates are no longer about reduction, but "linkage."[11] For the empirical purpose of constructing better explanations, it is increasingly clear that the distinction between micro- and macro-levels is at best an analytic one, marking a continuum of theoretical concepts that figure in an adequate explanation rather than a dichotomy between distinct levels of social ontology. But the consensus should not be overstated. There is no absence of reductionistic theories and explanations, particularly in the work of some proponents of two of the research programs discussed in this book: while the theory of communicative action is committed to linkage, rational choice theory and ethnomethodology have often been interpreted as radically individualistic, especially in their criticisms of other theories.

However, this residual individualism is not so much a metaphysical as an empirical presupposition of their research programs. Taken in this way, the macro–micro linkage becomes an *empirical* question. The reductionist programs of rational choice theory and ethnomethodology stand or fall on whether or not they can construct the best explanation of various empirical phenomena relative to other theories, especially those phenomena for which strong explanations in macrosociology already exist. Each program can refer to core cases of successful reductions: whereas rational choice models itself on the reduction of the aggregate effects of market behavior to microeconomic laws, ethnomethodology argues that many previous claims of conformity to norms and rules have been successfully reduced to highly reflexive "micro-management" of interactions by knowledgeable agents themselves. How far can these reductions be extended to other behaviors and activities? Besides such empirical questions of adequacy, there are also pragmatic questions about different levels of explanation. What are the uses of different types of explanation at different levels? Do certain types of explanation fulfill certain purposes better than others?

In the rest of the chapter, I would like to treat the micro–macro link as just such an empirical and pragmatic question, rather than as a metaphysical or ontological one. First, I will approach the issue by examining the current round of debates about traditional functionalist explanations in the social sciences. While it is all well and good to criticize the many bad functionalist explanations in the social sciences, this criticism does not undermine the many good ones. Their conditions of adequacy can be precisely stated in a pattern of explanation, for which there are many existent exemplars. Second, I will turn to each of the research programs that I have discussed so far and examine the micro–macro assumptions that guide their research and explanations. I will then try to suggest different types of equally valid micro–macro linkages, in particular problems related to culture and social systems. Finally, by considering the problem of bureaucracy as dealt with by many different approaches, I want to show the different purposes to which micro- and macro-explanations can be put and how these purposes enter into the ways that it is possible to assess their adequacy.

The Individualist Challenge to Functionalism

Traditional functionalist explanations in sociology and anthropology are undeniably holistic. According to their usual procedure, an institution or a practice may be explained in terms of its function, the benefits or purposes which it contributes to the maintenance of the social whole. In general, a functionalist explanation works by showing that a practice or institution has certain effects or consequences, the results of which are beneficial to the society, even if that effect or consequence is not intended by any of the actors. "Function" was one of Aristotle's four causes, and such purposes certainly form answers to "why" questions by clarifying "that for the sake of which something exists." Functionalist explanations abound in sociology, if not in all the sciences:[12] Durkheim explained rituals in terms of their effects of increasing solidarity among members of a group; Marx explained law and other parts of the superstructure by showing that they stabilize the relations of production; anthropologists from Malinowski on have explained a multitude of sometimes bizarre practices, such as witchcraft and sorcery, by the way supernatural sanctions help maintain the established moral order. Such functionalist explanations imply that societies are like organisms, seeking to maintain a self-stabilizing equilibrium and endogenously producing the proper beliefs and practices that maintain the system of relationships. Functionalist explanations of this sort typically relate micro-level behavior or patterns of action (rituals, social institutions) to the large macro-level order and thus provide a good test case for thinking about them in terms of micro–macro linkage rather than reduction or autonomy.

Functionalism has now fallen into ill-repute, at least since the cogent criticism of its bad forms by Merton and Stinchcomb and more recently by Elster.[13] As Merton notes, in its heyday functionalism became a "universal postulate." Any standardized piece of cultural or social behavior was attributed a positive adaptive function to the point of empirical vacuity. Like methodological individualism, functionalism is a research program and a heuristic postulate for inquiry. It is easy to show the non-empirical character of some of its explanations. Indeed, many statements produced as explanations in this broad program tend to be as much true by definition as Hempel's general laws. The critical portion of Merton's article is full of empty and absurd explanations like one taken from Kluckhohn's *Navaho Witchcraft*: "The at present mechanically useless buttons on the sleeve of a European man's suit serve the 'function' of preserving the familiar, of maintaining a behavior." But, as Merton goes on to note, this is true of any pattern of behavior whatsoever and thus fails to explain it. As Merton puts it, "Although any item of culture or of social structure *may* have a function, it is premature to hold unequivocally that every such item *must* be functional."[14]

Even granting that an item is functional, that is not the end to problems of explaining it in terms of its function. Explanations like Kluckhohn's also commit what Elster and others call the "functionalist fallacy": even if a pattern of behavior is shown to have certain consequences, it may not exist because it has such consequences. The same is true of collective purposes and interests as well: an institution or belief may serve a particular interest of a group, but that interest may not explain the belief, as we saw in the case of Shapin's explanation of phrenology in chapter 1. The supposedly arch-functionalist Durkheim already formulated something like this fallacy in his *Rules of Sociological Method*: "To show how a fact is useful is not to explain how it originated or why it is what it is."[15] Political institutions, for example, are not to be explained simply because they benefit the ruling class (although they usually do) or because they promote the development of the forces of production (which they do not always do). Institutions may or may not fit such a purpose, and even if they do they may be better explained by other purposes or causes.

For a purpose to really explain the institution or practice, it must fit stringent requirements: in Merton's terms, it must be "indispensable" to the social system that it maintains or benefits.[16] It would seem, then, that functionalist explanations require a detailed description of the requirements for a system's self-maintenance. Yet, there is an indefinite number of ways to fulfill any given purpose or function through various customs, beliefs, or institutions. The same item, too, may serve any number of functions or have any number of beneficial consequences. The problem with functionalism is an explanatory indeterminacy that is typical of macro-level explanations: by basing explanations on consequences and benefits for the group, "one will be able to generate an indefinite number of 'explanations' of the same explanandum."[17] The question remains whether or not such indeterminacy is really a "fallacy," or whether it is an unavoidable feature of certain types of explanation, as much as causal indeterminacy is a feature of intentional explanations. We have seen in chapter 1 that not only do intentional explanations also suffer from indeterminacy, but that even the introduction of "mechanisms" keeps them indeterminate in much the same way that purposes and functions are. Such low-level generalizations only indicate a possible context in which a particular intention might be a plausible explanation of an action.

What critics like Elster call "the functionalist fallacy" is not a fallacy at all, or even an explanatory deficit. Rather, it is a problem to be overcome in developing an informative pattern of macro-level explanation. Functional explanations require the existence of functional properties that are supervenient upon other non-functional properties; the same functional properties can be realized through any number of states with different non-functional properties.[18] Most explanations in the social sciences have this same feature, since even instances of intentional action are not necessarily identical with each other, but stand in a relation of supervenience to the properties of the states through which they are realized. Greetings are supervenient upon all the different vocal sounds and gestures that make up all the variations of recognizing others and initiating interaction. Individualists, therefore, are no better off than functionalists in their intentional, purposive explanations. This difficulty leads to embedding intentional actions in larger social contexts in order to explain them, and one such context is functional. Here the problem with the explanation goes in the opposite direction: from macro-functions to micro-level instantiations. Establishing this relation requires specifying the social actions through which the function is realized. All good functionalist explanations integrate intentional factors as one of their conditions of adequacy, thus linking micro- and macro-levels.

While Merton and Stinchcomb argue that such weaker functionalist explanations are valid, Elster attempts to show that most, if not all, functionalist explanations fail to meet this condition. Functionalist explanations are not only empirically inadequate, but on this view also the result of a category mistake of applying intentional predicates to macro-social phenomena, seeing purpose and sense in large-scale patterns. This might be called "the fallacy of misplaced intentions," and is uncovered by comparing a proffered functionalist explanation with one that shows the supervenience of the functional property upon some causal process (a "feedback loop") that realizes it.

Elster gives the following five conditions that all functionalist explanations must meet.

The Pattern of Functionalist Explanation

"An institution or behavioral pattern X is explained by its function Y for group Z, if, and only if,
(1) Y is an effect of X;
(2) Y is beneficial for Z;
(3) Y is unintended by the actors producing X;
(4) Y or at least the causal relation between X and Y, is unrecognized by the actors in Z;
(5) Y maintains X by a causal feedback loop passing through Z."[19]

Elster gives a few examples of functionalist explanations that do satisfy these conditions, usually because there is some individualist causal mechanism operating in the background. For example, competition assures the survival of profit-maximizing firms in the market, even when this is not their explicit goal.[20]

However, most standard functionalist explanations fail, usually by committing the category mistake of "objective teleology" that is needed to cover over the absence of a causal feedback loop. "Functionalist sociologists argue *as if* (which is not to argue that) criterion (5) is automatically fulfilled whenever the other criteria are"; that is, whenever there is an unintended and unperceived beneficial consequence, some causal process is at work.[21] While the requirement that the effect be unintended and unperceived may be unique to functionalist explanations, something like criterion 5 is crucial to all valid macrosociological explanations: what is important is not the requirement that the macro-property be supervenient upon a *causal* process, but that it provide *some* clear linkage between the macro-level properties or consequences and the micro-level of social actions.

Elster's criterion 5 is too specific even for functionalism. First, it is too narrow in its requirement that the causal mechanism must be independent of actors' intentions. Surely, functions can be fulfilled through agents' intentions; the point is that they can also be fulfilled even contrary to their intentions, if macro-constraints are strong enough. Second, it is also too specific, in that it requires that there be only one instantiation of the process that connects the behavior X to the overall benefits and consequences of Y. Instead, there may be very many different processes and mechanisms by which the same benefit is produced. This causal indeterminacy is not a defect of functionalist explanation but a consequence of the level at which the explanation is formulated. The functional properties of a practice or pattern of action are supervenient upon other non-functional properties (such as the intentions of actors or other causal properties of individuals and their relations), and in this case not reducible to them. In general, supervenience is always a relation between two terms: whatever has B (the subvenient property) has A (the supervenient property). However, not all things that have A are B. (For example, the survival of a firm may be due to technological innovation rather than profit maximization.) An explanation can employ supervenient terms so long as it shows that there is some, but not always the same, subvenient base the properties of which realize it. But there can be many such realizations, all of which are token instances of the same function; this overdetermination is sufficient motivation for a theory to move to a macro-functional level. While universal functionalism is certainly false, it is more reasonable to say that the same explanation can refer to a number of different causal loops or processes, the exact nature and number of which is an empirical question. Such functionalist explanations are not category mistakes but rather incomplete: they must be filled out by an indefinite variety of micro-processes that substitute for Elster's criterion 5. So long as something like supervenience holds, it is possible to ramify the levels of explanation beyond simply individuals and their functions.[22] Universal functionalism does result in inadequate explanations and fails as much as individual reductionism in recognizing indeterminacy. As in many false dilemmas, both the epiphenomenal and reductionistic strategies of collectivism and individualism fail to resolve micro–macro indeterminacy.

Many functionalist explanations do fail precisely for reasons that Elster's pattern makes clear. Radcliffe-Brown's explanation of ancestor cults as producing solidarity fails, since such effects depend on the production of "ritual attitudes" in the group. As Mary Douglas points out, not all rituals produce the right sort of subvenient attitudes.[23] But there are numerous examples of such explanations in terms of solidarity that do work, including her own explanations of beliefs produced by witchcraft and by conspiracy theories. Such beliefs have the consequence of maintaining group membership and participation, despite rising costs.[24] She suggests that Merton's own analysis of the latent function of Hopi rain dances for maintaining solidarity is equally successful. Given the problems of collective action like free riders, it is hard to see how the cognitive components of maintaining social order could be explained without some form of functionalism to show how culture or "a thought-world constructs the thought-style that controls its experience."[25] Cultural anthropology has been giving this sort of analysis for decades, showing the linkages between beliefs and actions, interaction and various levels of social order and structure.

In the spirit of reductionism, Elster's argument works by showing how biology meets his methodological prescriptions while the social sciences do not. On closer analysis, Elster's appeal to evolutionary theory falls short; it is no less variable and historical than anthropology. "Fitness" does not reduce causal processes to a single type; every token instance of fitness is not identical with every other, except in having the property of fitness. As Levine, Sober, and Wright point out, if such expectations do not hold for biological explanations, "there is no reason to believe ... that any simple property corresponds to the general category 'fitness,' that the same mechanisms explain the fitness of, say, a frog and a giraffe."[26] Nor should we expect that every beneficial effect on survival rates should have the same causal loop, any more than every macrosocial phenomenon will have the same micro-instantiation. Such social phenomena are supervenient upon a variety of different actions and interactions, as much as a particular belief is upon a variety of different neurological or electronic hardware.

Whether or not the concept of supervenience captures the nonreducibility of functionalist explanations is not at issue here. The problem is one of completeness for both macro- and micro-explanations. What Levine, Sober and Wright say about macro-level explanations applies to all explanations at any level: "Since every macro-process must have a micro-realization, the elaboration of the possible micro-foundation lends credibility to macro-arguments."[27] So it is also with micro-level explanations, which gain credibility when the micro-level processes can be elaborated so as to fit into a larger social, ecological, and historical context within which beliefs and intentions are relevant explanatory features. Recent developments in the explanation of cooperation in rational choice theory have added such contextual features: social movements, for example, must mobilize available resources in order to form organizations and achieve collective goals.[28] These features are, however, parts of the macro-context for the explanation of cooperative behavior, and are not explained by the intentions of individual actors.[29]

Both micro- and macro-level explanations are by themselves incomplete and indeterminate in complementary ways: macro-explanations require "micro-translations," and "micro-foundations" require stable and enduring social contexts within which individual factors can be identified. Whether we call this "supervenience" or "structuration," in Giddens' phrase, the main problem remains that such explanations must establish relations between various levels of analysis in order to resolve their indeterminacy. Both micro- and macro-level explanations must therefore be extended in the direction of the other, if they are to be explanations at all. Theories or research programs that do not permit such extensions quickly degenerate into prescriptive metaphysics. In the next section, I will test whether such limitations stand in the way of any of the research programs in intentional social action developed so far. When faced with anomalies, rational choice theory and ethnomethodology often fall into unnecessary indeterminate and *ad hoc* explanations, due precisely to their own false methodological prescriptions.

To explore this question I will turn to two different areas of linkage and reduction in macro–micro explanations in contemporary research programs: cultural practices as structuring contexts of action and agency, on the one hand, and well-integrated social systems as structures that are relatively independent of agents' intentions, on the other. In each area, I will present different extreme micro- and macro-explanations and then show how a more complete explanation might be constructed on the basis of linkages. The case studies that follow show why the methodological goal of micro-reduction in rational choice theory and ethnomethodology is misguided and dooms their explanations to incompleteness and indeterminacy. Although the theory of communicative action pursues such linkages, its major attempt to theorize about them is not fully successful. Few successful explanations are currently available, since social theory has for so long sought to be holistic or reductionistic rather than complete.

Macro and Micro Links: Culture, Norms, and Agency

Durkheim's famous dictum, "treat social facts like things," formulates one distinct program for macro-level theories of society. Rather than denying the difference between social and natural facts, what Durkheim had in mind was the way in which social facts also constrain individual action in various ways. The influence of norms on action offers the exemplary case for Durkheim: they constrain social action rather than causally influence it. In fact, Durkheim defines social facts in two ways: by their relation to individual actions and by their generality among all members of a social group. A social fact is "every way of acting, fixed or not, capable of exercising over the individual an external constraint" and "which is general throughout a given society, while existing in its own right, independent of its individual manifestations."[30] Critics like Stephen Lukes have pointed out the multiple and even contradictory senses of constraint operative in such passages in which Durkheim explicates and applies his own dictum. Lukes finds three separate criteria of social facts: externality (in that they exist outside of the individual); constraint (in that they act in a variety of different ways from sanction to structural limits); and generality plus independence (in that a fact must be general in the group and identifiable independently from individual actions and beliefs).[31] The last feature identifies the fact as social, while the first two show how such facts constitute individuals and their identities. As stated, the definition is fraught with ambiguity: cultural constraints like norms are *both* internal and external to the agent, often sanctioning, yet internalized and interpreted. Moreover, social constraints operate in a variety of ways, even within a class of phenomena like norms: sometimes they act as limits, sometimes as conditions of success or failure, and so on. Durkheim employs "constraint" in such a variety of ways that it simply becomes an unanalyzed name for the influences of society on the individual.

Does this ambiguity mean that there is no clear distinction between social and psychological facts? Such problems have less to do with the methodological goals of the distinction as with Durkheim's overly strong holism, with his insistence on the "independence" of social facts. In his later writings, Durkheim moved toward linkage and argued that norms "attract" individuals to certain goals once they are internalized as moral ideals. Rather than supporting the independence of social facts, the distinction only shows the incompleteness of many individualist explanations, much as functionalism found that intentional explanations could not fully explain regularities of behavior. It is just such regularity that Durkheim has in mind with his criterion of generality: the general and repetitive character of certain patterns of action is in fact the defining feature of social structure, according to one of the widely held definitions. It is therefore a theory of social structure that is to provide the extension of individualist explanations into wider contexts, including the patterns of interaction called cultural practices. Structure is supposed to explain how these patterns are regularized and reproduced.

The upshot of Durkheim's view that independent social facts and structures are needed to explain regular action can be seen in his arguments against individualist contract theories: he challenged their entirely conventionalist assumptions about the formation of society, however hypothetical they may be. Contracts cannot be the basis of a stable social order, Durkheim argued, since they relate only to individuals' self-interests and could produce only "transient relations and passing association."[32] Even for contractual relations to be stable, there must be a "non-contractual element of the contract" that makes the contract binding, an integrative order of binding cultural obligations.[33] This non-contractual basis is the *conscience collective*. But rather than discuss Durkheim's theory, I will consider more recent versions of the idea of collective cultural order in Bourdieu's holistic notion of a *habitus* and Habermas's idea of a lifeworld.

The "pre-contractual basis of the contract" was supposed to

explain how patterns of interaction can persist and a society can integrate itself through recurrent social practices. Social theorists have called this aspect of social order "social integration," the cultural structure in which the coordination of action takes place. Individualism, they have argued, cannot account for the obligatory character of social norms, the interconnectedness of actions in practices, and the persistence of actions across generations. While the actions of individuals sometimes may change a practice, most do not. Most actions in fact produce and reproduce much the same context within which they are embedded, and the theory of social integration is the attempt to explain how these processes take place. Speaking a language is one such structure: in formulating my beliefs and intentions in a language, I accomplish my purposes by generally reproducing its grammatical structures and rules, which form a social order that is not the product of any single individual's intentional actions.

The classic anti-individualist discussion of cultural structure and practice is Mandelbaum's analysis of the difference between "cashing a check" and "signing a piece of paper."[34] How can we discuss Mandelbaum's distinction without Durkheimian independence? Contemporary social theorists have emphasized the mutual knowledge and shared norms that make the practice identifiable to anyone within a culture. But if the regularized modes of action and relationships that make up this social practice need not always depend on the individual agent's own understanding of them, how can we talk of shared knowledge or culture? This is precisely the problem that Bourdieu tries to solve with his notion of a habitus as the pre-reflective, implicit dispositions shared among participants in a cultural practice. Habitus is then part of a theoretical account of a certain type of cultural structure that permits enduring relationships and modes of action, even enduring strategic relationships.

It should not be surprising that the appeal to this same sort of prereflective orientation has already figured in the analysis of interpretation and the concept of the background. In this context, the background or habitus is an explanatory construct, a collective cultural structure and set of beliefs and norms within and against which agents perform their actions and pursue their goals. As prereflective and non-explicit, it takes on a normative and conditioning force that is neither external nor objective, neither internal nor subjective. According to Bourdieu, this constraining force manifests itself in an agent's dispositions, the range of behavioral possibilities that we all have in common. Bourdieu writes, "Habitus is the product of the work of inculcation and appropriation necessary in order for the products of collective history, objective structures (e.g., language, the economy, etc.) to succeed in reproducing themselves more or less completely, in the form of durable dispositions in the organism (which we can, if one wishes, call individuals) lastingly subjected to the same conditioning and hence placed in the same material conditions of existence."[35] Socialization is the process by which this inculcation works and this prereflective domain is "appropriated" as a whole.

For Bourdieu, both individual subjectivity and mutual association are produced through sharing a habitus, which does its work without the explicit regulation or sanctions which constrain only negatively. As in functionalist explanations, habitus is indicated by its effects: the coordination of plans and purposes in a regular pattern "without in any way being the product of rules ... [and] without presupposing a conscious aim or an express mastery of the operations necessary to attain them."[36] It is, to paraphrase Kant, "purposiveness without purpose"; or, in Bourdieu's own terms, it is "collectively orchestrated without being the product of the orchestrating activity of a conductor." It is the Leibnizian solution to the problem of other minds: preestablished harmony, here in the dispositions of other agents. As with Durkheim's use of constraint, Bourdieu's explanation of internalized normative order requires a wide and ambiguous use of the term disposition: as generative principle, structure, and inclination.[37]

Bourdieu denies that habitus is the only proper explanatory principle for the practical order. It fails to apply to formal domains like law or to strictly regulated actions like rituals based on traditional precepts.[38] But he believes that still leaves a vast domain of actions governed by "generative and implicit schemata" rather than explicit discursive rules. For many of the same reasons that I gave in chapter 2, Bourdieu argues that rules rarely explain many aspects of social practice, even in "rule-governed" practices like gift-giving and kinship relations. Among the Kabyle people whom Bourdieu studied, there is even a preferred marriage pattern, that between parallel cross-cousins. Bourdieu contrasts the "official kinship" of the traditional rules with the "practical kinship" of what is actually done by people acting strategically. Practical kinship is supposed to provide a good case study for the explanatory power of habitus, which begins by looking at what people actually do rather than what they say they are doing.

What we find by looking at the infrequency of preferred marriages is that the rules do not act as constraints in a very strong sense. Rather, what is really operating is not the official culture but implicit schemes and "second-order strategies" that regulate improvisation within the set of possible marriages. The second-order strategies are designed to achieve a variety of purposes and strategic goals which are pursued in marriages, including wealth, power, and recognition, all of which must appear to fall within the officially sanctioned rules and representations. Bourdieu gives a straightforward functionalist explanation for the preferred marriage pattern, showing how it reinforces the integration of the family unit through a causal loop of interconnecting ties and relationships. But other marriages may better accord with the symbolic and material interests of the group, so that they are "regulated improvisations" within the habitus for purposes like strengthening ties outside the group or maximizing power and prestige. Habitus is therefore the "pre-strategic basis of strategy," and as such it still tends to reproduce the same conditions that make the strategic moves possible in the first place and that makes them identifiable as moves at all.

But does habitus really have any explanatory role in this account of preferred marriage? Bourdieu justifies his claim that it does by contrasting his explanation with one that employs the "official rules" and one that employs "objective probabilities" of utility maximization. Official rules are followed infrequently enough that when they are it must be explained; similarly, even when actors are calculating strategically, the various possibilities are not in any sense weighed equally. Rules and utility are referred to only when interests fail. "To eliminate the need to resort to rules," writes Bourdieu, "it would be necessary in each case to establish a complex relation between the habitus, as a socially constituted system of cognitive and motivating structures, and the socially structured situation in which agents' interests are defined and with these the objective functions and subjective motivations of their practices."[39] Norms do not do the explaining as much as do these objective and social conditions, the larger contexts and sediments of past interactions within which agents find themselves. But how does it improve matters to define agents in terms of a prereflective habitus rather than an official culture? The only answer that Bourdieu gives is surprisingly like the old answer for rules and norms: the habitus acts to constrain and limit action much like Hempel's set N, now inculcated as dispositions. Inculcation shows us to be "conditioned" by "objective teleologies" built into the social world like purposes are built into tools.

This conditioning character of the cultural habitus governs the calculation that agents make of their own success. This fact supplies Bourdieu with his gloss of Hume's well-known statement about desire and possibility: "We are no sooner acquainted with the impossibility of satisfying any desire than the desire itself vanishes."[40] In Bourdieu's terms, it is more likely that the desire would not be formed in a habitus in which it cannot be satisfied. Is this the most plausible account of Hume's phenomenon? Elster has used rational choice theory to explain it as "sour grapes." Elster appeals to a cognitive mechanism in which one adjust one's desires to what is obtainable, like the fox in Aesop's fable who declares the unreachable grapes to be sour anyway.[41] As the Stoics saw, this phenomenon raises paradoxes for the ordinary concept of freedom as doing what one wants: in that case, one becomes free by eliminating certain desires rather than by satisfying them; one would be more free if one's desires were properly conditioned in Bourdieu's sense. Elster's explanation works by showing how such irrational preferences are the result of the mechanism of "adaptive preference formation," a form of the reduction of cognitive dissonance between beliefs (about what is attainable) and desires (what one wants to obtain). Does Elster explain the phenomenon better than Bourdieu?

If good micro-explanations can be related to the macro-level, and vice versa, and if we avoid the unnecessary prescriptions of holism and individualism, then it is not simply a matter of determining which of these two explanations is intrinsically superior. Rather, Elster's explanation fills out what is entirely missing in Bourdieu's concept of inculcation: the micro-level of motivation and cognition of an agent under the constraints of the social situation. Holistic "conditioning" of dispositions and desires by a habitus is too underdetermining to be really an explanation at all. Except for differences in skill and differences among various classes or groups in a society, this conditioning seems to produce no clearer picture than the explanations inspired by official rules. It is hard to see how habitus is really an empirically useful link between cultural structure and any micro-level explanations of action, except in a one-sided causal-like macro-to-micro link from shared habitus to individual dispositions. Bourdieu's actors are not the "rational fools" of decision theory in pursuing their strategic goals; they have normative and moral commitments that they can reflect upon. Still, they are dopes about the frameworks in which they acquire prereflective dispositions and that they mysteriously take as given in their strategies. This elimination of a real cognitive component to Bourdieu's explanations is one of the dangers of macro-level theories of social norms as causal conditions of agency itself. Not all such accounts, however, succumb to this same anti-cognitivist consequence, as can be illustrated by Habermas's concept of the lifeworld as background and context of social action.

Habermas's lifeworld is similar to Bourdieu's habitus in that it concerns the shared and taken-for-granted presuppositions of social action that enable actors to interpret each others' actions and to participate in common institutions. It is also like habitus in that, as background, it is never completely under control or transparent to the agent. The lifeworld is the socially shared and structured whole that forms the basis for practices of communication and their rational achievements, including knowledge-producing practices. Among its many uses, Habermas employs the concept to discuss the Weberian idea of rationalization as a process by which a cultural domain ceases to be merely taken for granted and becomes the subject for explicit and formalized knowledge in institutions like law and science. It is this possibility of a reflexive relation to the lifeworld that makes it a more useful concept for explanations: it shows how holistic cultural structures may be indeterminate and yet constraining conditions for social action.

In explicating the theoretical uses of his concept, Habermas distinguishes between "formal" and "empirical" concepts of the lifeworld, or the "communications-theoretic" from the "everyday" lifeworld. The formal concept is entirely lacking in content: it designates that social acts presuppose some preinterpreted, holistic context. The lifeworld in this sense is a transcendental condition of possibility in that it enables speakers and actors to perform tasks of interpretation and communication necessary for social action, such as sharing a common definition of the situation. This context is a "resource" for such acts, a set of "shared interpretive patterns" to draw upon in communication. The empirical lifeworld consists of the shared set of interpretive patterns of a particular linguistic and cultural community. Even at this level, the lifeworld is holistic in its encompassing and unproblematic character. As Habermas puts it, "qua lifeworld, it cannot become problematic; it can only fall apart."[42] Like the prereflective habitus, the lifeworld always remains "behind us" and in the background, so that the social scientist examines it indirectly by reconstructing the implicit know-how and shared frameworks of competent actors.

For Habermas, the holistic character of the lifeworld refers to its character as a horizon or context of meaning, not to any particular element in it such as "preferred marriage schemes." As opposed to Bourdieu, Habermas consistently rejects any causal-like vocabulary to describe the micro-macro linkage. *Qua* background, the lifeworld is not simply underdetermining, as Bourdieu would have it (making us "variants" of the class or group habitus so prominent especially in his work on taste, *Distinction*)[43] but rather indeterminate. The point is the same here in this context as with the background for interpretation: macro-cultural structures like shared contexts and inheritances from the past are not determining limits but are enabling constraints that permit multiple possibilities.[44]

This important difference between the two concepts can be seen in the ways in which Habermas may extend his macro-cultural theory to permit a variety of micro–macro linkages, including the cognitive and reflective ones not available to Bourdieu. Indeed, Habermas's theory makes it possible to explain why it is that some lifeworlds permit a wider range of actions, greater contestation of cultural beliefs and values, and more self-awareness than others. Furthermore, his analysis clearly separates the perspectives of the observer and the participant: while lifeworlds are experienced holistically, they need not be analyzed as such. Finally, lifeworld constraints do not act as a determinate limit on explicit, formal knowledge, as particular contents and structures lose their taken-for-granted character and become themes for institutionalized efforts at knowledge and collective efforts to change beliefs and attitudes. To specify holistic cultural limits already shows the capacity to overcome any one of them, to reveal their alterability and contingency.

So far I have discussed only one direction of linkage: from macro-structures to micro-conditions of action. Few theorists have developed the other direction of linkage, since most micro-oriented theorists are methodological individualists who want to deny the autonomy of social facts and structures. I shall consider these criticisms again in more detail in the next section. An analysis of systemic social order, and hence of subjectless and anonymous social structures that are quite different from the holistic features of cultural practices, may be more susceptible to such objections. In the cultural sphere, ethnomethodologists and rational choice theorists also want to deny the necessity of appealing to macro-level collective norms, since such appeals assume something like a collective subject or group cognition. But rather than being a question of the ontology of groups, it is a problem of linkage: can macro-level explanations be extended to include the actions which produce and reproduce practices and structures? If that is possible, what more does the macro-level add to the full analysis of action and interaction among individuals? What is added is greater explanatory completeness, as a closer examination of the shortcomings of a reductionist program like ethnomethodology indicates.

According to the ethnomethodological research program as developed by Garfinkel, social order is achieved and maintained entirely through reflexive, accountable action rather than through regulating social norms. The normative macro-level analyses of a standardized action like a greeting "generally have acknowledged but otherwise neglected the fact that by these same actions persons discover, create, and sustain this standardization."[45] As noted in the analysis of the explanatory pattern of ethnomethodology in chapter 2, its fine-grained descriptions pick out those features of action by which cognitively and morally competent actors produce and reproduce some aspects of social order. If one of the classic definitions of social structure is "stable patterns of interaction," Garfinkel's analyses might be seen as providing an account of the empirical processes by which such patterns emerge and stabilize at the micro-level. Garfinkel does not so much link the micro–macro levels as he does replace all macro-level explanations with micro-level descriptions. Such patterns can be explained entirely on the micro-level as contingent accomplishments. However, such "radical indexicality" is as deeply ambiguous in its explanations as Bourdieu's holism.

For Garfinkel, the very idea of social structure is as useless as the philosophical concept of "the meaning" of an utterance. Instead, all social scientific explanations should be restricted to context-dependent terms in their analysis of "settings," "occasions," or "situations." The problem is that, when applied to "standardized actions," this caveat becomes ambiguous. For example, in the quotation above, actions are said to be both created and discovered. Which aspect is more important? Even the arch-structuralist Saussure held that *langue*, the system of relations that make up a language, was nothing but an abstraction useful in analyzing *parole*, the events of speech. Only the verb "create" suggests anything "radical" about the indexicality of most standardized action, and the view that agents fully create the situation in which they find themselves leads to an extremely punctual view of social interaction, of disconnected individuals connected by a thousand implicit conventions. The verb "discover," however, does suggest a way to link the micro-analysis of action with features of social action recurrent and inherited enough to call cultural structures.

Ethnomethodology needs this ambiguity between agents' "creating" and "discovering" shared order if it is to avoid the impoverishing consequences of indexicality. Another strategy that ethnomethodologists often use is to attribute explanatory features to the setting itself, rather than to the situated reflexive social actors. Here again the problem is with the characterization of order as a merely contingent accomplishment. Contingency need not imply that the features that explain an action or sequence of actions is unique to it. Once this is admitted, contingency in no way contradicts the idea of social structure; features of the "setting" are simply structures of the shared lifeworld within which action takes place. The real disagreement is only about whether these structures are a closed set of pre-defined possibilities or an open-ended space for elaboration and interpretation. For all Garfinkel's claims, ethnomethodological descriptions do not bear out a rigidly micro-level approach: every time actors are called "members of settings," we find analogues to cultural structures and constraints, about which some participants are myopic dopes. Perhaps one of the most striking examples of this Durkheimian use of the concept of setting can be found in the following claim by Garfinkel and Sacks about "competent language users": "an actual occasion with no text will furnish its members."[46] To cite another example: Cicourel claims that "procedures," not actors, "structure unfolding action sequences,"[47] making order somehow the accomplishment of the setting rather than of the agents in the setting. A more self-conscious strategy of linking action and structure, micro- and macro-levels of description would be far superior to these odd formulations of hidden macro-level structures. If these criticisms are correct, then there is no real opposition between ethnomethodological analyses of practical reasoning and of social structures and cultural norms, so long as these are reflexively accessible to individual agents.

Other individualist accounts face similar problems that require similar linkages if they are to be adequate. Elster has recently attempted to give a different individualist account of social norms as an alternative to rational choice mechanisms. Typically, rational choice theory has treated norms as sanctioned general rules in order to avoid the free rider problem discussed below. However, sanctions and side payments also have costs. Why should resources be invested in sanctions, particularly for sanctioning those who do not sanction others, and so on? Instead of the usual rational models of norms as coordinating mechanisms, Elster proposes non-cognitive and affective psychological mechanisms like envy and jealousy. His examples favor non-rational practices like blood feuds based on codes of honor that have no obvious beneficial consequences.[48] While some norms may in fact be non-rational, there is no reason to accept this as a general account of all norms or to think that the beneficial consequences of more rational moral practices and beliefs explain them. Both ethnomethodology and rational choice theory can provide the material out of which micro–macro linkages can be formed, resulting in much more complete and adequate explanations than either program alone can provide. Indeterminacy is by itself a good reason to reject both holistic and individualist one-sided explanations of norms or any other social phenomenon: structures neither determine nor condition actors simply to reproduce them, nor do actors simply create or constitute the conditions under which they act. Instead, action and structure are linked and mediated in diverse ways, the variety of which a good social theory is supposed to organize conceptually and explain empirically.

Mediating Macro- and Micro-Explanations: Social Systems, Institutions, and Actions

In the previous section, I discussed aspects of social situations or processes that might be called their cultural structure: they are those contexts of action that (1) persist and are inherited from the past, (2) provide a basis for shared understanding and are not necessarily changed by individuals, and (3) constrain beliefs and actions without determining them. I argued that overly holistic accounts of these contexts of social action have explanatory deficits to the extent that they remain unconnected to the purposes and interpretations of individual actors; at the same time, individualist reductions of them fail and often smuggle in macro-level concepts in the ambiguities of their explanations.

Are there other types of macro-level explanation related to different types or aspects of social order? In contrast to explanations of the cultural and normative order, many social theories have developed explanations that refer to the holistic interrelationships typical of modern, complex societies: the systemic order of functional interdependence between parts of a whole that are not directly dependent on the shared beliefs and norms of actors. This contrast between "system" and "social" integration, as sociologists have called it since Lockwood's ground-breaking discussion,[49] can be developed along a number of dimensions.[50] First, the two forms of integration can be distinguished according to "the degree of interdependence of action," along a continuum from cultural constraint as the weakest to system dependence as the strongest form. Cultural constraints can best be seen in the conditions for the coordination of practices or in explicit accountability to the expectations of other actors. Greater degrees of interdependence require a far greater predictability of outcomes and consequences than is permitted in simple cultural integration. Indeed, it is the existence of such stronger constraints like those of the market as a system of interdependent actions that makes economics a more determinate science on the macro-level; some degree of predictability is a condition of a market order. Second, greater interdependence also follows from another characteristic of systemic order: complexity. Complex webs of interrelated actions allow spatially and temporally distant actors to affect each other, often without their knowledge. Certainly, some modern social systems like the world economy are so complex that all of the interrelationships within them may not be surveyable by most actors; yet, a certain type of order is created and sustained by individual acts of buying and selling. From an historical perspective, it may be that the break-down of the more local cultural order was a necessary condition for the spread of such a world system, since cultural order limits the scope of interrelationships to those that are created out of shared practices. Third, system and structure can be distinguished only as contrasting analytic levels, which can then be empirically connected in a variety of ways. As Giddens puts it, "Patterns of social relationships only exist insofar as the latter are organized as systems, reproduced over the course of time."[51] The converse is also true: systems exist only if they are organized in social institutions. In the case of modern markets, states, and corporate organizations, their breadth, complexity, and scale all require this level of macro-analysis, although all of them have interconnected macro- and micro-cultural levels of order as well. As the variety of "corporate cultures" in Japan and the United States shows, there is no one-to-one relationship between these forms of order.

Even if connected to culture and action, it is precisely the complexity of systems that gives rise to a fourth and most highly problematic feature: their relative autonomy from any particular set of cultural norms or beliefs. This notion of independence admits of degrees, with the most extreme version of it found in Habermas's description of systems as "blocks of norm-free sociality." On this view, some aspects of social order, specifically material reproduction, may become "uncoupled" from the norma-tive or cultural order. The primary examples of such phenomena are markets and bureaucracies, each of which also begins to have effects upon the cultural order out of which they have emerged; these "reifying" effects are part of the evidence for their relative independence. A second, more moderate position merely contrasts two different processes of integration, as was Lockwood's original intention in distinguishing social and system integration. System integration may exist even in the absence of any agreements or normative consensus presupposed in the Durkheimian tradition of the sociology of culture. As opposed to cultural integration, "conflict may be endemic and intrinsic to a social system without causing any basic structural change."[52] Rather than by achieving consensus, system integration works by means of both the orderly and the conflictual relations between *the parts* of the social system, not relationships among actors. The third position does not demand the autonomy of systems and sees their order as emerging from the "unintended consequences" of individuals in their actions. Thus, systemic order can be explained though the presence of the "invisible hand," and its complexity arises from the aggregation of such unintended and intended consequences of individual actions.

In the case studies in this section, the decisive issue for the adequacy of an explanation is how the macro-level explanation captures this relative independence and dependence of systems on action and actors' orientations, while retaining their complexity and scale. Marx's explanations of historical change are as much the origin of this type of systemic explanation as Durkheim's collective consciousness is for macro-explanations on the cultural level. Marx explained large-scale historical change as a process that goes on "behind our backs" and "independently of our will." Do such claims exclude empirical linkage between micro- and macro-levels of explanation? How does the linkage work if not through "our will," through the intentions and purposes of agents? Central to establishing valid macro-level explanations is the problem of the structure's persistence in repeated and different contexts: are macro-structures independent only from some of the agents' intentions or from all intentions of all agents? If it is the latter, then systems cease to be social in any sense and come to confront agents as natural forces and causes, like the wind.

The notorious passage in which Marx develops his concept of systemic explanation does not directly concern the problem of social order but instead the orderliness of history and historical change. The passage develops the "guiding thread" of historical materialism and consists of a theoretical statement about the relationships between the "forces" and the "relations" of production.

The basic statement of historical materialism has two different parts: the second treats the historical causality of "the forces of production," and the first addresses structural aspects of the "social relations of production" which have one of Durkheim's main features of social facts, their externality. "In the social production of their life, human beings enter into relations that are indispensable and independent of their will, relations of production which correspond to a definite stage of development of their material forces."[53] Both the basic pattern of change and social relations are said to be non-intentional: social relations are already established prior to any individual will, and the processes of change form a pattern that transcends the direct intention of any individuals or groups. These non-intentional social relations, which we might call "institutions," become a "fetter" or an external constraint upon individuals pursuing their strategic purposes and must be altered through collective action. This process of collective action can change the relationships that make up the social system, its institutions, its patterns of domination in interaction, and the conditions of social production.

Read in this way, historical materialism is a theory about the processes of change internal to social systems: it holds that societies are integrated systemically through their material production and reproduction, and change when these processes break down and change. Marx gives primacy to the "material conditions" of production in explaining changes in social systems, analytically distinguishing the forces and relations of production. G.A. Cohen argues that Marx gives further causal priority to the forces of production, leading Cohen to characterize Marx's theory of history as "technological determinism." This "primacy thesis" identifies technology as the macrosocial causal power operating "behind our backs," in which cultural factors play only a functional role of inhibiting change and stabilizing the social system.

Like most truly Hempelian social science, the deductive laws of Cohen's version of historical materialism turn out to be either false, if general, or if true, not general. A close examination of Marx's more detailed treatments of particular instances of large-scale change in European history reveals an awareness of a much more complex, multi-causal process at work. For example, the transition from ancient to feudal society does not seem to be caused or even accompanied by any significant technical innovations whatsoever. Even in the transition to capitalism, rapid technological change did not occur until *after* capitalism was firmly in place; the immediate changes were cultural and political, with the rise of Protestant Christianity and the emergence of the modern administrative state. But rather than undermining historical materialism as a thesis about technological change, this multiplicity supports it so long as we interpret it as a theory about the nature of the systemic character of society and how it may change. As in the case of evolutionary theory, it leaves open which of the systemic features explain any such initial changes and its basic mechanisms; the theory only provides a framework in which historical explanations can be plausibly advanced. Indeed, it is the diversity of self-destructive processes in social systems that Marx highlights in his explanations of change, not the way systems maximize productive capacity. As Richard Miller describes the historical character of historical materialist explanations, "It is no part of the theory to describe general conditions in which basic internal change does, inevitably or usually, occur."[54] Rather than being general, Marx's macro-level explanations are historical narratives which consist of showing how the events in one part of the social system begin to fall out of step with the others as a stable society is about to change. Such change is not inevitable, as long periods of stasis in history indicate, making macro-level explanations as indeterminate as teleological explanations of social action. Even when conditions are present which make it possible, a society may not undergo such a basic transformation for a variety of contingent reasons.

Historical materialism does not, however, merely construct explanations case by case, as Miller's view seems to indicate. Contrary to both Miller and Cohen, it employs an extendable pattern of explanation of historical change in which systemic societal factors are identified as decisive factors for potential conflict and change. The theoretical framework serves to identify the possible locations for the emergence of processes of social change in large-scale social entities – that is, in the "modes of production" which are interrelated social systems: change is related to conflicts within and contradictions between parts of the social system. Lockwood traces Marx's concept of change to the breakdown of "system integration," not just to technological change or even conflicts between actors and groups over power. "One might almost say that the 'conflict' which in Marxian theory is decisive for change is not the *power* conflict arising through the relationships in the productive system, but the *system* conflict arising from 'contradictions' between 'property institutions' and the 'forces of production.'"[55] Such contradictions become manifest in the destructive consequences of technical change in capitalism, not in capitalist limitations on technological innovation. To make such a systemic explanation plausible, it is necessary to include structuring institutions (like the market and the state) and the motive force of the collective intentions of group actors (capitalists and workers, each pursuing their own goals and strategies) who operate within the framework of the system's structure and interrelationships. Technological innovation and change is explained by these factors; it is the explanandum, not the explanans.

According to Marx in *Capital*, the very success of economically motivated technical innovation contributes to the crisis tendencies of capitalist development.[56] For many Marxists, this tendency operates "independently of our will," entirely at the macro-level as a consequence of systemic relationships in the mode of production. But technical innovation is pursued by the capitalist to increase productivity and reduce wages; at the same time, other capitalists are pursuing the same innovation, resulting in a drop in the price of a commodity along with wages, leading to a new round of innovations. Thus, Marx seems to be providing a "micro-analysis of macro-patterns,"[57] rather than simply explaining one macro-pattern (technical innovation) by another (increase in average profit). However, Marx is also not simply reducing such macro-patterns to micro-motives, as rational choice Marxists assert. Certainly, part of the explanation relies on the maximizing behavior of individual capitalists. However, the explanation ultimately rests on institutional facts about the interdependency of such choices in market situations and shows the systemic consequences of individual strategies; without such interrelated consequences, no downward spiral is created. Hence, such micro-analyses require that there exist a stable set of institutions which aggregate choices and interrelate actions. Those institutions cannot themselves be explained by the choices and actions of individuals within them, since their structures create consequences that undermine many of these same goals and objectives. Indeed, capitalist choices turn out neither to be maximizing nor optimal, since certain technical innovations would undermine conditions of scarcity necessary for market relations to exist. (Such systemic limits include not just quantity but also qualities such as durability, as light bulbs show; for Marx, this demonstrates the collective "irrationality" of markets as systems.) Thus, neither micro-foundational nor macro-structural explanations are sufficient by themselves. Marx's explanation works only by connecting both of them in a complex analysis that has at least three levels: a large-scale description of interdependencies within a social system (capitalism) with its major structuring institutions (markets and state administration) and the actions of individuals in structurally identifiable groups (classes) making choices whose consequences are defined within this system (seeking to maximize profits and wages, to reduce suffering, and so on). Within the system that makes up all these levels, technical innovation is shown to produce the opposite of what the individual actors believe it will. Indeed, the whole point of the explanation is to show that the perspective of individuals and their intentions is insufficient to explain the ultimate consequences of technical innovation: lower profits and lower wages, which produce greater instability throughout the social system. Systemic factors are ultimately more fundamental to the explanation of breakdown and change, although individuals pursue their goals and interests constrained by them.

As it stands in *Capital*, Marx's explanation of technical innovation in capitalism is at least complete. Its adequacy is shown in the empirically verifiable linkage between micro- and macro-levels. Hence, using this explanation as an exemplar, an adequate pattern of macro-structural explanations includes at least three statements.

Pattern of Macro–Micro Explanation

(1)   The structure of interdependencies and relationships within the social system (S) must be described and modelled as accurately as possible.
(2)   The conditions of action and agency (A) in S must be specified, including the goals that actors pursue and the knowledge necessary to participate in it.
(3)   The description of the intermediate level (I), such as that of social institutions or practices, must analyze those recurrent processes or practices that link S to A.

One-sidedly individualistic and holistic explanations drop one or more of these factors. It has certainly been one of the great contributions of "rational-choice Marxism" to provide a good account of statement 2 of this pattern, where conditions A have been absent in the older, collectivist versions of historical materialism. Too often it has, however, attempted to reduce the pattern to this single level, claiming that macro-patterns on the other levels are simply the aggregate consequences of all individuals acting according to their motives and interests, leaving out I as a condition of aggregation that may permit further macro-descriptions of S as well. Elster's complaint against functionalism is that it also leaves out I, since causal loops that are repeated social processes generally designate institutions. Rational choice also tends to leave out I for different reasons, leaving their micro-explanations of macro-phenomena as being aggregates of individual actions radically incomplete. How does this aggregation occur? How is the framework of choice reproduced so that choices can be iterated?

If such a micro-to-macro explanation is to work, it is necessary to describe precisely how the system of action functions in such a way to structure incentives so as to make aggregation possible. This is the job of the institutional level of analysis, here of the market (statement 2 of the pattern, where market functions such as coordination and competition serve as the intermediary level, I). As James Coleman has argued, a micro-analysis only begins from incentives and preferences; "it also contains, implicitly or explicitly, a model of the institution, process or structure" through which the activity to be explained takes place.[58] To give an example used by Parsons to criticize exchange theory: generalized exchange and aggregation require the institutionalization of a medium, in this case money. Such media are required to maintain and steer the interconnections among the parts of the social system, and yet are also rooted in the value-orientation of individual actors.[59] Given the importance of his analysis of money as a medium and of its reifying effects on the beliefs and desires of individuals in capitalism, Marx must have agreed.

Micro-to-macro explanations of this sort can be made for institutions other than markets, such as in the analysis of voting in political institutions. As I argued in chapter 2, voting is a notoriously difficult phenomenon to explain on a purely micro-level. Reductionism leads to serious explanatory shortcomings. Suppose voters elect an inconsistent slate of officials, where representatives from the same district hold opposing views on many issues. This apparently irrational outcome could be explained in terms of the irrationality of individual voters. Yet, such irrationality, as in the case of irrational preference rankings in political choices, may have more to do with institutional failures than the failure of agents to be rational. In large representative democracies with an underdeveloped, media-controlled public sphere that undermines most forms of participation, individuals are not required to be consistent or even to develop reflectively explicit preference rankings in most large-scale voting systems. Institutional limits on choices, such as monetary barriers to small parties, may also result in voters accommodating their preferences to narrowed existing alternatives. Institutions and their structures are thus unavoidable in explaining many forms of contemporary social behavior, and these institutions must themselves be explained in larger-scale macro-patterns.

In light of this general pattern of micro–macro explanation, it is now possible to return to the original question: how can social systems have explanatory properties that are relatively independent of individuals and their beliefs and actions? Within an institutional framework, actions can have intended and "unintended" consequences, and in particular, consequences which result from the interrelatedness of actions in an integrated social system. Markets create one such not-directly-intended institutional order, deemed "the invisible hand." Most invisible hand explanations refer only to beneficial consequences of unintended interrelationships, as in Adam Smith's idea that the market turns "private vices" (intended, self-interested motivations) into "public virtue" (unintended mutual benefit). In the same way, markets are often said to produce greater efficiency, such as less surplus and fewer shortages. However, the invisible hand also has what Russell Hardin calls its "malevolent backside." Markets can produce shortages under certain conditions (such as those famines that are not related to supply). Not only can it not be assumed that public benefits will always result, but it is also true that some goods may not be achievable within its structure. It is an empirical question how such consequences work, since they can only be identified in terms of an account of the structure and function of various institutions within which intentional action takes place.

This example of social actions in market economies also demonstrates a further point. The fact that a consequence is unintended does not mean that it operates independently of the original intentional action. Even Marx thought that the way markets operated was in part dependent on what people believed about them, and he was fond of pointing out the many false beliefs that capitalists have about them (such as confusing capital and money). According to Marx's functional account, the many false beliefs that people have about their economic life provide them with motivations to participate in it and in turn cause them to reify many areas of social life, that is, to see them as beyond their control or influence. "Reification" is a paradigm case of the negative effects that social systems have upon actors, the critical analysis of which must now include the effects of macro-structures like capitalism and state bureaucracy.

In *The Theory of Communicative Action*, Habermas tries to give a comprehensive theory of such reifying effects of social systems, complete with each level of the pattern of macro-explanation: social systems, institutions and the cultural order of action, and interpretive practices and beliefs. According to Habermas, the modern systemic order of markets and bureaucracies is "invading" or "colonizing" the lifeworld, thus adversely affecting the domain of language and culture whose function is to reproduce society and to socialize its members. This description implies that system and lifeworld can be distinguished from each other, either as different empirical domains of social reality that are causally influencing each other or as opposing, empirically identifiable processes of integration. Although sometimes ambiguous in his descriptions, Habermas usually gives the latter description: whereas the lifeworld marks a form of social order based on linguistic interaction, normative consensus, and shared cultural knowledge, systems are based on functional interdependence and abstract media like money. If systems are "blocks of norm-free sociality," then they acquire a kind of independence and relational integrity more akin to natural than to cultural objects, albeit as an objectified second nature within the larger social order. Habermas develops this idea as an historical thesis about the emergence of social systems in modernity and its pathological effects: not only does the cultural order typical of traditional societies break down, but parts of the social order acquire independence from the normative orientations of participants, with all of the consequences that Marx termed "reification": turning human beings and social relations into things and adversely affecting their non-objectifying practices, as when the imperatives of the insurance industry and the defense bureaucracy begin to dictate the character of medical practice and the goals of scientific research.[60]

At first glance, Habermas's colonization thesis seems to be an exclusively macro-structural explanation, explaining one macro-pattern (cultural fragmentation and the disruption of socialization) by another (the spread of bureaucracies and markets). Indeed, Habermas does borrow the exclusively macro-concepts of Parsons' and Luhmann's systems theories, neither of which uses all the elements of the pattern of explanation that I have outlined here. Does this borrowing make for explanatory deficits, or only an "overly reifying vocabulary"[61] in describing social systems (S) as part of statement 1 of the pattern? A closer examination of the explanations employed in the colonization thesis shows that Habermas does make the requisite empirical linkages between the various levels of good macro-to-micro explanations: his explanations refer to the macro-level of social system S, to institutions typical of them (I), and to the micro-level of action and belief-formation (A). Properly reconstructed, Habermas's explanation of the colonization of the cultural lifeworld by the advance of social systems like markets provides a good example of an adequate macro–micro link for the purposes of showing the dysfunctions of the social system and its undesirable unintended effects.

In explaining how systems "invade" and "colonize" the lifeworld, Habermas must show how each level is both autonomous and interconnected. In one of his more successful "reconstructions of historical materialism," Habermas uses Marx's base–superstructure distinction to establish both sides of this distinction. Put simply, just as in Coleman's discussion of micro-to-macro explanations, Habermas appeals to institutions and the social processes that go on within them to explain how macro-to-micro relationships are established. As superstructure, systems must be "anchored" in the lifeworld through institutions, and it is these institutions that make up their base.[62] For a social system to function, there must be a balance or fit between it and its institutions that makes this interdependence possible. In markets, this fit must be between the systemically organized sphere of material production and new cultural institutions such as civil law and bureaucratic offices. The interdependence of system and lifeworld in institutions makes "increases in [system] complexity dependent on the structural differentiation of the lifeworld."[63] Furthermore, it is just this link to institutions that permits the spread of systems in the form of the monetarization and juridification of social relationships – that is, the increasing capacity of institutions of law and exchange to define the character of social relationships is what has the dysfunctional structural effects and bad unintended consequences.

If this explanation is correct, then the lifeworld is not simply a passive medium for the causal effects of systems; rather, it is adversely affected by such systems if, and only if, it is inadequately rationalized and inadequately differentiated. If it is less complex and rationalized in its sphere than systems are in theirs, it fails to be the more encompassing order that makes it a "base" for the systemic "superstructure." In this situation, the anchoring institutions do not necessarily resolve the problems and side-effects of the systems that they support; social systems are not in automatic equilibrium, and institutions often fail to fulfill the purposes that actors believe they have. In particular, actors discover that the political institutions fail in this respect, since they become adapted to imperatives of systems, not to actors' orientations and purposes. In such cases, Habermas speaks of the "uncoupling" or "detaching" of systems from the lifeworld, in order to capture how their institutions come to be systemically rather than culturally integrated. In this case, the complexity of systems are no longer balanced by the rationality and differentiation of institutions in which actors express their needs, regulate their interactions, and pursue their purposes. This lack of balance tends to increase as systems begin to take over more and more functions that the anchoring institutions were supposed to perform, leaving actors little room for activity that is not formally regulated by juridical codes or defined by the distribution of monetary resources. Even so, systems can still be channelled through undetected cultural structures that have not been replaced by monetary and juridical relationships, as the case of the continued influence of gender roles on areas of family law and labor markets indicates.[64] Habermas wants to point out that culture does not exhaust the ways in which the contexts of social action can narrow the extent of an action's rationality.

Habermas's interpretation of markets as systems provides an alternative foundation for a critical concept of reification. Rather than using a Marxian theory of value, reification is explained in terms of a macrosocial theory of markets as institutions. If complete, such a pattern of macro-level explanation can incorporate other similar analyses of the basic structures of modern society with adverse effects and dysfunctional consequences, in particular the Weberian analysis of bureaucracy. Bureaucracy and bureaucratization have been repeatedly analyzed by sociological theory, including all the research programs that we have discussed in this book. However, their analysis has suffered from problems of macro–micro linkage that have resulted in both incomplete explanations and pessimistic practical diagnoses of possibilities for change which echo Weber's pronouncements of "the iron cage." For this reason, the comparison of different macro- and micro-explanations of bureaucracy will provide a good case study with which to conclude this chapter.

Case Study: Bureaucracy as Social Order

Given their complexity and scope, markets have guided most of the discussion of systemic order. But the modern social order would not be possible without bureaucracies as well. Such an intentionally guided coordinating institution is necessary because of the complexity and differentiation of society into various spheres and subsystems. In fact, Weber saw markets as one of the chief conditions for the emergence of modern, large-scale bureaucracies (defined as the ideal type of "rational, legal domination")[65] since markets strip away all other forms of legitimate power and replace personalized loyalty with abstract rules and formal organization. The rational character of bureaucracies consists in the way such formal organizations create efficiency and calculability in the performance of routine tasks. Bureaucratic organization can be compared to other forms of decision making, in the same way that machines can be compared to non-mechanical forms of production. As Weber describes the contrast, "Precision, speed, unambiguity, knowledge of files, strict subordination, reduction of friction and of material and personal costs – these are raised to the optimum point in the strictly bureaucratic organization."[66] Bureaucracy is defined as a formal, well-defined hierarchy of offices, executed by knowledgeable "officials" who make a career out of their service in the organization. Bureaucratization cannot occur without knowledgeable actors who know their tasks and the structure of the organization and act purposively and rationally within it.

Because of its flexibility and efficiency, bureaucratic organization spreads into all areas of life and subsumes individuals and their actions under the domains of various organizations. With its growth and development, bureaucracy takes on the quality of "an objective force of an apparatus operating autonomously, above their heads," as the functional consequences of markets operate "behind their backs."[67] Weber compares a bureaucracy to an animate machine or objectified intelligence "with its specialization of trained skills, its division of jurisdiction, its rules and its hierarchical relations of authority."[68] Like some mechanical Leviathan, bureaucracies expand and bring more aspects of social life under the control of parts of their centralized, formal organizations until society becomes an "iron cage." While Weber sees this more as a tendency than an inevitable outcome, most modern organizations become bureaucratic in form, adopting its impersonal, centralized, and formal structure.[69]

Ethnomethodologists tell quite a different story about social order and bureaucracy, showing how even here actual and not ideal–typical order emerges at the micro-level of actions and interactions within organizations. Far from being an "animated machine" populated by experts and regulated by entirely formal rules and procedures, a micro-analysis of existing bureaucracies shows a fluid and shifting "negotiated order," to use the symbolic interactionist Anselm Strauss's term for one such bureaucracy, the modern hospital. Besides being formal organizations, bureaucracies are settings in which interactions and conflicts occur; indeed, many of the members do not even know all the rules that they are supposed to be enacting, and most follow only those which they deem feasible. By doing empirical, micro-level descriptions of actual behavior in these settings, ethnomethodologists show that the idealized picture given by macro-level theories of bureaucracy and bureaucratization are empirically inaccurate and incomplete. For example, in his analysis of filing systems at a psychiatric clinic, Garfinkel did not find any efficient or formal technique, but rather "good organizational reasons for bad clinical records."[70] Such records cannot be understood as an account of what "really" went on during a patient's treatment. Only when one discovers the folder's actual purpose does it make sense: it is not "the whole record" but, as Garfinkel puts it, "the unformulated terms of a potential therapeutic contract." Other studies show enormous discrepancies between the official goals of the organization and the negotiated order that constrains what can be achieved. Wieder's study of a half-way house (discussed as an example of the explanatory pattern of ethnomethodology in chapter 2) argues that official goals and procedures do not explain what happens in interactions between clients and staff. Rather, what does guide interaction is a "code" of behavior of which both are aware and in terms of which they hold each other accountable. While the code undermines official therapeutic goals, it does permit the resolution of conflicts by maintaining separate spheres of activity and separate identities for clients and staff.

Further doubts about the picture of the "iron cage" can also be raised from the micro-analyses of organizational behavior in rational choice theory. The structure of formal organization cannot eliminate uncertainty at the level of individual tasks and how they are carried out. Higher-level administrators cannot predict what lower-level administrators will actually do or even how they will produce their decisions. This uncertainty gives rise to unanticipated and constant coordination problems within bureaucracies, including redundancy and inefficiency. Moreover, the more complex an organization is, the more difficult it is for any administrator to survey everything, especially if the cost and efficiency of information gathering itself is taken into account. On the Weberian, formal description of bureaucracies as social systems, one might think of each member of the organization as maximizing the efficiency of her behavior. But the behavior of the administrator is not optimizing but instead is *satisficing*: she does not seek either to maximize efficiency or to achieve optimally the organizational goals, as much as she seeks to solve problems as they come up.[71] The analysis of such satisficing decision-making strategies shows that decision making in bureaucracies is not all that different from the procedures employed by social actors in everyday life. Administrators do not approach the Hempelian ideal of the engineer who acts with full knowledge of all the available alternatives. Rather, their choices are ordinary judgments under uncertainty.[72]

Micro-analyses of decisions and frameworks of action within organizations do not support the thesis of an historical tendency towards the "iron cage" of a fully rationalized world. There are definite internal constraints on formal procedures and efficiency that are related to uncertainty, coordination problems, and the ability by competent actors to reinterpret and renegotiate an order that turns them into objects of administrative decisions. The micro-level of social action is always sufficiently indeterminate to be never fully calculable; the "totally administered" world is a social scientific fiction. A close examination of markets might find the same looseness in the micro-order. This outcome is, however, not as entirely comforting as it might seem, since it does exclude the possibility of reification in formal organizational settings.

A closer examination of Weber's thesis shows that a macro-level analysis of bureaucratization is entirely consistent with micro-level indeterminacy, particularly if the tendency is interpreted in light of Habermas's colonization thesis. The whole point of seeing bureaucratization as colonization is to show the negative unintended consequences that bureaucratic organization has on *other*, non-formal aspects of social life. Simply showing that the formal structure of a bureaucratic organization is itself reinterpreted and renegotiated by competent members does not undermine the thesis at all. Even when they are indeterminate, negotiated orders, bureaucracies may still have pathological effects as they regulate institutional processes in areas like politics, education, or research. Both markets and bureaucracies must themselves be institutionalized; as Weber notes, bureaucracies are institutionalized in the modern state and mediated through the recognition of the political order as legitimate. Here, too, the institutional anchoring of the system provides a macro–micro link, as well as a location in which the bad consequences and pathological effects will be felt and contested.

As in the case of markets, the treatment of bureaucracies as social systems makes sense only if there is a steering mechanism analogous to the institution of money. Both Habermas and Parsons think that "power" in certain forms fulfills this role. Such media have functions and properties sufficient to replace language as a "steering mechanism" for social interaction, in this instance guiding interactions between parts of the system rather than between persons (who are now placeholders in a hierarchy of formally defined relations).[73] Like money, power must circulate and be accumulated, ready to be alienated and used as a resource: power "redeems" claims made in commands and is stored in the relation between the various positions in the organization. In this way, it is not tied to the personal prestige of an individual, but can be generalized up and down the organization in variable contexts of decision making. Organized power requires both legitimation and institutional form and "therefore calls for a more demanding normative anchoring than money."[74] Micro-analyses can show what these demands for legitimation actually entail: legitimation requires that organizations are not only systemically organized but culturally ordered as well.

Organizational theorists since Michels and Weber have also noted the futility of internal problem solving in bureaucratic organizations: to solve a problem, further mechanisms of hierarchy and control are created, including meta-tasks of controlling the organizational process itself and solving problems created by problem solving. Outside the organization, bureaucratic problem-solving techniques, particularly second-order ones, can have even more negative consequences. One such consequence can be analyzed as the "colonization" of the cultural order, that is, the replacement of the normative order and its integrative mechanisms of shared understanding with a systemic order and its integrative medium of power. As bureaucracies shape practices, they may make them more technical and inaccessible to everyday knowledge, as illustrated in the case of medicine. In hospitals, death becomes a bureaucratic event, not a culturally defined passage. Bureaucracies can also shape the nature of medical practice itself through cost–benefit analyses. In the United States, the insurance industry increasingly determines how and when people will be treated, provoking strong political reactions and legal challenges. One such reaction is the "deprofessionalization" of health care through the use of self-care or self-medication. Many other cases of both organized and silent contestation of bureaucratization can be given, including the adaptation of the educational system to the occupational system or the debate about standardized tests in the United States. The pathological effects show up both at the macro-level in the failures of the education system to perform its function and at the micro-level in relations defined by the social roles of teachers and students, children and parents, and in particular between members of bureaucracies and their clients. These reifying effects occur regardless of whether or not bureaucracies are themselves normative and negotiated orders.

Habermas's account of bureaucratization must therefore focus on the differences between the social processes involved in different sorts of order and integration, and in differences between language and other media, in the interactions occurring in each setting. Fragmentation, the loss of meaning, and anomie can be discovered at the micro-level. As Habermas puts it, "Systemic mechanisms suppress forms of social integration even in those areas where a consensus-dependent coordination cannot be replaced, that is, where the symbolic reproduction of the lifeworld is at stake."[75] This mechanism can explain major problems and consequences of modernity, traditionally one of the themes of macrosociology, including inadequately formed personalities in socialization and inadequate collective forms of life, such as political institutions. Persistent cultural problems are the result, not the iron cage – problems which may lead to widely felt crises and lack of legitimacy for institutions.

As developed by Habermas, the idea of the colonization of the lifeworld provides the framework for empirical research into various social problems. An interesting application might be the administration of "family law," where courts intervene into the culturally structured world of the family and legalize its relations. Certainly, some effects of this process may be progressive, including the reduction of domestic violence against women and children. But the legal system seems grossly inadequate for resolving many types of conflict in this setting: it turns family members into objects of negotiation between experts within a complex web of often unintelligible laws, requiring that lawyers negotiate with each other and with judges without the full knowledge or participation of those involved. Participants are not treated "as having the capacity to represent their own interests and to regulate their affairs themselves."[76] At the same time, however, law does introduce universal standards and requirements of public justification, often by breaking down traditional patterns of domination and power within the "private" family sphere. These ambiguities may be due to an incompleteness in this analysis of reification and colonization at the micro-level. At what point does the process become invasive? Similar problems plague Habermas's analysis of the bureaucratization of political parties, which also tend to get out of the control of their members. When do they cease to be representative bodies and become governed by the imperatives of the social system? One function of representation and parties has been to reduce complexity, something Habermas recognizes as necessary for large-scale social order. But at some point, such bureaucratization simply adds more complexity, and organizations like parties cannot fulfill their original functions. Habermas's explanations require some fuller description of what threshold is necessary in order for the explanations to be complete rather merely general descriptions of two interrelated macro-patterns.

In the case of the political and cultural consequences of bureaucracies and markets, Habermas's analysis is complete enough to suggest a solution to counteract these tendencies and resolve these problems: increasing democratization is a way to more fully rationalize institutions, in order to balance and counteract the expansion of systemic mechanisms of order. Democratization restores the interpretive texture of social interaction under modern conditions. According to Habermas, "new social movements" are now emerging whose explicit goal is to increase the scope and range of democracy, movements like grass roots citizens organizations, feminism, and the ecology movement. These movements contest the invasion of the lifeworld and attempt to engage in collective actions in order to produce new institutions that would enrich the lifeworld and its cultural space for action. Habermas does seem Weberian enough to have doubts about whether any institutional change is sufficient to deal with massive and complex systemic order: "In modern societies there obviously exists an asymmetry between the (weak) capacities for intersubjective self-understanding and the (missing) capacities for the self-organization of society as a whole."[77] However, if my analysis of the pattern of macro-level explanations is correct, this pessimism is a consequence of some of the unwarranted assumptions of Weber's original thesis: it does not make sense if bureaucratization itself has institutional limits and if bureaucracies can be contested at their micro-foundations. A more adequate account of all the levels of the explanation of systemic order leads not only to better explanations, but also to greater awareness of possibilities for change and locations for struggle. On the theoretical level, it is clear that Habermas wants to use the concepts of systems theory in order to avoid an individualistic reduction of social order to face-to-face interaction. However, this requirement does not mean that systems are separated from institutions and human action. Explanatory incompleteness can lead not only to theoretical deficits but also to impasses on the level of practice and often to an unwarranted pessimism.

The completeness of Habermas's theory is shown precisely in its practical implications for collective action. The practical side of good macro-theories introduces a new feature in the analysis of social scientific explanatory practice: its explanations can be critical. Habermas not only shows why certain phenomena exist in modern society, but how they might be changed and contested by participants. Since Marx, macro-level explanations have always been linked to social criticism, except in the hands of theorists who emphasized models of social equilibrium like structural-functionalism. Such large-scale explanations often contradict agents' own beliefs and self-understanding of their own practices. How can they fail to correspond to agents' own self-knowledge and yet still be correct? These basic problems of critical social science raise an even more fundamental epistemological question about the social sciences as a whole: what type of knowledge do the social sciences provide, if one of the features of such complete explanations and theories is that they are inherently critical?

5

Criticism and Explanation

Since Quine's pragmatist challenge to the two main "dogmas of empiricism,"[1] a rhetorical ploy common in the philosophy of science has been to add a third or perhaps a fourth dogma to be disposed of. As I argued in chapter 3, Donald Davidson's criticism of the "final dogma of empiricism," the distinction between scheme and content employed by conceptual relativism, is relevant to problems of interpretation and rationality. Davidson's own criticisms of explanations in decision theory have shown the fruitfulness of this less empiricist, more pragmatic orientation in the social sciences, although Davidson succeeds more at clearing up false theoretical pretensions than in giving an independent account of non-Hempelian explanation.[2] But perhaps the most deeply ingrained and subtle dogma of empiricism in the social sciences is the distinction between fact and value and its related methodological counterpart, the distinction between explanation and criticism. Such a distinction relies on the naturalistic picture of science as a gradual accumulation of various "facts" or law-like regularities, in which values have no significance except as subjective expressions of approval or approbation. Indeed, "the empirical criterion of significance" was also the basis of Hempel's view that an explanation of rational action could easily separate descriptive from evaluative concepts of rationality, where explanations had to employ only the former and needed to exclude the latter if they are to qualify as scientific. I argued in chapter 1 that while systematic regularities can indeed be found (say between urban life and high suicide rates), these regularities cannot inductively generate social theories. Once complex rational and interpretive factors are permitted in explanations of social action, a clear logical distinction between the descriptive and evaluative uses of concepts becomes even more difficult.

According to the old logic of the methodology of social science employed by both Weber and Hempel, evaluations were to be excluded from scientific explanations for two reasons: first, they introduce "normative biases"; and, second, they cannot provide the basis for empirical–causal explanations.[3] Explanations should strive to be "neutral" with respect to all evaluative judgments, whether positive or negative. But interpretive constraints and causal indeterminacies make it difficult to eliminate all such "biases" and achieve the standpoint of the neutral observer of Hempel's model; even so, I have shown that adequate explanations are still possible. In this chapter, I want to show that once we reject this "neutral" view of determinate explanation, the empiricist exclusion of criticism and evaluation in the social sciences must be rejected as well.

Since there is no simple "logical" distinction between "is" and "ought" in explanations of intentional actions, it is possible to show that each of the explanatory patterns discussed so far has critical potential, along with social scientific interpretation and macro-explanation. In short, I want to argue that *any* theory can be critical, although the practitioners of the particular research program need not employ its explanations for explicitly critical purposes. However, not every pattern of every theory is critical in the same way, nor are they necessarily useful for "radical" social criticism, that is, for criticisms aimed at some basic transformation of existing social relations and structures. At the same time, I see no reason why a radical critical social theory cannot employ any form of explanation for its own purposes, so long as it can locate it as part of a larger and more complete account of the contemporary social order, a "diagnosis of the times," or a "critical history of the present," to list just a few of the titles for such a comprehensive critical theory.

For all his emphasis on the need to use reasons in explanatory contexts, Weber held fast to the seemingly anticritical doctrine of the "value-neutrality" of the social sciences. I shall not go into the complexities of Weber's view here,[4] but rather use his view of the role of values in social theory to raise certain difficulties that any critical social theory must face. In fact, it should soon be apparent that value-neutrality in Weber's sense does not exclude the possibility of social criticism, but rather only limits its scope. In his methodological writings, Weber repeatedly criticizes the positivists of his day, particularly those economists who argued that all that social science should do is construct abstract models and predictive causal explanations.[5] Even if Weberian social scientists do not make value judgments (*Werturteile*), their analyses must still be value-related (*wertbezogen*) and hence can clarify the values themselves, their consequences, and the means necessary for achieving them.[6] While it is often not clear how this is possible without making judgments, such explanations and analyses might change many of our value-related beliefs. Amartya Sen's work on hunger in welfare economics offers a good contemporary example of value-related social science: he gives an adequate causal analysis of famines, which shows why they can occur even when there is a large available food supply. Contrary to our beliefs, famines have little to do with supply and the availability of food, but rather have to do with the breakdown of social entitlements to goods and of the complex social interdependencies that make economic life possible.[7] Thus, a value-oriented causal analysis such as Sen's can be both practical, in that it suggests new strategies and remedies, and critical, in that it suggests the falsehood of prevalent beliefs about hunger and poverty. Sen's analysis is critical and practical in the good Enlightenment sense of ameliorative social reform, and it points in a clear direction of social progress, if its remedies are adopted.

Much of social science is practical and value-related in quite a different sense. It is practical in a technical sense: its explanations supply better means to solve problems. Many economists simply accept the patterns of scarcity in the world, and explain hunger as a technical problem that can be solved by a better system for the distribution of food. But, from Marx forward, many social theorists have attempted to develop a stronger notion of the critical and practical purposes of social science. Certainly, Weber had knowledge of this tradition, and yet he argued for a much more limited conception. Why? The answer goes to the heart of the problem of the indeterminacy of social criticism: criticism, he argued, is theory-laden and theory-dependent, and this circularity limits what social science can do. As in the case of the hermeneutic circle, I will argue that this "critical circle" is not a vicious, but a reflexive, aspect of indeterminacy. Like the theory-laden character of observation in the natural sciences, it has broad ramifications, particularly for the nature of social scientific knowledge itself. Indeed, one of the main issues here is epistemological, that of the nature and limits of theoretical knowledge in the social sciences. Limits on criticism are often limits on theory, as is the case for Weber.

The non-trivial character of this circularity can be seen by examining Weber's attempt to exclude certain types of values (which he called judgments) in his explanations of social phenomena. According to Weber, reference to values is necessary in an explanation of social actions because they are end-directed: explanations of actions have a "subjective" component in that they can be made intelligible only in light of the ends and orientations of actors. As a social action, criticism itself is also oriented to a particular end: the critic seeks to change the attitudes and beliefs of members of a society so that they will adopt new ends and orientations. But for what end that purpose is pursued (socialism, perhaps, or the Messianic age) is a matter of "decision" for a critic, a decision among a competing plurality of "gods and demons" available to modern actors in the context of a disenchanted world.[8] The context of social criticism in the modern age is one of irreconcilable and competing values. As a result of the disenchantment of the world, no more substantive value rationality can be achieved and values are ultimately a matter of mere choice or decision.[9] Both Weber's theory of rationality as purposive and his description of the pluralism of values in modernity place insuperable limits on the social scientific critic, who is the product of that same modernity. Criticism is simply another form of struggle between social actors and their competing interests and "gods." As Weber puts it, "Every meaningful value judgment about someone else's orientation must be a criticism from the standpoint of one's own Weltanschauung; it must be a struggle against *another's* ideals from the standpoint of one's own."[10] In the absence of means for rational adjudication and ultimate value axioms, the social scientists, *qua* social scientists, also have nothing more to contribute once the clarification of values and means of achieving them have ended and "positive criticism" has begun. This skepticism about criticism is true if, and only if, many other aspects of Weber's social theory are correct: his theory of action, his conception of values and norms, his view of modernity and disenchantment, his theory of rationality, and his "diagnosis of the times."

Consider the opposing theoretical commitments of a different, more positive assessment of the possibility of normative social criticism in modernity. In *The Theory of Communicative Action*, Habermas uses Weber's theory of rationality as a foil for the development of a critical social theory of modernity. Teleological, means–ends orientation is only one form of rational social action, and technical knowledge is only one form of scientific knowledge and is not typical of the social sciences. Furthermore, use of the concept of norms, not values, is the proper way to characterize the moral aspects of social reality in that it points to the structuring of social encounters by shared knowledge, expectations, and rules. Criticism is therefore not an act of struggle among "gods and demons" but an act of communication, mediated by moral–practical rationality and discursive political institutions like the democratic public sphere. Far from making the social situation of the critic one of irresolvable conflict, modernity has brought with it new contexts for the resolution of conflict and universal normative procedures to which the critic can appeal. Participants in these institutions no longer accept moral conventions and meanings as "social facts" and are capable of revising their own ends and beliefs. Habermas's "diagnosis of the times" and other components of his social theory all make social criticism possible in the social sciences, whereby social scientists become self-reflective participants in institutionalized processes of social learning and discourse about one's social life. I will return to Habermas's views later in the chapter, when I discuss the role of explanation in social criticism. Here I want to show only what these differing views reveal about the "critical circle" of fact and value.

The contrast between Weber and Habermas can clarify one main point – namely, that the distinction between facts and values is an outcome, and not a presupposition, of the commitments of a social theory. One of the main presuppositions of naturalism was that the distinction could be made in an a priori, theory-independent way, between what is knowledge (accumulated facts) and what is not (preferences and values). Of course, placing this distinction in doubt raises anew questions about the status of knowledge gained in the social sciences and how that knowledge might be verified. Each of the research programs that we have examined has advanced its own standards of evidence for the particular statement in its explanatory patterns. More generally, the research programs seem to yield little in the way of results that fit the Baconian adage that "knowledge is power," especially compared to other areas of research that have a place in administrative institutions. But rather than technical knowledge, perhaps it is better to see such "new" social science as providing a modern form of practical knowledge: it helps us reflect better on our situation and improve things not by controlling a domain of phenomena but by changing beliefs and attitudes. The capacity of explanations to supply critical insights then becomes a crucial epistemological test for non-naturalistic social science. While this insight may, under appropriate circumstances, increase human freedom, it is not necessary for it to do so in order to be practically verified.

Not all these research programs have been formulated with explicitly critical purposes in mind. For example, according to some of its practitioners, ethnomethodology denies the possibility of social scientific criticism. However, each of their patterns of explanation contains premises that make it possible to use their explanations for critical purposes. Good examples of the critical potential of each type of explanation already exist: the detailed accounts of the social construction of scientific facts in certain ethnomethodological approaches to the social study of science; applications of rational choice theory of beliefs and desires to the theory of ideology and irrationality; and the development of a normative concept of "distorted communication" using the theory of communicative action. This list takes only exemplary and well-developed cases and in no way exhausts the critical potential of each program and its form of explanation, and it can be expanded to other explanations. Indeed, I will argue that *any* sufficiently developed form of explanation can be used for social criticism. Hence, there is nothing unique about the methods and theories of critical social science, except that they have made their purpose explicit, as, for example, in the case of the Marxian theory of value. Typical critical social science in its past forms has been oriented primarily to macrosociological theories, as is clear in the overall Marxian program. But there is no reason to think that criticism is confined to such theories alone, or even primarily based on such social theories at all: just as there can be explanations that do not refer to theories, as in the case of narratives, so, too, interpretations can at times be critical without explicit theoretical commitments. There are still important differences between criticisms that are informed by theories and those that are not: interpretive critics are limited to the internal perspective of participants of the practices they criticize, with all the normative and epistemic limitations that might be the price of increased persuasiveness and rhetorical effectiveness. The critical social theorist, too, can adopt the interpretive stance in order to articulate, as Marx put it, "the ideals and aspirations of the age."

An Exemplar of Critical Explanation:
The Theory of Ideology

Even while any explanation can be employed critically, there is a long tradition of philosophical and methodological reflection on explanations and theories whose purpose is to be critical. Many philosophers in this tradition of critical theory have argued that there is a set of features specific to theories of this type (such as "totality"), or a particular ("dialectical") method appropriate for producing them. The decline of naturalism, of which the orthodox Marxist philosophy of science is one variety, raises suspicions about privileging special methods or theories as warrants for knowledge claims; what goes for natural science should go for critical social science as well. In the manner that I have argued throughout the book, I want to show how evaluations of the adequacy of various critical theories is nonetheless still possible. Some theories that do make critical claims, like the "post-modernism" of certain analyses of science, can be shown to be inadequate when compared with theories that better fit similar critical purposes – in this case, the treatment of scientific communities in feminist theory and in the theory of communicative action. Like macro-level explanations, one of the main problems is that critical theories are often incomplete, although this incompleteness is in many instances motivated by problems with critical social science that the theorist wants to avoid or resolve.

In order to discuss the criteria of adequacy for critical theories and explanations, I will first elaborate some of the standard features and desiderata of critical theories in general relative to their goals. I will then turn to an exemplary case for the history of this social scientific practice: the theory of ideology. Indeed, the theory of ideology employs one of the standard linkages between macro-level social and economic structures and micro-level descriptions of actors' beliefs and knowledge-producing practices, mediated through social institutions like the state and organized religions.

From the time of his early pronouncement of the need for a "ruthless criticism of everything existing," Marx's writing represents a sustained attempt to find the methods and basis for such a complete critical endeavor.[11] Marx's historical social theory (the historical materialism discussed in the last chapter) provides a theoretical basis for his criticism of capitalism beyond the mere "critical criticism" offered by the left-Hegelians. This explanatory social theory, however, does not exhaust the critical resources of many of Marx's writings. *Capital*, for example, is a multi-genre work of social criticism, using a variety of interpretive and explanatory techniques: Marx develops, among other things, a theory of the developmental tendencies of capitalism towards recurrent and cyclical crises, a theoretical account of working time in the theory of the value of commodities, and detailed and novelistically crafted documentary accounts of the life-conditions of workers in the nineteenth century. *Capital* also employs techniques of ideology critique, particularly in its analysis of the "fetishism of commodities"; Marx wants to explain why it is that members of capitalist societies endow certain things (commodities) with subjective and social powers (of producing value on their own). This explanation of the beliefs necessary to participate in market relations is a particular instance of a general theory of ideology, which explains how people produce false beliefs about their own practices under conditions in which one group dominates another.

A theory of ideology is a critical theory about the formation of social beliefs. For Marxists with Eleatic tendencies, it works by presenting a simple contrast between the "true" beliefs of historical materialist social science and the "false" beliefs of unscientific participants, a contrast between the way of knowing and the way of seeming. In light of the theory of forces and relations of production outlined in the last chapter, the historical materialist can explain the false beliefs of actors both causally and functionally. The economic structure of society, or base, causes the superstructure, the prevalent set of beliefs that agents have, particularly those of law, morality, and theology. The beliefs that become widely shared in a society are the ones that fulfill the function of promoting and maintaining the social relations of production, that is, the relations of domination between classes. As Elster and others have pointed out, Marx usually only sketches these relationships between actors' beliefs and their position in the social structure, so that the Marxian theory of ideology offers good examples of incomplete and inadequate macro-level explanations of how our beliefs are formed in processes that go on "behind our backs." However, some instances of ideology critique in Marx are fairly complete.[12]

What makes this a critical theory of belief formation? The critical features of such an explanation of beliefs can be seen by contrasting Marx's theory of ideology with that of Mannheim.[13] Like Marx, Mannheim constructed his explanation in terms of large-scale relationships between the content of beliefs and their social context and origin, claiming that "ideas are always bound up with the existing life-situation of the thinker."[14] Unlike Marx,

Mannheim's accounts claim to be neutral and non-evaluative. Mannheim bases this neutrality on the reflexivity of his theory: once all thoughts relate to some "life-situation," then the critic has no place *hors de combat* to stand and pass judgments. By contrast, Marx's theory does not see the situated and historical character of thought as a limit upon social criticism. While he accepts the reflexive character of his theory, he attempts to turn its theoretical paradox of being situated in an historical epoch into a fruitful circle for practical knowledge that would empower agents to overcome their cognitive limits. Marx's critical and non-paradoxical reflexivity is possible only if the theory of ideology accepts extra burdens and standards of proof for its explanations.

If it is to discharge this burden, the critical theory of ideology must add features to its theories and explanations. In *Critical Social Science*, Brian Fay gives a fairly good list of its requirements: any critical theory must be "scientific, critical and practical," to which a post-empiricist philosophy of social science must add "self-reflexive" in its form of justification. The scientific character of these theories requires that they offer "comprehensive explanations of wide areas of human life ... subject to public, empirical evidence."[15] These explanations are critical insofar as they imply negative evaluations of the present social order; they are practical by promoting an understanding of social conditions that can become a basis for their transformation. As opposed to mere problem solving, critical theorists usually identify their goal as "human emancipation," the overcoming of conditions that restrict human freedom and cause human suffering, a goal that cannot be achieved within present social arrangements. Their explanations must not only further this goal, but also be reflexive: a critical theory must be able to account for its own social and historical conditions of possibility as well as for its potential emancipatory effects and consequences. These conditions have too often been assumed in dogmatic social criticism and objectivistic understandings of theory, and Fay's account of critical social science does not incorporate recent attempts to make such reflexivity an explicit criterion of adequacy, as, for example, in Habermas's conception of the relation of theory and practice.

Marx's theory of ideology fulfills all these requirements for critical adequacy, even reflexivity. However inadequate it may be when compared with more recent efforts that I will discuss later in the chapter, the theory offers a causal account of the factors producing and sustaining dominant ideas. The systematic mechanisms it discusses include reflective practices like moral theory and theology and are open to historical verification.[16] In light of its causal and functional analysis, alternative practices for self-reflection can be constructed with different social roles, such as promoting those beliefs necessary for collective agency and radical transformation.[17] The critical theory of ideology therefore offers not only an account of the processes which relate large-scale social structures and historical trends to agents' beliefs but also analyzes conditions under which beliefs can be changed and a more truthful inter-pretation of social practice generated. Far from being detached from any social setting, the theory shows that engaged social criticism is possible: the critic reveals contradictory aspects of the social situation and articulates the aspirations of those who live within it and are capable of changing it. The effect of the critique of ideology is not to free actors entirely from the causal influences of social structures on their beliefs, but from particular causal influences and functional connections. The critic seeks to replace those causally formed beliefs that integrate members of a society and coordinate their practices with ones that have the function of creating collective identification and solidarity among oppressed groups. The critic of ideology can also suggest what beliefs might emerge under different social conditions.

As a critical and scientific theory, Marx's theory of ideology is subject to criticisms regarding its verification. In order to overcome functional indeterminacy, it requires good causal accounts of cognitive and social mechanisms of belief formation. It is clear that the explanatory patterns of all three research programs can con-tribute to increasing the explanatory power of such a micro–macro link. In what follows I will consider such recent accounts of belief formation in Elster's cognitive theory of ideology, Latour and Woolgar's reflexive examination of the construction of the belief that there are "facts" in science (similar to that done by ethno-methodologists), and Habermas's account of ideology as "distorted communication." All of these explanations can be used as the basis for a practical and critical theory of social beliefs, whether their intention is critical in Marx's sense or not. In all of these cases I want to raise issues of explanatory adequacy as well as issues about their practical verification and consequences. In con-sidering social criticism inspired by rational choice theory and ethnomethodology, I want to show that their explanations can be used for often quite contrasting critical purposes. Indeed, while any explanation may be employed critically, the political and moral direction of that criticism may be indeterminate and diverse.

This broad specification of the critical potential of social science raises some interesting questions. First, who is the social critic? Certainly, not all, or even most, social critics are social scientists, although some very important critics have been. In *The Company of Critics*, Michael Walzer describes critics in terms of their social function: a critic is anyone who makes complaints about the present social order, a designation which might include even a fundamental Christian preacher who condemns the "Babylonian" morality of modern society.[18] If social scientists are critics, they are critics in their public activities, interpreting rather than explaining their culture, using their theoretical categories as new Emersons and Musils. Here, my concern is with the critical activities of social scientists *qua* social scientists, although some of their interpretations can be critical in this regard. Second, are there unique features to emancipatory – as opposed to other – forms of criticism? Many theorists in emancipatory critical traditions have claimed that critical explanation must have specific theoretical features or follow a specific method.[19] Horkheimer held that critical theories do have such unique features and could be distinguished from "traditional" theories in their object-domain and purpose: "The critical theory of society has for its object human beings as producers of their own historical way of life. . . . Its goal is the emancipation of human beings from the relationships that enslave them."[20] A closer examination of the actual practice of these same critics does not bear out such a claim to uniqueness: Marx creates abstract models of capitalism much like the economics of his day, documents child labor and life quality statistics, and engages in a variety of ordinary forms of theorizing and evidence gathering. Horkheimer himself calls for an "interdisciplinary approach" and tries to incorporate the results of various newer theories of culture, and he even had members of his institute do survey research. This claim to uniqueness does, however, serve a more philosophical than social scientific purpose: a broader definition of critical theory leaves no tight fit between theoretical and political orientations. Certainly, in Horkheimer's statements above it is the emancipatory direction of critical theory that is most important. But the lack of a *unique* emancipatory direction provided by theory is a philosophical consequence that we should be willing to bear, since some of the political problems of all emancipation movements in this century center on this lack of diversity. This ineliminable plurality is also an implication of the circularity and indeterminacy of criticism in explanatory contexts. This conclusion does not endorse all political directions as equal: there are still questions concerning the adequacy of the theory as a form of reflexive practical knowledge that articulates aspirations and ideals as well as provides critical insights. It is this practical dimension of social science that serves to test orientations, to see if they are genuinely liberating rather than simply conforming to some theoretical goal defined in advance of practice.

Rational Choice Theory as Critical Explanation

While Hempel often argued against Weber's methodological writings and against his requirement that social action must be explained as "intelligible," his analysis of the structure of explanations of rational action clearly distinguishes fact from value, evaluative from descriptive concepts of rationality. As I argued in chapter 1, the descriptive approach to rationality neither improves the empirical content of explanations of rational action nor does it clarify what rational dispositions are apart from the beliefs and desires of the agents. Further, the best developments of Hempel's approach in rational choice theory use both normative and descriptive statements in their explanatory pattern, as I argued in chapter 2. It is precisely the normative statements of its explanatory pattern that contain the critical potential of rational choice explanations. These ideal or normative sides of the theory can be developed through rigorous extension of the standard "thin" conception of rationality: either by analyzing the intrinsic rationality of beliefs and desires, or by arriving at a "broader" characterization of the relationship between the two than mere consistency and maximization. In both ways, the explanatory pattern can be developed into a critical, normative theory of the micro-foundations of rational action in beliefs and desires.

The possibility of even this modest form of social criticism has not always been recognized within the research program of rational choice. In the heyday of naturalism, rational choice theory was basically utilitarian and at best attempted to elaborate institutional proposals that would increase average or total net utility. As the need to turn to revealed preferences shows, such norms foundered on the problems of the measurement of interpersonal utility, leaving only a weak principle that any change in institutions should be Pareto optimal (that is, increase the utility of at least one member of society without decreasing the utility of others).[21] Pareto optimality is hardly a rallying cry for social criticism: in the absence of a clear norm for ranking desires or comparing welfare, rational choice must discover a more indirect, less large scale form of social criticism than utilitarianism, generally one that does not raise its problem of interpersonal comparison. In critical contexts, rational choice theorists typically have used their pattern to reformulate explanations made by critical theories in the past, usually ones that have made dubious holistic assumptions that can be corrected and made more rigorous on individualist grounds. One such critical theory is the Marxian theory of ideology discussed in the last section, a theory that tries to show the interested and irrational character of certain self-deceived desires and beliefs. Marx, too, was little concerned with the actual content of ideological beliefs and desires, claiming for instance that they "have no history."[22] Instead, he focused on the macro-social causes of such beliefs and desires and their function in maintaining the structure of domination in a society. Jon Elster, among others, has argued that such holistic and functional explanations are not only inadequate but can be replaced with "endogenous" rational choice theoretical redescriptions of the same phenomena entirely on the individual or micro-level: these explanations appeal to specific cognitive mechanisms that produce self-deceptions and "deviant" desires. Certainly, Marx's macro-structural explanations are incomplete in the sense discussed in the last chapter; but it still remains an open question whether or not Elster's own entirely micro-account of ideological beliefs and desires is adequate as a form of critical explanation. In what follows, I will concentrate on his explanations and criticism of ideological beliefs, although similar considerations apply to his comparable account of ideological desires.

Elster defines ideology as a set of deviant beliefs "that can be explained through the position or (non-cognitive) interest of some social group."[23] The explanans of such an explanation is a set of irrelevant causal influences on the process of belief formation in individual agents, influences which can be either "hot" or "cold," "psychodynamic" or "psychologistic." Thus, Elster places the theory of ideology squarely in a long tradition of social–psychological explanations that employ a contrast between standard and deviant cases, beginning with Aristotle's notion of *akrasia* (psychologistic or cold influences) and Freud's notion of the unconscious (psychodynamic or hot influences). While Elster thinks that the tradition has overestimated "hot" motivational over "cold" cognitive mechanisms, his explanatory pattern requires the traditional normative distinction between "normal" and "pathological" cases, where the norm is a "rationally caused belief." Elster defines the standard case of a rationally formed belief as follows: "A belief is rationally caused if (i) the causes of the belief are reasons for holding it and (ii) the reasons cause the beliefs *qua* reasons, not in an accidental manner."[24] By contrast, a deviant belief is shaped by the wrong sorts of causes or processes of formation, and thus has an irrelevant causal history. For this theory, a precise account of the formation history of a belief and the cognitive mechanisms that produced it are crucial to explaining it as ideologically deviant: the criteria of relevance are established through the standard causes of similar, well-justified beliefs. Even if the ideological belief is true, as some are, it is not rational; if it is caused in a deviant way, it cannot be well justified, as in the case of a logical fallacy accidentally producing an unjustified, yet true, belief. In fact, the analogy to logical fallacies is quite apt, since many of the "cold" cognitive mechanisms of ideological belief formation are versions of inferential errors, like the confusion of parts and wholes.[25] Such cognitive mechanisms, and not the influence of collective social structures, produce ideological beliefs. For example, Elster explains the Calvinist belief in predestination as the false generalization of market determinations of prices.[26] The social position of capitalists leads to such a cognitive distortion of other beliefs. Similarly, opposition to marriages for love in traditional societies is justified by the lack of success of such marriages within such a culture, again where social position in a culture without such a practice leads to the acceptance of a belief for reasons which do not cause the belief *qua* reasons.

Elster's studies of ideology and other forms of social irrationality abound with interesting mechanisms and plausible causal histories of particular beliefs, all based on a richer, broader view of the rationality of beliefs that includes questions of justification. For example, agents change their preference rankings when confronted with different situations: if my car breaks down, I may spend $20 on a cab to go to a concert, but if my car is working, I will not spend the same amount on buying a second ticket if I lose mine. This sophisticated norm of consistency shows that the mechanism of "preference framing" will not produce consistent, autonomous preferences.[27] What is important here is not so much the individual case studies, but whether or not Elster's individualist theory can fulfill the critical tasks which he sets for himself. In this regard, there are three unresolved difficulties. First, Elster offers a general account of "deviant" beliefs, but no specific account of ideological beliefs: his mechanisms may produce erroneous and irrational beliefs that may not be collectively shared and hence not ideological. Ideology is certainly a sub-species of deviant beliefs, but it must also have some distinguishing features. The features that Elster mentions (positions and interests) play no role in his explanations, since various cognitive mechanisms do all the work. One could imagine following Elster's individualist program by giving a complete account of all formation mechanisms for ideological beliefs; still, at the end, one might not be able to clearly identify which among the irrational beliefs are candidates for being really effective ideological beliefs for members of any given society. In this regard, it is also not clear how Elster's Davidsonian framework makes it possible to determine which beliefs are ideological, since a belief must be taken to be true if it is to be understood. Second, and more importantly, it is hard to see how the theory of ideology could ever be systematic: the identification of various mechanisms would always be an *ad hoc* affair. The same problem arises in formal logic, where formal concepts of consistency and validity do not in any way capture what makes some invalid arguments appealing and others absurd. Elster might answer the charge by saying that his theory is based on a generalized concept of "cognitive dissonance," as employed in the work of social psychologists like Festinger, Nisbett, and Ross. Dissonance does seem to be more fruitful than mere consistency or maximization, but it is hard to see why the avoidance of dissonance should be so pervasive a part of social psychology, or that consistency is really a guiding motive in all belief formation. Many religions simply accept and do not resolve the dissonances of their traditions, and many ideological beliefs, like the currently widespread belief that markets always produce greater efficiency, cause more rather than less dissonance.

The third problem is more telling for the explanations of ideology that Elster offers. Even if we know what mechanisms might produce an ideological belief, it is still unclear why such irrational beliefs would ever become widely held, particularly if we endow actors with enough second-order reflective capacities that they not be "rational fools," in Sen's phrase. Why should a whole culture of cognitively equipped and reflective agents, who are neither dopes nor fools, commit collective logical fallacies (especially when various systems of logic are widely available in the culture) or be compelled to engage in dissonance reduction (when they can come to reject their beliefs and learn new ones)? Elster rejects the usual way out: instead of a theory of hegemony whereby the ruling class or dominant group controls discourse and promotes its own ideas, he favors the view that ideological beliefs "arise spontaneously and independently in the minds of many individuals."[28] Certainly, not all social explanations of beliefs need to be externally caused, and many ideological beliefs among oppressed groups are produced by their own members, as the anti-feminism of neoconservative women reveals. But these facts are true only of a certain category of ideological beliefs, particularly unreflective and less socially organized beliefs like Marx's "fetishism of commodities" and "religion of everyday life," which seem to result "spontaneously" simply from participating in practices. But that such beliefs arise "spontaneously and independently in the minds of many individuals" is something to be explained, not assumed (for the sake of making the theory of ideology safe for methodological individualism). Indeed, even Nisbett and Ross, to whom Elster often appeals, argue for a conclusion quite opposed to the spirit of Elster's theory: when beliefs are socially rather than individually formed, many deviant beliefs can be corrected in public, particularly if processes of belief formation become explicitly and formally organized as in scientific practices. Social processes of knowledge gathering and debate in formal settings go well beyond the typical inferential strategies that often make individual beliefs erroneous, by "using normative principles often conspicuously absent in everyday life."[29] Even though these formal processes and institutions can also produce deviant beliefs and maintain community-wide biases, as some feminist philosophers of science have convincingly shown about the natural sciences,[30] the possibility of such a highly reflective social practice makes it implausible to appeal to unchecked, "endogenous," and spontaneous beliefs that mysteriously and harmoniously produce the same widely shared unjustified beliefs.

This lack of any explanation of how deviant beliefs come to be widely accepted and shared throughout a culture also leads to practical and normative deficits in Elster's theory. If it is unclear why beliefs are accepted or shared, it is also unclear how the critic could change these beliefs at all, or in what way practices should be changed so as to avoid such formation processes. At times, Elster gives hints of stronger normative criteria at work independently of his explanatory strategies, as when he contrasts non-autonomous preferences with reflective character formation.[31] But no social analogues to such processes are forthcoming, although Nisbett and Ross offer just such an alternative in the mutual testing and explicit reflection on beliefs and belief-formation processes typical of formal-scientific institutions. Indeed, many beliefs are formed this way already, both inside and outside of institutional settings. Here, too, feminist criticisms of science as a belief-forming institution seem more adequate than Elster's critical approach, in that they offer a range of corrective proposals: the rethinking of what our culture identifies as knowledge, the inclusion of excluded voices and perspectives, the introduction of egalitarian procedures, the explicit thematization of restrictions on knowledge gathering and its effects on our first- and second-order beliefs. Without these practical and corrective dimensions to the theory, Elster's account of deviance fails both practically and reflexively. A critical theory of ideology must not only account for itself as a practical activity, but also for the possibility of success in changing deviant formation processes. Nisbett and Ross see the social level of formal procedures as correcting psychological tendencies; this option is not open to Elster's critical theory, restricted by his commitment to individualism.

This sort of theory does not exhaust the uses of micro-level explanations of beliefs and desires in social criticism. While rational choice theory has recently been put in the service of reconstructing Marxian social science, it has traditionally been associated with neoclassical economics and with more conservative and libertarian political goals.[32] Indeed, for a long time rational choice theory might have been the leading competitor to Marxian social theory: it is a type of theory that is not directed at radical transformation but with the Hobbesian goal of preserving a social order compatible with the greatest amount of individual liberty, which is assumed to be part of the self-interested motivation of rational agents. Rational choice theory has been used to criticize many attempts to achieve collective goods, from collective action to democratic participation. Such concepts as a "general will" are shown to be deeply restrictive of liberty and supposedly impossible without "the sword of Leviathan," to use Buchanan's phrase. Thus, decision theory applied to social choice problems of aggregating preferences has been used to uncover the hidden operation of force and coercion in modern, centralized political institutions and to point out the illusory character of many communitarian political ideals tied to the radical democratic tradition.

Using such results of social choice theory, William Riker tries to show the superiority of "liberalism" over "populism," of a weak view of democracy consistent with the existence of ruling elites over a strong view based on political participation.[33] Riker's argument is based on the application of the minimal criteria for rationality of all rational choice explanations: utility maximization and consistency of preferences. In light of those assumptions, Arrow's theorem proves that for any set of random preferences, there is no consistent ordering that represents an optimal solution.[34] Riker interprets this result to mean that no rule or procedure, such as voting or representation, could arrive at a non-arbitrary set of outcomes for any given distribution of preferences. The result is that practical questions cannot be decided rationally except by a small elite, who would rule as tyrants if not for periodic plebiscites. Riker and others think that their view of politics is also what is implied by the lack of a solution to the "collective action problem." Even if people happen to share interests or preferences in common, it is still not necessarily in the individual's interest to act collectively given that all have an interest in solving problems at no cost to themselves. Thus, besides a problem of preference orderings, democracies face "free rider problems."[35] On this view, it is hard to explain why people vote, much less invest scarce resources like time in political activity, since it is improbable that anyone will cast the deciding ballot.[36] Political behavior in complex societies simply becomes irrational, and the purpose of political arrangements is reduced to engendering mass loyalty rather than making fair and just decisions. A consequence of this theory is that non-rational factors are ultimately explanatory, if we are to explain political phenomena in economic terms.

The problem is that in his criticisms Riker lacks any reflexive awareness either of their theory-dependency or of their improbable assumption that we are all "rational fools." The limits of this criticism can be found in its theoretical basis: Arrow's theorem, for example, applies only if we assume fixed preference rankings. Democratic practices, on the contrary, could be oriented to changing preference rankings through rational discussion and deliberation. Thus, the formation of a popular will is not impossible for any assumptions about rationality and reflective preference ranking. Further, such discussion suggests an analogy to a cognitive learning process which would lend further empirical support. In applying probability theory to the decisions made by juries and committees, Condorcet found that the reliability of decisions made by majority rule was always greater than that of even the most competent single member of the group. Thus, Riker's attempt to apply the paradoxes of social choice and collective action to democracy succeeds only if we grant dubious theoretical assumptions about rationality and politics. This analysis shows the problems that emerge from the use of theoretical results in social criticism: their use may itself be subject to criticism as ideological, particularly if the criticism attempts to persuade members of a society to adopt a particularly narrow view of their practices. One task of the philosophy of social science is to show how such theories are being used and why such uses of them fall short of the critical purposes of reflexive practical knowledge.

Ethnomethodology as Social Criticism: Demystifying Science

Because of its phenomenological background, ethnomethodology holds to a methodological ideal of pure "documentary" description, sometimes at the cost of a lack of awareness of interpretive problems. It has also tended to emphasize the active character of social judgments, particularly in implicit inferential or practical activities, rather than avowed beliefs or self-conscious justifications. Contrary to the intentional explanations of rational choice theory, in ethnomethodology what is important is what members of a setting actually do, not what they think they do; detailed descriptions of what people are actually doing often lead to revealing explanations of unnoticed aspects of everyday activities. The critical potential of such explanations lies in the fine-grained, detailed descriptive statements of the pattern, which show how everyday activities are constructed and maintained by the "work" of their members. Although ethnomethodologists often deny any irony or revision in their descriptions, these details often contradict what agents themselves believe about their own activities. In such cases, description itself can become critical, despite methodological strictures that the social scientist report only "what's going on." In particular, ethnomethodology can show the constructed character of what agents often take to be "natural" or eternal facts. Thus, ethnomethodological description has an alienating, defamiliarizing effect, like the gaze of an ethnographer from another culture on our own practices. In it, what is immediate now becomes mediated, what is familiar becomes dependent on a web of shared expectations. Thus, the method of ethnographic description turned inward provides critical distance, and it is this creation of distance that is the critical strength of ethnomethodology. It is also its weakness.

The critical effect of defamiliarizing and deflationary criticism can be seen in some of Garfinkel's early studies. Garfinkel's studies of transsexuals shows the social construction of gender by knowledgeable and accountable social actors. The transsexual Agnes (who is about to undergo a sex change operation) is herself an acute ethnographic observer of this practical activity, resulting in her quite skilled and precise performance of gender expectations; she does all this despite her own belief that gender is a "natural fact" and her great desire to be perceived as "normal." As Garfinkel puts it, Agnes shows how "normals make sexuality happen in commonplace settings as an obvious, familiar, recognizable, natural and serious matter of fact."[37] The stance of the social scientist is only Agnes's stance made explicit, reporting on the "moral–natural order of sexuality" as maintained in so many mundane actions. As a hypothesis of the research program, Garfinkel's account of this "fact" can be generalized to all social "realities," distancing us from them as real or given and discovering them to be constructed and maintained. Melvin Pollner has tried to show exactly the procedures we use to maintain a sense of a world in common, one result of which is his denial that there are really any logical or empirical grounds for deciding between two competing views, or "reality disjunctures." Reality is not an objective fact,[38] but a "tribal" construct decided by membership qualifications as much as anything else. Thus, in Garfinkel and Pollner's descriptive studies, critical distance is used to support a radically nominalist strategy in showing the socially constructed character of the "objectivities of everyday life." Studies of practical activities in laboratory settings apply a similar notion of description to scientific practices and provide a new, non-causal basis for the sociology of science, one not subject to the same difficulties of the interest-based explanations of the strong programme.[39]

As opposed to Elster's cognitive–individualist analysis of ideology, ethnomethodologists have attempted to extend this criticism of false objectivities to formal scientific settings in a series of laboratory studies of "laboratory life" as a location for the construction of "scientific facts" and for the maintenance of the social networks whose members recognize their objectivity. This attempt is as old as phenomenology itself. Husserl already undertook such a deflationary criticism of scientific naturalism in describing its activities as historical constructs, claiming in *Ideas* that the usual view of facts is nothing but pure "mythology." Further, in the *Crisis of the European Sciences*, Husserl attempted to show the historical and abstract character of our current Galilean view of the natural world; he contrasts the abstract constructs of physical theory with the lived experience of everyday life.[40] In place of Husserl's description of intentional consciousness, recent attempts to demystify scientific facts as constructs rely on micro-level ethnographic descriptions of the activities that go on in scientific laboratories, descriptions that consciously eschew the normative categories of epistemology. Whereas Husserl wanted to avoid a particular ahistorical, realist view of science, the stated intention of ethnographic approaches to the sociology of science is to replace epistemology and its "idealized view of scientific activity" altogether, in the same way that molecular biology replaced outdated vitalism.[41] While claiming to be "materialist," this approach is not concerned with macro-structural causation through "interests," but with the local and contingent production of facts in their micro-settings – for example, in laboratories.[42] These are quite strong and quite critical claims: this avowedly descriptive approach is meant to do nothing less than change our false beliefs about science, or as Woolgar calls it, "the ideology of representation."[43]

In *Laboratory Life*, Woolgar and Latour describe their analyses as an "ethnography of the sciences," using methods of participant observation in an actual laboratory setting, in this instance, research in biochemistry at the Salk Institute. The term "anthropology" or "ethnography" here is defined as taking a particular perspective – that of the stranger. As Woolgar describes it, ethnographers of science "adopt the perspective that the beliefs, assumptions, and discourse of the scientific community must be perceived as strange."[44] It also denotes a basic method of accumulating dense empirical details, primarily consisting of descriptions of the oddities and vagaries of the practice of science, "science in the making." Latour and Woolgar argue that science in its finished and polished form tends to "occlude" the character of the process of making scientific knowledge, as much as finished commodities occlude their origin in human labor. Like ethnography, this description of science in the making tends to "apprehend as strange those aspects of scientific activity which are readily taken for granted."[45] In employing the methodological equivalent of the symmetry principle, observers of "science in the making" refuse to accept the self-descriptions of scientists as much as do anthropologists who "refuse to bow before the knowledge of a primitive sorcerer."[46] It is interesting to note the model of anthropology Latour and Woolgar employ: they are not interpretive anthropologists, but must claim to know more than the native's point of view, occluded as it is by naive cultural beliefs about the "authority of science." I will argue that this lack of any interpretive dimension represents not only a crucial empirical difficulty for their explanations of scientific practice, but also an insuperable obstacle to effective and convincing social criticism of science and its authority. Even if the distance of the anthropologists permit them to explain the sorcerer's rituals in terms of what they are "doing" in their social context, this same distance usually means that the terms of the explanation make criticism of them impossible.

Just as in the ethnomethodological studies of gender and shared reality, Latour and Woolgar's studies find the process of the construction of facts in the laboratory to be a contingent and negotiated order, in no way distinct from everyday practical activities. This contingent order is obscured from view by the results of "finished science," as opposed to "science in the making." Both aspects of science form the two sides of Latour's Janus-faced figure of scientists at work, each frozen in its rigid gaze away from the other. Far from being well organized and coherent, science in the making "in fact consists of a disordered array of observations with which scientists struggle to produce order."[47] Once these sociological micro-foundations of scientific order are seen through by the ethnographic gaze, we can "deconstruct" the very idea of "hard facts" and "objects," which now are "nothing but inscriptions." It can also be shown that the "norms of inquiry" play little role in explaining actual research, in which scientific information is not public knowledge but capital used to produce more information. The really operative norms are prestige, honor, and status within a particular social network, not the disinterested search for truth; norms like objectivity are more rhetorical devices than determinants of scientific activity.[48] All these criticisms result from defamiliarizing scientific practice and disillusioning us about its ideal character as a supposedly well-warranted body of knowledge obtained in an open democratic community. Unlike the participants, the more jaundiced anthropologists of science prefer the monochromatic picture of science in the making and never seek to discover whether the Janus figure is capable of moving its gaze back and forth, like most competent participants in a continuous activity. However, the ethnographic observer sees only the motions of science being made, its claims to truth turned into the unexamined assumptions ("black boxes") upon which further inquiry is based and greater resources and prestige are accumulated.

It would take considerable space to justify any of these descriptive or critical claims about really existing science. Let me instead focus on a particular claim that is recurrent in both *Laboratory Life* and *Science in Action*: the description of the political character of truth claims in science, of the process by which some claims become authoritative and immune from criticism. This description violates the common belief codified in Merton's idea of "the republic of science" and embodied in Galileo's famous statement about the emerging new experimental science of his times: the new physical sciences are different from the older theories, Galileo claimed, because "here a thousand Demosthenes and a thousand Aristotles would be left in the lurch by any average man who happened to hit upon the truth for himself."[49] Latour treats this claim as Marx does many similar claims about capitalism that need demystifying: "the economy is self-equilibriating," "profit comes from exchange," "technology makes the day's toil easier and shorter," all of which can be criticized through explanations of how commodity production in real capitalist societies actually works. The last claim about technology is most apt here, since Marx begins his chapter in *Capital* on the factory system with Mill's puzzlement about why machines have not made life easier for workers. Marx refutes the claim that they do by a tremendous accumulation of documentary detail about the conditions of factory work and machine labor, a powerful documentary criticism that works without recourse to any sophisticated theory. Latour tries to show just as descriptively that no average man is going to refute any of the claims made by a modern Aristotle or Demosthenes, who has a particle accelerator and other instruments with which to produce facts and to raise the costs of making objections and engaging her in debate.

Latour and Woolgar demystify Galileo's view of scientific discourse through a close analysis of the textual process by which truth claims come to be accepted in the sciences. Science, in their view, is not a democratic and consensual endeavor but rather a highly competitive and antagonistic one, as can be seen in the defensive and rhetorical methods of writing a scientific paper to be objection-proof. In good ethnographic fashion, Latour and Woolgar suggest precisely how to revise our familiar perspectives to understand what is really going on in science: reality, or in their terms, "out-there-ness," is a consequence of scientific work rather than its cause. Reality is produced through having a claim accepted and embedded in other claims and other scientific papers; it is a product of reflexive accountability of social action in the scientific community rather than any "fit" with the facts. After a period of contestation, a particular fact becomes accepted by being cited by others, by becoming an unquestioned assumption, or "black box," that becomes increasingly less likely to be reopened. More than that, during the period of contestation, instruments and other resources are accumulated as resources to defend the claim, all of which produce various "inscriptions" that count as the "facts." In this way, instruments make argument and debate more and more costly. "The equal world of citizens having opinions about things becomes the unequal world in which dissent is not possible without a huge accumulation of resources which permits the collection of relevant inscriptions."[50] As in Foucault's work on the human sciences, natural science is also seen as a product of power and knowledge, of a politics of truth. Since all claims are dependent upon particular contexts and networks for their recognition, the conclusion of the ethnography of science is not only that the republic of science is a fiction, but that "facts" are nothing but the "necessary illusions" of the social practice.

Foucault provides a good point of comparison for this type of analysis, since his claims for the interlocking of knowledge and power in the human sciences are more adequate and even more radical. As opposed to Latour and Woolgar, Foucault's explanations make no reference to the intentions of human scientists, most of whom turn out to create and spread social networks of biopower while seeking humanitarian reforms. The creation of ever-extending networks of power and knowledge work not because scientists do not follow the norms and ideals of their practice, but precisely *because* they in fact do so. In Foucault's ethnographic gaze on the present, such networks of knowledge and power are also revealed only by adopting an adequately external perspective, with similar nominalist results about moral ideals like progress or reform. In many respects, Latour and Woolgar attempt to make many of the same points about the natural sciences, by showing, for example, that Pasteur's experiments required that all of France become his laboratory. At the same time, they remain inconsistently wedded to an internal ethnographic perspective; they do not want simply to exclude the normative stance, along with Foucault, but to show it to be an illusion. Their internal descriptions must be accurate if they are to function as explanations: the details of the account must be the same as those routinely produced by scientists themselves as they explain the persistence of error, appeals to authority, the lack of accurate data, and the informal character of science. Thus, according to Latour and Woolgar, one test of the validity of their explanations is that participants' and observers' accounts must be *identical*, not simply entirely different and external as in the case of Foucault's use of power to explain the human sciences. Latour and Woolgar suggest this standard in defending their efforts from critics: "Is there any essential distinction between the nature of our own construction and that used by our subjects? Emphatically, the answer must be no."[51] This claim is not, however, supported by the studies themselves. What is critical about these studies is the defamiliarizing perspective that gives weight to aspects of scientific practice usually dismissed by participants as trivial or unimportant and shows their actual significance. However, the external and internal perspectives continually work at cross purposes: one is the real explanation, the other simply illusion. This clash puts Latour and Woolgar's criticism on the horns of an irresolvable dilemma: *either* they go the way of Foucault and Durkheim and deny any explanatory import to intentions and beliefs, *or* they must really produce an identical and internalist account, in which case there is no demystification or deconstruction of beliefs about facts. In either case, no adequate explanations of science are produced. Certainly, no adequate criticisms are advanced that would change anyone's beliefs, since they are simply not addressed or comprehended.

The explanatory and critical deficits of the anthropology of science can be seen in one of Latour's own examples. Latour recounts Wood's well-known efforts to falsify Blondlot's theory of N-rays; Wood simply removed a crucial part from Blondlot's apparatus, and yet it continued to produced the supposed N-rays. Latour tries to explain this falsification as a rhetorical move by which Wood deprives Blondlot of the resources necessary to make his claim persuasive. But why does the removal of the piece cause this problem? Here the refusal to refer to theoretical norms and content simply impoverishes the explanation. This poverty can be seen by contrasting it to Foucault's explanation of power in the human sciences: rather than denying any role to norms in the explanation of these practices, Foucault shows that their political effects are produced through the very operation of these same norms, not by their being ignored or absent. Latour and Woolgar can make their criticisms stick only by being highly selective about the aspects of participants' knowledge to which they appeal, by limiting their descriptions to ones available to everyday knowledge.[52] Such limitations leave the ethnography of science open to competing descriptions, which like Foucault or perhaps Habermas (in a different way) might show the explanatory importance of political and normative elements, of the self-reflective and ideological components of the same activity. Like old Victorian anthropology of other cultures, this ethnography works by turning the natives into dopes about their own activities and leaves much of what goes on in laboratories simply incomprehensible to the social scientific stranger who has not done enough interpretive work to enter into the community and its forms of discourse.

Laboratory studies do present a source of potentially powerful criticism of many beliefs about scientific knowledge and authority. But these criticisms are only as good as the explanations upon which they are based. After having the underbelly of laboratory life exposed in these studies, it is not at all clear how we should change our beliefs about science or its practice. If facts are "false objectivities" and representational knowledge is "ideology," then it is clear that we should change both. After the practice of socially constructing facts is explained, Woolgar would have us come away believing that "representations in science are no different than representation elsewhere."[53] Does this mean anything more than that science is part of our web of beliefs? Or is some more radical conclusion called for? If so, the norms and goals of that critique must be much more explicit, as Longino makes her egalitarian and democratic norms explicit in her demands for an "oppositional" natural science.[54] Such norms cannot emerge under the assumptions of this type of ethnography. It is as yet unclear how those disabused of their false beliefs about science and representations are supposed to treat scientific practice: are we now simply to become more self-consciously Machiavellian about power and authority? Or does such criticism open up new alternatives for science as a reflexive and practical activity? Whatever those alternatives are, they must be found in a different pattern of explanation with different interpretive and normative assumptions. It was in response to a similar directionless "critical criticism" of the left-Hegelians that Marx turned to social theory in his attempts to articulate and defend a richer critical perspective.

Criticism and the Theory of Communicative Action: Ideology as Distorted Communication

The patterns of explanation that we have examined so far have critical implications and consequences, even if they were not constructed for the purpose of social criticism or in light of standards of critical adequacy. Since Habermas's theory of communicative action is both meant to be a critical theory and to provide an explicit normative basis for social criticism, it is not surprising that it better fulfills all the requirements for critical adequacy. As is typical of the logic of critical explanations, his theory of communicative action is both explanatory and normative. Its analysis of the presuppositions of successful social interaction can be used to construct a theory of socially "deviant" or ideological communication and speech; that is, a theory about how power and domination influence social relationships mediated through language and speech. In order to show why the theory has a critical character and then how it can perform some of the same functions as Marx's theory of ideology, it will be useful to make the normative features of its explanatory pattern explicit and then apply it to a phenomenon of social communication already discussed here: discursive decision making in democratic political institutions.

The explanatory pattern of the theory of communicative action contains a core set of critical–normative features upon which its criticisms can be constructed. Criticism itself employs the same cognitive abilities of speaking, acting, and judging, each of which can be analyzed in terms of the ideal conditions of their successful employment. These conditions in turn indicate the complex requirements and norms manifest in "standard" cases in which these capacities are used rationally; pathological or deviant cases violate these norms and conditions and fail to be rational. Each ability manifests aspects of comprehensive communicatively employed rationality, while deviant cases form the basis of a comprehensive theory of irrationality in social settings. If rationality has to do with "how speaking and acting subjects *acquire and use knowledge*," irrationality is manifest in deviant cases and in failures at such acquisition and use.

According to Habermas, ideology is in general distorted communication; that is, it is the irrational employment of communicative abilities in such a way that they undermine the possibility of successful communication and reproduce conditions of power and domination. Ideology is not simply the set of prevalent false beliefs that are caused by social structures, those basic and constitutive patterns of interaction in which domination is produced and reproduced. Marx's formulation of the distinction of base and superstructure and its mono-causal view of production as determining social activity are inadequate to account for the role of linguistic interaction in structuring social life.[55] The theoretical recognition of the structuring effects of communication as well as of production also helps solve a problem unresolvable on individualist grounds alone: how similar beliefs "independently and spontaneously" become widely held. While a comprehensive theory of ideology must also include ideological beliefs, desires, and actions, interaction seems to be the location in which collective forms of irrationality are manifest and repeated, primarily as stable restrictions or barriers in communication. Such restrictions indicate the presence of "systematically distorted communication,"[56] recurrent and systematic violations of the conditions for the rational employment of communicative abilities. If for Marx ideology was "thought" distorted by the division of labor, for Habermas it is communication distorted by power and domination.

In his treatment of distorted communication, Habermas has tended to emphasize violations created by confusions among the various modalities and types of action. Indeed, distorted communication is primarily explained as the substitution of strategic forms of action in place of communicative interaction.[57] Oddly enough, this formulation does not fit the purpose that Habermas describes for his theory: it employs criteria for ideology conceived more in terms of a contrast between standard and deviant cases of action than in terms of communication; certainly, such dissonances in modalities of action – that between goals and means, context and intention – form the core of a theory of ideological action, and represent a generalization of the cognitive forms of dissonance discussed in Elster's theory to the level of action. However, as a theory of distorted communication, it is limited in scope and identifies only one of many possible mechanisms for the production of ideology. For a full theory, it is necessary to turn to a more generalizable aspect of the theory of communicative action than its intentional component: its formal analysis of speech acts that makes explicit the conditions and rules of successful communication between speakers and hearers. The problem is whether or not such a highly formal analysis of a system of anonymous rules can be made critical enough to apply to actual situations of domination.[58] The formal analysis of speech does not do this critical work by itself, but rather can fulfill this function only if it is fit into the overall pattern of explanation of the theory of social action.

Like the theory of rational choice, the theory of communicative action is an ideal theory that can both describe and explain rational behavior of a certain sort. In this case, however, its norms of rationality are derived from the structure of acts of communication, not from the means–ends structure of instrumental action and its norms of maximization and consistency. The normative structure of speech is uncovered in an analysis of a standard or "normal" case: someone saying something to somebody.

S (speaker) says (performative verb) p (some semantic content) to H (hearer).

Habermas calls this the "internal structure of speech,"[59] a basic structure that may be employed by speakers for numerous purposes. Communicative competence consists of the ability to put together these components into a whole utterance that fulfills various social functions of communication.

Although not necessarily complete, Habermas constructs a typology of such basic functions of language use, a typology that consists of the various possibilities for connecting the component parts of a meaningful utterance. Utterances can fulfill expressive, interactive, and cognitive functions.[60] The first type of utterance communicates intentions or desires: it connects *meaning* and *intention* by fulfilling conditions of sincerity. The interactive type connects *meaning* and *action* and establishes relationships between speaker and hearer. As Austin put it, such utterances do things with words: they accomplish something by their very performance, such as the way a promise binds the speaker to the hearer in future interaction. The cognitive employment of speech connects *meaning* and *validity*: assertions play such a role in argumentative speech, or, in general, in any discourse that makes claims to represent a state of affairs in the world. From these successful cases it is possible to infer the violations that make for unsuccessful cases in which the connections between these parts of the utterance are not made. Perhaps the paradigmatic case is the pragmatic paradox of double bind utterances or statements, like the command "Don't read this sentence!" The act of writing such a sentence undermines its own conditions of success; meaning is not connected to any action, despite the nature of the command. Such an utterance wears its distortions on its sleeve, as it were, but other cases are more subtle. A promise, for example, becomes "deviant" and hence ideological not by commonplace occurrences of being violated, but by social relations of power that fail to make it binding. Similarly, self-expression is not ideological so much when it is insincere as when it cannot be made publicly effective, when the speaker cannot bring his or her needs and desires into the public sphere, as is the case for the poor and oppressed. Such restrictions on communication distort the public processes by which beliefs and decisions are formed, skewing them in favor of dominant and privileged groups. The available means of interpretation and public expression then give rise to pathological forms of self-expression and might result in collectively irrational deliberations about needs.

Once the formal analysis of ideological speech is developed, the theory of distorted communication can then be applied to various practices of communication in society, in particular to public, discursive practices such as science and politics, arguably the location of the formation of ideologies even for Marx. On the basis of this theory, one might construct explanations of the frequent violations of rational and democratic norms in scientific practice that are quite different from those of Latour and Woolgar. Instead, Latour and Woolgar seem to require that theorists reconceive the practices in ways independent of participants' norms; Habermas's model, on the contrary, would show that the violation of such norms does not entail their irrelevance, but rather indicates the ways in which power and domination restrict and influence inter-action in discursive communities. Since the political dimension of such discursive practices is at stake in Habermas's explanations (and hence a normative politics of truth), such explanations could empower rather than undermine participants' attempts to better fulfill their ideals of greater democracy and self-reflection. Expla-nations using a theory of distorted communication are not simply "disillusioning" and "demystifying," but aid practical reflection on how to change structures of communication in institutions. For Habermas, the Mertonian "republic of science" is not merely a fiction, but something which needs to be brought about by changing the existing institutional form into the democratic politics of scien-tific truth.

The place to begin constructing such a critical politics of truth that warrants normative–practical rather than merely deflationary criticism is by turning to the nature of politics itself and to the role of normative ideals like democracy and consensus in politi-cal institutions.[61] According to such a normative theory, democ-racy refers to an institutionalized process of communication in a society, through which participants publicly deliberate and make collectively binding decisions. What makes such decisions demo-cratic is the process of communication by which they are formed, their open procedures rather than their determinate outcomes. Ideology, by contrast, restricts and limits such processes of com-munication, so that they issue in agreements that preserve existing relations of power. The critique of ideology in this case does not simply deny that norms are functioning within the institutional setting of political discourse but rather tries to correct patterns and structures of communication that violate them, all for the sake of greater democracy. However, none of this guarantees that the results of science or politics are any less false, since theories and decisions may still be unwarranted.

In the political sphere, such a critical theory uncovers and ex-plains distortions and restrictions on democratic communication across the full range of linguistic functions, using the formal theory of the internal structure of utterances as a heuristic guide. Practi-cally, the analysis of these restrictions or barriers shows how they undermine institutional goals by violating the conditions of suc-cessful discourse within democratic procedures. Theoretically, it corrects the absence of the criticism of formal–institutional settings in individualist theories of ideology. I will here confine myself to discussing the explanation of a few such barriers to institutional-ized discourse in political settings.

One of the most obvious sources of distortion in politics is the character of the institutional arrangements in which public discourse takes place, which make effective participation and full interaction impossible. Communication can be distorted when the institution fails to create a framework in which all have an equal chance to speak and to affect the decision. Bachrach and Baratz have called one such effect of power "the mobilization of bias," in the case of the way bureaucracies tend to filter issues out of the democratic process, often before discourse or deliberation has even begun.[62] Inequalities among participants can also affect their capacities for effective self-expression, as can the creation of costs for entering into public discourse, like the privileging of the modes of expression, styles and vocabularies of dominant groups. Further, widespread beliefs about the relation between politics and values can restrict democracy, particularly self-reflective beliefs about the nature and scope of democracy itself. Indeed, it could be argued that decisionistic and non-cognitive views of democracy, such as those of Riker, are themselves ideological or at least serve ideological purposes. In their concern to restrict the subject matter and outcomes of democratic discourse, such theories tend to justify the hasty adoption of overly restrictive democratic arrangements, such as leadership elites, for supposedly empirical reasons. Thus, this list suggests ways in which each of the social functions of communication can be distorted in restricted democracies.

Besides explaining how it is still possible to have power and domination influence discursive settings despite democratic laws and procedures, Habermas's theory also permits the critic to make clear suggestions about how such institutions can and should be changed. First, competent and reflective speakers have the abilities to correct such conditions. Even in cases where the distortions are systematic and unperceived, and where the capacity for self-expression is limited, the critic can appeal to the self-reflective communicative capacities of speakers through direct and indirect discourse aimed at opening up restricted discourse.[63] Thus, the competence of all the participants involved can potentially be used to produce publicly shared insights. As an analysis of the presupposition of participating in certain institutions might show, the rational capacity for learning is built into these institutional and communicative situations, and critics in such settings can attempt to "initiate processes of self-reflection" through communication with those whom they are criticizing.[64] The theory of distorted communication simply makes explicit the results of the acquired capacity for self-reflection built into these abilities and social settings. Once these insights are formed and shared, actors may form groups for collective action to change their institutional structures, such as the way social movements challenge and contest inadequately democratic decisions made by powerful groups. Participation in these movements in turn further develops communicative abilities among less powerful groups and provides the wider public space for learning and innovation necessary to change the arrangements and rules that people use to govern their own lives. The practical direction of the criticism of distorted communication is clear: it is undertaken to initiate processes of self-reflection, whose result is some process of collective change and learning directed to greater collective autonomy and rationality.

If its explanations are properly expanded and developed, Habermas's theory of distorted communication is a complete and adequate critical theory. It employs a well-warranted pattern of explanation that can both explain and revise the beliefs and attitudes of participants about their practices. It is practical, in that it suggests how the institutions it negatively evaluates can be changed for the better and provides justifications for such changes. It is self-reflexive about the position and purposes of critics, showing the basis of criticism in communicative capacities and actual situations of interaction. Habermas might be able to argue that his social theory is also a product of these same capacities and situations, now institutionalized in the public discourse of social science. At the very least, discursive institutions of all types cannot do without the self-reflection that social theories make possible if participants are to test their results and consequences, revise those decisions that are not just and fair, and learn how to change the structures of institutions that reproduce power and undermine their own ideals.

In sum, then, the explanatory patterns discussed in this book all have some critical potential. This is no accident: while all of them take the beliefs and desires of actors into account, their explanations are not exhausted by them. Next, I want to show how two quite different, if not contrary, aspects of social science are also potentially critical: macro-level explanations in which beliefs do not play a central explanatory role, and interpretive social science, in which the agent's point of view is reconstructed. Under certain conditions, both types of explanation can be critical.

Interpretation and Holistic Explanation: Critical and Non-Critical Forms

In each explanatory pattern, it was possible to identify at least one statement that provides the basis for social criticism, whether it be a practical norm of action, a finely detailed description of a setting, or the rational potential of an ability. As the problems with Latour and Woolgar's explanations and criticisms of science demonstrate, explanatory adequacy and critical adequacy are interconnected. Similar considerations apply to interpretation and macro-level explanations: if we look at the features of exemplary cases of both, we discover that those features which make each of them adequate also make each potentially critical. As we saw in chapter 3, interpreting other people's actions has a moral dimension: such interpretations are social acts that take place in a dialogical situation in which the interpreter accepts responsibility for the accuracy and consequences of her interpretations. Only if we are willing to allow their beliefs to call ours into question can we enter into a dialogue that is sufficient to garner the evidence necessary to interpret their way of life. This same moral responsibility may involve criticizing ourselves and others, as well as proposing new possibilities of interpretation. Similarly, as we saw in chapter 4, an adequate macro-level explanation has a micro-level linkage: it is precisely in forging these links to agents' beliefs and self-interpretations that macro-level explanation not only becomes complete but also critical. If interpreters do not accept such responsibility and if macro-level explanations do not offer such linkages, they become non-critical, as is the case for most of what passes for social science in macro sociology and interpretive disciplines like cultural anthropology.

Because of the character of their concepts and activities, social criticism is more precarious in these forms of social scientific analysis, which range from the most practical and embedded in the case of interpretation to the most theoretical and abstract in the case of macrosociology. The features relevant for criticism in each case directly contrast: as Clifford Geertz has put it, interpretive concepts are "experience-near," while those of macrosociology are "experience-distant." The latter offer the "thin" descriptions of general theories, while the former's descriptions are "thick," rich in the textures of lived experience. Thin descriptions do not depend so directly on the meanings and cultural significance of actors' own interpretations; they apply to general and multiple contexts and are thus less local and context-bound. As Geertz puts the contrast in terms of how anthropologists use both types of concepts, "An experience-near concept is, roughly, one that someone – as patient, a subject, in our case an informant – might himself naturally and effortlessly use to define what he and his fellows see, feel, think, imagine and so on. . . . An experience-distant concept is one that specialists of one sort or another – an analyst, an experimenter, an ethnographer, even a priest or an ideologist – employ to forward their scientific, philosophical and practical aims."[65] Social stratification is an experience-distant concept of social science; "caste" is an experience-near concept, at least for Hindus. As the second sentence in the above quotation indicates, Geertz in no way restricts ethnography itself to experience-near concepts; rather, the point for an ethnographer is to find adequate connections between the two as part of what it is to understand their categories in our terms. The interpretive task is to understand other people's experience-near concepts "well enough to place them in illuminating connection with experience-distant concepts theorists have fashioned to capture the general features of social life."[66] Like interpretation, criticism also aims at such illuminating connections between explanations and the social experiences of different groups within a society, mixing experience-distant concepts with experience-near descriptions in their explanatory patterns.

As opposed to such more developed and integrated patterns, both interpretive and macro-level social science can easily lose their critical force, as they become too experience-near or too experience-distant. On the one hand, structural, functional, and systemic explanations can be simply too independent from lived experience to be connected back to agents' beliefs and attitudes. In this case, social science adopts so entirely an external, third-person point of view that it has no foothold from which to change internal, first-person beliefs or goals. On the other hand, interpretations can be so immersed in the texture of ongoing social life as to fail to provide even the slightest distance for a criticism of it. In this case, the categories of social science are insufficiently distinct from the subjects studied to provide anything like critical illumination or insight. Quite apart from these difficulties, both forms of non-critical social science fail even as explanations and interpretations and do not possess any reflective character in their theoretical or practical knowledge. Such failures occur even when theories claim to be reflective, as in the case of Latour and Woolgar's unconvincing attempts at demystification. However, exemplars of critical interpretive and macro-level social science are available, and they exhibit how critics can use the resources of both experience-near and -distant concepts to coordinate both internal and external perspectives, all the while becoming neither too engaged and embedded nor too detached and distant.

Michael Walzer's recent writings represent a sustained effort to validate a contextualist, experience-near, internal, and non-detached form of social criticism. His two main targets are the overly abstract and universalist principles of moral philosophy (such as theories of justice) and the overly independent and objectivistic theories of social science: both project the false Romantic and Enlightenment figure of the critic as detached hero. Walzer is not alone in criticizing this heroic figure. Critical theorists in the Frankfurt School have also criticized this vision of criticism as based on the fictions of the transparency of the social world and the epistemic superiority of theoretical understanding. Certainly, if the critical insights of theories are to be communicated, they cannot be justified as "a view from nowhere." As involved and connected, critics slip into the position of a participant, arguing and interpreting along with their reflective peers about the nature of common social practices, shared norms, and authoritative texts. However, as Walzer himself admits, even while engaged criticism does not require any special access to objective truth, it does still require a certain type of distance that is typical of innovative and good interpretations. "Criticism does not require us to step back away from society as a whole, but only to step away from certain sorts of power relationships within a society."[67] The critical distance of an innovative interpreter is less than that of the theoretical observer: as opposed to the outsider or stranger, Walzer measures the distance of a critic "in inches." This metaphor describes not only what actual critics do, but it also describes what the ideal critic must be like.

Walzer directs much of his criticism of ideals of detachment against the retreat of Marxist social theory into claims of scientific neutrality and objectivity. This raises questions about the target of his criticisms in social science as a whole. Does this description fit newer social theories? Walzer assumes that newer social science still remains tied to this vision of objectivity; however, the patterns of explanation that I have discussed in this book represent a quite different form of practical and reflexive knowledge, one that participant critics might find useful and insightful. In *The Company of Critics* Walzer gives a list of such engaged criticisms, to which he might add his own work, *Spheres of Justice*, in which he offers a powerful and unifying criticism of the complex demands of justice and equality within our modern political traditions. Once consideration of the adequacy of this interpretation for particular areas of social life is raised, social science has much more to contribute. Walzer asks us to regard this interpretation of justice and community very much like the best reading of a poem: "The best reading is not different in kind, but in quality from other readings: it illuminates the poem (or here justice) in a more powerful and persuasive way."[68] But unlike a poem, some of the systemic features of complex economies may require an explicit theoretical perspective in order for critical demands of justice to find their mark and become persuasive.

Walzer's descriptions of actual critics disclose the variety of ways and the diverse contexts within which interpretations become critical. There is no royal road to effective criticism: it involves complex cultural activities like making moral complaints and prophetic appeals, selecting submerged aspects of traditions, and expanding forms of discourse, all of which seek to transform beliefs and attitudes. Where Walzer begins to distinguish among critics is on questions of effectiveness. "Success in criticism," he writes, "has more to do with the place or standing of the critic than with his theory of society or political ideology."[69] This is certainly true of a critic, such as a politically oriented theologian, who employs a given cultural practice and its shared meanings in order to offer new and innovative interpretations of it. But if we are really to judge critical success as Walzer asks us to, most of the critics in his book do not fit the bill. Few succeeded in changing anything. Indeed, the line between distance and detachment is never a clear one. Although interpreters do not employ experience-distant concepts but often poetry and fiction instead, some of their interpretations are quite foreign to their cultures. Some critical interpretations even need to create their own new audiences. This is true even of the rhetoric of *The Communist Manifesto*, which was oriented to the future working class and had very little immediate effect.[70] Furthermore, there is no reason to believe that theories and abstract norms cannot also become the common coin of shared meanings in various practices, and reformist and revolutionary movements in modernity are replete with many such instances.[71] Thus, Walzer's concept of the ideally engaged critic is empirically false for the domain of interpretive critics that he favors; it is also overly exclusive and ignores the ways in which theories and even abstract principles (like human rights) become shared meanings in new institutions and practices. Given problems of interpretive adequacy, it is not clear how a critic interpreting in light of a given set of meanings determines which are the results of power and which are not, especially without the reflective aid of a theoretical analysis of the effects of power. Even if the critic is concerned with effectiveness and success, she need not start from the assumption of an existing commonality with those whom she criticizes, but may try to create new ones, along with the accompanying moral sensibilities and capacities.

Walzer's arguments for the necessity of internal criticism follows from his conception of interpretation, a view that commits a form of the strong holistic fallacy that I analyzed in chapter 3. By equating the scientific critic with the cross-cultural critic, Walzer confuses limits and constraints and implies that participants are so involved in their practices that distance and detachment are impossible to imagine. Nonetheless, reflective distance is a regular accomplishment of competent actors, particularly actors who live within many different practices and with overlapping shared meanings, features that are typical of complex and multicultural societies. More importantly, even engaged interpretation is an active and intertwined process which should not necessarily be modelled on participating in continuous traditions. Extricating oneself from those aspects of cultural traditions and inheritance tainted with power requires a complex moral and cognitive judgment about various competing claims concerning the nature of a practice, claims which may be both internal or external to the participants' standpoint. It is in the gap between the actuality and possibilities of a practice that critics can open up the space for revisions of practices. Thus, the view that critics should be internal is not justified by what it means to be a competent and modern participant, especially since Walzer's original purpose was to avoid the theoretical equivalent of being ethnocentric about one's own form of life.

This analogy between criticism and ethnography can be pursued further, since the ethnographer traditionally represents a legitimately detached figure. Nonetheless, the interpretations of good critics and good ethnographers are remarkably similar. Both the critic and the interpreter are constrained by current beliefs; but neither is limited by them, since not even enthnography has to describe these beliefs in the same terms as the natives would. Critics need to presuppose a complex set of relationships between themselves, their audience, and their culture: even in relatively simple societies identities are complex, with shifting perspectives of multiple allegiances, memberships, and reference groups typical of mature members. In any case, the claim that an internal perspective is somehow necessary in both ethnography and social criticism leads the interpreter into a potentially infinite regress of smaller and smaller cultural circles and identities, all of which are supposed to possess resources enough to change themselves. Given the potential for irrationality, I cannot share Walzer's transcendental belief that this is always possible.[72] Internalism is often a recipe for moral failure and "the easy comforts of being ourselves," to recall Geertz's criticisms of Rorty's relativism. In the absence of these non-empirical guarantees, Walzer's notion of interpretive criticism does not adequately capture its own reflexive conditions of possibility, which should not require that the critic be trapped within the resources of his or her own particular culture and its audience, unenriched by other cultures and theories.

Walzer is certainly correct that acts of social criticism do not always depend on the theoretical discoveries of the social sciences, although he is wrong in his repeated insistence that it consists entirely in "elaborating existing moralities and telling stories." His persuasive examples of the abuses of social science caution critics about their claims for the superiority of experience-distant concepts. At the same time, one of Walzer's targets, Marxism, has offered rich resources for interpretations of social life, as artists from Diego Rivera to Berthold Brecht illustrate. Certainly, macrosocial theories have been used to maintain the power of elites and existing social structures by analyzing the requirements of the existing social system and how best to fit individuals and their actions into a coordinated system. Taylorism is just one such integrated micro-to-macro analysis of production as an efficient system of coordination. On this model, social science solves problems and corrects system malfunctioning through the technical knowledge of system integration that helps elites maintain control. Such technical knowledge need not consider the self-interpretations of those managed and controlled, except as inputs and potential problems. The Orwellian expert knowledge of theories of delinquency and efficiency are exemplars of non-critical holistic theories that are more concerned with controlling and managing society than with articulating and clarifying the "wishes of the age."

Even the most holistic, macro-level explanation, however, has critical potential. That structural and functional concepts can be put to critical use is most evident in perhaps the greatest work of critical social science: Marx's *Capital*. In it, Marx gives a holistic account of the structure and functioning of capitalism as a system of production and commodity exchange, developing a simple abstract model of the complex relationships that make up the conditions for its continued existence. The critical pay-off of such an analysis is not in providing technical knowledge of how this complex system can be maintained or made more efficient, but in practical and diagnostic knowledge of how it breaks down. Marx's ultimate aim at the macro-level is to provide a theory of capitalism's crisis tendencies, emerging as the result of economic actors and classes pursuing their goals and interests within a set of institutional structures and constraints. Since these crises are "systemic," and hence tied to the very identity of capitalism as a system of commodity production, any measures taken to correct them, such as technical innovation, government intervention, and the concentration of capital, only deepen and widen the difficulties. Thus, the system integration of production, in which many actors relate to each other through the unintended consequences of their actions, breaks down as the market mechanisms of coordination can no longer contain its driving force, the process of accumulation. The analysis of these crisis mechanisms culminates in volume 1, chapter 25 of *Capital*, in which Marx develops the spiral effects of accumulation crises and actors' attempts to correct them. In this case, a complete macro-level analysis of crisis serves to explain the inherent conflict of a collectively irrational social institution.

While such crisis theories provide obvious critical insights into non-equilibriating social systems, two aspects of them are distinctly practical and reflexive. First, crisis theories are related to a certain type of narrative, a narrative of transformation from the present to a better future set of social institutions, following some fundamental event that changes the identity of society. As Habermas has pointed out, the original Greek usage of "crisis" denoted a turning point, as when we say a patient is in "critical" condition. In such dramatic narratives of the type that Aristotle said tragedy is made, crises are resolved only if "participants win back their freedom from the mythic power of fate through the formation of a new identity."[73] Crises are not just external events, but are related to actors' perceptions and interpretations: "Only when members of a society experience structural alteration as critical for continued existence and feel their social identity threatened can we speak of a crisis."[74] Because of this relationship to agents' experience, systemic crises may be distinguished from lived crises, and a critical explanation tries to show how the two may be brought into relation with each other. The systemic crises of capitalism are the manifestations of its breakdown: the falling rate of profit, unemployment, stagflation, and environmental effects, all of which halt the ceaseless process of accumulation. In contrast, lived crises refer to the historical experiences of individuals who undergo such systemic breakdown and include in this case the suffering of workers which Marx so carefully documented in all its brutality. Such experiences provide the transformative motivations that Habermas speaks about as necessary for winning back one's identity and autonomy: experiences of exploitation, brutality, and injustice can have a transformative effect,[75] and are the crucible out of which new social relationships and identities are formed.

Throughout his writings, Marx challenges non-critical explanations of the structure and functioning of capitalism, from "invisible hand" explanations of the benefits of the market to views of capitalism as automatically self-equilibriating. His critical claims are supported by arguments that show the superiority of his explanations in accounting for all the evidence and piercing the veil of appearances to reveal the reality of the way capitalism functions. Marx credits many of the explanations of classical political economy for going beyond the mere appearances and crude illusions of everyday life: "Nevertheless even the best spokespersons of classical economy remain more or less in the grasp of the world of illusion which this criticism has dissolved . . . and then they all fall into inconsistencies, half-truths and unsolved contradictions."[76] Thus, the critical aspect of his explanations helps to make them more adequate. The documentary evidence of the lived crisis of the working class serves an epistemological and a theoretical function: it serves as empirical evidence that the classical model is wrong and that his diagnosis is correct.

Nonetheless, perhaps the greatest weakness of Marx's explanation is its failure to achieve a thorough coordination of these perspectives of lived and systemic crises. The documentary chapters of *Capital* serve primarily a theoretical function, and Marx does not adequately reflect upon whether they supply practical verification as well: he simply takes the objective facts of the overwhelming suffering of workers to be sufficient motivation for transformative collective action.[77] Under current conditions, the practical verification of a critical analysis of capitalism is more difficult to come by, as the conditions giving rise to potential lived and systemic crises have changed as well. To meet these changing requirements of a critical theory of accumulation, Habermas generalizes the idea of system integration and system crises so as to indicate multiple locations for the occurrence of lived crises and their indicators, conflict and struggle. Even as systems become "detached" from the lifeworld, they are still subject to crisis and contestation, now including tendencies towards anomie, the fragmentation of life, the failure of the state to solve certain recurrent problems, the breakdown of socialization, and much more. Like Marx, Habermas contrasts his critical explanation to non-critical ones employing similar concepts and argues for the empirical superiority of his own theory. As opposed to non-critical forms of holism, Habermas's theory depicts systemic order as causing crises in other areas of social life and as being open to challenge by collective actors – that is, by social movements that are organized around the unresolved problems and consequences of systemic breakdowns, such as the destruction of the natural environment and the failure of the state to manage economic growth and unequal distribution of wealth and opportunities.

Such generalized crisis theories face difficulties in practical verification which Marx's less mediated, more objectivistic theory did not. It is now no longer possible to count on the obvious effects of system malfunctioning to supply motivating reasons for transformative action. In this situation, many critical social theorists argue against putting crisis theory at the center of social criticism, usually for two reasons. First, currently existing moralities do not provide resources to make lived crises sufficient to cause changes in social identity. Existing moralities have little integrative force or capacity to compel change; as Habermas puts it, "Bourgeois consciousness has become cynical."[78] Second, historical experience makes it increasingly uncertain that crises will be resolved in a progressive direction. The experience of fascism is a striking illustration of the dangers of such periods of incomplete change. For this reason, Habermas has attempted to rethink the problem of emancipatory change on the model of social learning, rather than as the proper resolution of a crisis. Progressive change embodies some learning process by which the identities that actors achieve in the emergent form of society can be shown to be cognitively and morally superior to the old one. If his analyses of the imbalances between system and social integration presented in chapter 4 are correct, then the basic problem of social change at present involves creating new and better institutions for social integration that could anchor systems more adequately in the lifeworld. As Habermas puts it, "If a socialist organization of society were the adequate response to crisis ridden developments in capitalist society, then it would have to be explained in terms of a process of democratization; that is, the penetration of universalistic structures into action domains previously reserved to the private autonomous setting of ends."[79] Such a practical goal relies on the communicative and cognitive competence of participants in modern complex societies for the capacities and motivations for social change. A critical social theory still can diagnose present obstacles to such a transformation (privatism, for example, or the depoliticization of the public sphere) and uncover locations (systemic breakdowns, invasions) in which challenges to the current systemic structures can occur. Such a practical–reflexive conception of critical social science occupies a middle position between stronger and weaker claims for what social critics can do: they can go beyond the internal limits of the interpretive critics, but cannot claim the superiority of the vanguard revolutionary who is external to the social order. If social change requires competent agents capable of social learning, then the social scientist is but one participant in this self-reflective process, initiated by the social experiences of problems that can only be resolved by basic changes in social identity.

Conclusion: Criticism, Verification, and Indeterminacy

In the last two sections, I have argued that there are no features unique to critical explanations as such, although some explanations may be less adequate to the practical purposes of social criticism. I have also tried to show that there are two different levels of verification for such explanations: as explanations, they are verified empirically by publicly available evidence; as criticism, they are verified practically in their capacity to supply agents with insights and motivations for change. That critical social science is not unique can be seen by the fact that it suffers from the same sorts of reflexive indeterminacy as all of social science: its analyses of social actions and practices are just as dependent on interpretations as any social science, and its explanations of norms and ideals just as dependent on theories of the roles that such factors play in social situations. But it also faces further practical problems of indeterminacy: Does the lack of agreement with the theory by the group it targets as a potential agent of change necessarily falsify it? Does the lack of success of the emancipatory movements and agents it selects as significant for forming new identities disconfirm its analyses?

Habermas recognizes this difficulty in his crisis theory. While a crisis theory must take the agents' viewpoints and aspirations into account, "a contemporary consciousness of crisis often turns out afterwards to have been misleading."[80] Further, the mere belief that there is a crisis is not sufficient to cause one. A good critical social theory must be able to tell the difference between crisis ideologies and the valid experience of real crisis. But how can such validity be confirmed or disconfirmed, given the indeterminacy of action, norms, and interpretations?

Some critics of this type of social science see no solution to the problem. For example, Raymond Geuss tries to demonstrate the failure of the two most often proposed and related criteria for such practical verification. First, a criticism is said to be correct if agents would accept it under ideal conditions (such as the absence of distorting causal influences of power or the false beliefs of ideologies). Thus, practical verification always has a counterfactual element. Second, a criticism is verified by the weight of empirical evidence publicly available to all, which eventually must convince people "in the long run." If critics need to create their own audience, verification may be put off until the historical future. Both fail, according to Geuss, because critical theories cannot escape problems of critical circularity and thus cannot state the agents' true interests and desires. Geuss argues that the critical circle, the old problem with critical social science for the empiricists, is ultimately vicious on either criterion.

Geuss admits that all critical theories have had to explain why many of the beliefs that agents have about their own practices and actions are false and against their own deepest interests: this fact puts a critical theory in the epistemic situation that participants also will not immediately recognize the truth of many critical explanations. However, if a critical theory is to be practical, agents must in some respect be the "final judges" of its statements about their own conditions of freedom and coercion, at least in the Peircean sense that the "final opinion" of the community would bear out the theory. "The agents are the final judges of their own freedom or coercion only in that there is no appeal from their perfectly free, fully informed and thoroughly considered judgement."[81] Thus, complete freedom and full information are ideal conditions under which agents would find the theory's insights acceptable, and some future may approximate these conditions more closely than the present. But such ideal conditions do not decide the issue: even if the theory can specify what these conditions are, "to use them at this point would seem to involve a circularity."[82] This is particularly true of the concepts employed to specify what the current conditions of coercion are, which may be at odds with the agents' own substantive interpretations of freedom and its role in social life. There is also no appeal to public criteria that are really independent of the theory being evaluated; thus, no criteria could be formulated in such a way as to be neutral between competing views about current freedom and coercion. Only a neutral standard for the successful achievement of emancipation might independently verify the theory's critical power and adjudicate conflicts about its interpretations; in the absence of such independent criteria, the "critical circle" is vicious.

The critical theorist might respond less globally by showing the warrants for particular normative claims made by her theory. Geuss overlooks the internal perspective of the critic, including the macrosocial theorist who has to connect her criticisms to the beliefs of the participants. The public criteria appealed to are not those of a value-neutral, independent standpoint, but convincing reasons that have to be offered case by case and that are part of the resources of the critic's theory. Thus, Geuss's criticisms are telling only if the critic uses her theory as an external standard rather than one which can internally account for agents' self-interpretations and yet have critical distance from them. Free and equal participation are not simply external standards of discourse but part of their very presuppositions. Critics can identify aspects of knowledgeable, reflective action that give their criticism an internal purchase and force, even if it is rejected. However, the better strategy is simply to accept the charges of circularity and show that they do not have the consequences for the enterprise of critical social science that Geuss thinks they have. Indeed, *no* social science that appeals to norms, meanings, and intentions has the kind of neutrality that Geuss demands; such a strong, empiricist requirement of publicity fails to apply to the situation of any explanation in any social science. If critical social science lacks criteria of adequacy, then all social science does: Geuss's requirement of independence is too strong for any interpretive or explanatory enterprise. One must also accept that appeals to the ideal conditions of reflective judgment of agents themselves do not solve the problem of disagreements. In this case, the theorist can still explain why these particular agents do not accept these particular theoretical redescriptions of their beliefs. Ideal conditions are a negative rather than a positive criterion of adequacy. A set of ideal conditions for agreement to a criticism supplies only a number of dimensions along which any actual agreement about needs and interests may be questioned and hence do not resolve problems of indeterminacy. The sort of conditions that Geuss discusses are not strong enough to provide any convincing solution to deeply held disagreements with critics, and even a stronger set of non-ideal conditions would be no less circular. Rather than appealing to ideal conditions, a critical theory must consider the reflexive conditions under which actual agents might agree with particular criticisms. Ideal conditions are simply too vague and counterfactual; they work only if they enter into the explanations of why the criticism is not accepted. Hence, the lack of acceptance of a critical theory is something that must be reflexively explained, along with its own conditions of possibility. Such reflexivity shows the critical circle to be fruitful, not vicious, although it does not guarantee that a particular criticism does not founder on such circularity or on simple rationally irresolvable disagreements.

The more fundamental challenge to critical theory concerns its very conditions of possibility, not its ideal conditions of acceptability. Such challenges have been offered most dramatically by Max Weber and more recently by Michel Foucault. Weber challenges the possibility of critical theory by arguing that rationality does not extend beyond the instrumental sphere; Foucault attempts to implicate all social science in practices of domination and constellations of power and knowledge. Both of these criticisms of criticism are themselves strongly theory-dependent – Weber on his non-cognitive account of norms and values and their place in a teleological theory of social action, and Foucault on a theory of "bio-power" that is diffused throughout modern society and that acts upon the body rather than upon belief-formation.[83] The adequacy of such genealogies of the origins and limits of social science can certainly be challenged, along with the theories upon which they are based. If the reason that critical social science is infected with power is that everything in modern society is, no reason has yet been given to reject it or deny the possibility of achieving its goals. Moreover, there are many types of critical social science and many types of social criticism, and it seems highly doubtful that all are captured by such large-scale criticism of social science. Indeed, Foucault himself offers us a model of a self-critical critical social scientist who, seeing the effects of norms and truth claims, provides strategic knowledge for dealing with the subtle mechanisms of power operating in contemporary institutions.

In *The Company of Critics*, Walzer outlines three basic tasks for social critics: "The critic exposes false appearances of his own society; he gives expression to his people's deepest sense of how they ought to live; and he insists that there are other forms of falseness and other, equally legitimate, hopes and aspirations."[84] While I accept these taks, I reject that critics must understand themselves as addressing a particular community in which they have membership: not only is it unclear how or why the critic should identify the boundaries of "his" people or "his" society, but the critic may have some audience besides a people or community in mind, an audience that may even be created only in the future if certain norms are accepted in the long run. Criticism is thus a cognitive and a moral act: by criticizing a society or an institution, the critic accepts the burden not only that the criticism is cognitively correct, but also morally responsible in the dialogical situation with the subjects of his or her criticism. This is part of the special reflexivity of a critical social science that combines both explanation and interpretation in a fruitful perspective on social life and practice. Each activity carries with it its own standards: the fallibilist standard of explanatory adequacy and the dialogical moral responsibility of acts of interpretation are regulative ideals through which critics come to terms with the indeterminacy of the critical circle. Critical social theory has always sought to combine such intellectual and moral responsibility in an integrated theoretical framework and in a political practice aimed at human emancipation.

Conclusion
Philosophy and the Social Sciences

Each of the problems of indeterminacy discussed in this book has at one time or another been the chief stumbling block for philosophical attempts to unify the social sciences. In each of the previous chapters, I have identified many different forms and cases of indeterminacy: those regarding causes, rules, interpretations, macro-structures, and criticism. Just as the last chapter on criticism discussed each form of explanation, it also had to address each form of indeterminacy. In attempting to make effective criticisms, social critics must confront multiple forms and contexts of indeterminacy: the indeterminacy of fact and value, the indeterminacy of criticism itself as a social action, and the indeterminacy of the explanations that she employs critically. Many critics have foundered on one or more of these problems. One of the primary negative goals of each of the previous chapters has been to show how major philosophers, theorists, and critics have failed to recognize and deal with these problems of indeterminacy in the social sciences, including Durkheim, Weber, Marx, Parsons, Taylor, and Winch, to name a few. Positively, however, both the post-empiricist philosophy of science and recent research programs in social theory have begun to develop solutions to these problems, solutions which do not so much overcome indeterminacy as take it for granted and make it manageable within empirically adequate and verifiable explanations.

The solutions to the various problems of indeterminacy that I have developed all work by offering adequate and detailed patterns of explanation with well-defined scope. The statements of the patterns specify the precise conditions under which the explanation is adequate. Because of their complexity, some of the problems of indeterminacy have multiple solutions, depending on the phenomena to be explained. In each case, no social theory exhausts all the possibilities. First, the indeterminacy of social action requires that explanations in the social sciences take into account the fact that knowledgeable social agents are not mere bearers of social forces or norms, but can change themselves and alter their circumstances. Adequate causal explanations of actions are still possible if we can discover the appropriate mechanisms with specific empirical scope; such mechanisms, however, are not general enough to permit predictions and may themselves be altered by agents who become aware of them. Second, rules are indeterminate insofar as they rarely define fully specific and exception-free conditions for following them. Nonetheless, agents themselves manage this indeterminacy in their interactions with others in a variety of ways: they may employ rules as interpretive frameworks, as mechanisms of co-ordination, and as reasons for having legitimate expectations of persons or for believing in the legitimacy of institutions. Each of these phenomena can be explained through a different theory of social action. Third, indeterminacy is part of the very conditions for the possibility of interpretation. Interpretation is thus un-avoidable in social sciences that take agents' beliefs and intentions into account. While such interpretive indeterminacy cannot be eliminated, it can be handled by clarifying various purposes to which different types of interpretation can be put and by making explicit the evidence for favoring one interpretation over another. Fourth, macro-level explanations are indeterminate in that they may refer to many different possible actions and processes on the micro-level. Indeterminacy in this case can be overcome if macro-level explanations are made complete: in these adequate macro-level explanations, cultural and systemic structures are linked to mediating institutions and to the micro-conditions of agency. Fifth, social critics can employ the different patterns of explanation to cope with indeterminacy; each of them contains statements that permit enough critical distance from practices and beliefs to form the basis for the practical knowledge needed to transform beliefs, attitudes, and identities.

Because of the range of these explanatory and interpretive prob-lems, social scientific knowledge takes a variety of forms and does not require unifying theories. The strategy of the post-empiricist analysis of explanatory practices given here has been open-ended. Instead of elaborating a model of social scientific knowledge in advance, I have tried to see what problems the social sciences face and how they are solved by the best available theories and explanations. This more pragmatic approach has its price: not only is it not appropriate to expect a grand theoretical unity underlying the variety of problem-solving explanations, but it is also not feasible to make prediction a goal of social science. Even so, there is no reason for skepticism about the social sciences, so long as their diversity and purposes are clear. As I argued in chapter 5, problems of indeterminacy force us to rethink the character of the social sciences as a practical, self-reflective, and historical form of knowledge. Social theories are not so much instruments for producing accumulable facts or controlling future events as they are the means by which reflective agents become aware of their circumstances and how they can change them. Once agents begin to explain and criticize their social world, they come to have a different practical relation to the historical processes that occur in it. While the social sciences do not necessarily free us from all the constraints they reveal, nor give us determinate control over future social events, they do help us to understand that part of history in which we live and which individual and collective actions may alter.

In this same pragmatic direction, post-empiricist philosophers of science have suggested that the idealized models that have been typical in philosophy need to be rejected and that science must instead be understood as a social and historical activity. On certain accounts of this turn to social practice and history, an historicist social study of the sciences is soon expected to replace epistemology and the philosophy of science. This idea that the social sciences are "successor disciplines" for philosophical reflection is one more in a long line of positivist misunderstandings of the relation of the sciences to social practices. In the past, philosophers expected the natural sciences to replace theology and metaphysics, or neurology to replace the Cartesian self of inner experience, or the science of value to replace moral reflection. Philosophy would then become at best what Locke called an "underlaborer" to these various disciplines, primarily concerned with providing conceptual and methodological clarifications of the proper way to do rigorous science.

The difficulty with this view of the relation of philosophy to the sciences is that it requires a form of determinate knowledge that cannot be expected from the social sciences, if it ever could from any science. The indeterminacy of the social sciences makes them poor candidates for successor disciplines to philosophy. Indeed, both have the same status as forms of practical and reflective knowledge. That is why I argued in my Introduction that many post-empiricists have a misguided view of the social sciences, giving powers to them that they deny to philosophy and the natural sciences. While the social sciences share the domain of practical knowledge with philosophy, the two are not identical. Whereas the social sciences do not replace philosophy, neither does philosophy legislate for the social sciences. As opposed to Locke's "underlaborer," Kant thought that philosophy could fulfill the role of being a "judge" for the sciences, a high priest of culture who validates their results and assigns each their proper sphere and methods.

The presuppositions of the Kantian idea of the relation of philosophy to the sciences has been increasingly attacked by historicism, Marxism, pragmatism, and hermeneutics, all of which show the inextricable ties that judging subjects have to contingent features of social life.[1] Like the post-empiricism which is their heir, all of these movements have argued that knowledge can only be understood through an historical and social perspective. With the end of the juridical and legislative notions of the philosophy of science, the way is opened for a new, cooperative relation between philosophy and the social sciences.[2] The "new" philosophy of science that I have argued for here does not stand above the battle as transcendental judge organizing social research. Rather, this philosophy of science is self-reflection within the context of problems raised by various social theories and explanatory strategies. Thus, philosophy needs to be transformed by the social sciences, by entering into their debates rather than generating its own independent set of problems. Such a relationship is already adumbrated in cooperation between moral philosophy and moral psychology, the philosophy of language and empirical linguistics, the philosophy and the history of science, and the philosophy of mind and cognitive science. Whether or not these particular empirical theories have a special status as "reconstructive sciences," as Habermas claims, is not the main issue.[3] Rather, what is significant is that through developing a working relationship with them, philosophical reflection becomes dependent on empirical claims and fallible knowledge. These interrelationships have already been especially significant for critical social science, as the explanations given in the various newer theories of ideology in chapter 5 illustrate. Here social psychology, linguistics, and macrosocial theory have all been organized systematically and used to reflect critically upon the content of social beliefs, how they are formed, and their role in maintaining social relationships.

This last example also shows that this cooperative relationship is not one-sided – it depends just as much on transforming our conception of the social sciences. Their normative and evaluative component is accentuated in the relationship, not just for the sake of philosophy but for the sake of good social science. Problems with eliminating such elements are apparent in Mannheimian sociology of knowledge and in recent sociologies of science: what they have in common is the attempt to eliminate rather than transform the remnants of the normative orientation of the philosophical tradition. Already in the 1930s, critical social theorists criticized this relativizing form of sociological explanation of beliefs. Certainly, it is necessary to explain how moral, political, and scientific theories and ideas "have developed with the life-processes of society."[4] All forms of knowledge are socially and historically conditioned, in a variety of ways. However, social science should not be concerned only with the dependent and limited nature of knowledge. Such a view results in skepticism, even for the reflexive and practical knowledge claims of the social sciences themselves. As opposed to Mannheim and other paradoxical and anti-practical positions in the sociology of knowledge, Herbert Marcuse argued that the social study of knowledge must preserve the ideal of truth, even while taking an historically conditioned perspective: "What is linked in past knowledge to specific social structures disappears with them; in contrast, critical theory concerns itself with preventing the loss of the truth that past knowledge has labored to attain."[5] Against the relativizing tendencies of the sociology of knowledge, a critical theory is normative and practical; it seeks to help us get on in the present. This goal requires not only that we preserve past knowledge, but also some emphatic, though transformed, conception of truth and reason if we are to have any critical relation to present knowledge at all.

Such a normative–reflective orientation towards practical knowledge of the present transforms both philosophy and social science. Let me conclude by citing several examples of this perspective that illustrate the possibilities of fruitful cooperation between philosophy and social science in various traditional philosophical disciplines: epistemology, moral theory, and political philosophy. The epistemological presuppositions of current sociologies of science treat truth claims in precisely the same way as the sociologies of knowledge that Horkheimer and Marcuse criticized. If anything, their skepticism is more radical. In place of this relativizing, anti-philosophical, and detached strategy, a practical–normative approach analyzes the ways in which participants in scientific practices attempt to eliminate such cultural biases and the obfuscating influences of power, however unsuccessfully. While certain aspects of current scientific practices need to be criticized, the ideal of an open scientific community with democratic institutions needs to be made practical and transformed, not simply eliminated as an unreflective fiction. A normative sociology of science could contribute to the practical knowledge needed to change current institutions in light of such practical and political ideals.[6] Similarly, moral theory needs to take into account the ways in which moral ideals are part of the process by which agents acquire an identity within an historical society. This social perspective implies neither that morality is purely ideological nor that it is the contingent product of relations of power, although at times it has been both.[7] If morality is a place for the critical reflection of a culture on its own practices, it can also transform such practices as new identities emerge out of current social problems and crises. Thus, the emphatic normative claims of morality can be redeemed if they can be located within possibilities of social learning and change. Whereas philosophy articulates these new identities, the social sciences explain and criticize how both the old and the new ones were formed. Finally, democratic theories need to consider the social conditions that make such political institutions possible. They cannot be made practical without a social theory that explains the current social forces, powers, and inequalities that undermine any attempt to expand the nature and scope of democratic institutions. The role of philosophy contributes a better understanding of the conditions of public reason in collective institutions, while social science can analyze the previous and current attempts to institutionalize such rationality in law, science, and political organization.[8] The theory of ideology is here again one location for cooperation between social science and philosophy, since it is a form of critical reflection about the rationality of the beliefs and decisions that such political institutions produce.

In all of these examples, social scientific explanations play an important role in critical reflection and in practical change. Since philosophy has always at least in part been this form of reflection, it can now bring the empirical knowledge gained in the social sciences to bear on the old Socratic task of examining one's life and culture. In their common critical and interpretive roles, both philosophy and social science help us to understand the beliefs, institutions, and structures that we inherit as members of a particular society living at a particular time. If the social sciences are such practical and reflective knowledge, then their goal is not somehow to capture the essential and invariant features of all societies at all times. According to practically oriented post-empiricism, they are best grasped as pragmatic and historical instruments for understanding the present and shaping the future. Ultimately, both philosophy and the social sciences succeed to the extent that they develop the means by which we transform ourselves and our relations to others. Both must be judged according to this purpose, by their contribution to the human struggle with the problems and indeterminacy of social life.

Notes

INTRODUCTION POST-EMPIRICISM, INDETERMINACY,
AND THE SOCIAL SCIENCES

1 See our editors' Introduction to J. Bohman, D. Hiley, and R. Shusterman, eds, *The Interpretive Turn* (Ithaca, 1991).

2 For a good account of what post-empiricism means and what gave rise to it, see Mary Hesse, *Revolutions and Reconstructions in the Philosophy of Science* (Bloomington, 1980); also Ian Hacking, *Representing and Intervening* (Cambridge, 1983).

3 See Charles Taylor's seminal article, "Interpretation and the Sciences of Man," in *Collected Papers*, vol. 2 (Cambridge, 1985), pp. 15–57.

4 See the volume edited by Martin Hollis and Steven Lukes, *Rationality and Relativism* (Cambridge, Mass., 1982).

5 Jürgen Habermas, *Toward a Rational Society* (Boston, 1969), p. 7.

6 On the concept of exemplar, see Thomas Kuhn, "Postscript," *Structure of Scientific Revolutions* (Chicago, 1970).

7 On this concept of a core applied to causality in general, see Richard Miller, *Fact and Method* (Princeton, 1987), p. 76. I do not see the core as a set of "elementary varieties," but as a specification, to the extent that it is possible, of the elements which make a particular explanation the token of a type, or a determinate of a determinable. Like Miller, I do not see the core as a definition but as well-defined empirical cases.

8 One way to achieve much the same result might be a "sociology of sociology," as Robert Friedrich and others have done. But this approach fails to capture the first-person features of self-reflective, normative activities, favoring instead macrosociological categories. For the same reason, I do not regard this book as an instance of "metatheorizing," to use George Ritzer's term.

9   See Donald Davidson, "Actions, Reasons and Causes," in *Essays on Actions and Events* (Oxford, 1980), pp. 3–20. For a discussion of this circularity, see Jon Elster, *Making Sense of Marx* (Cambridge, 1985), p. 461ff.

10 See K. Baynes, J. Bohman, and T. McCarthy, eds, *After Philosophy* (Cambridge, 1987),

11 Jon Elster, *Solomonic Judgments* (Cambridge, 1989), p. 1.

12 See the discussion of Ryle in Clifford Geertz, "Thick Description," in *Interpretation of Cultures* (New York, 1972), pp. 3–32.

13 See Max Weber's methodological introduction to *Economy and Society* (Berkeley, 1978).

14 Charles Taylor, "Understanding in the Human Sciences," *Review of Metaphysics* 34 (1980), p. 26.

15 Many of these debates have revolved around issues of verification.

16 W.V.O. Quine, *Word and Object* (Cambridge, Mass., 1960), pp. 53 and 73.

17 In discussing what he calls "the Wittgensteinian paradox," Kripke contrasts Wittgenstein's analysis of the indeterminacy of rule following with Quine's thesis in terms of assumptions about behavioral evidence. I discuss the paradox below in chapter 2. See Saul Kripke, *Wittgenstein on Rules and Private Language* (Cambridge, Mass., 1982), pp. 14–15.

18 See Arthur Fine, *The Shaky Game* (Chicago, 1986), p. 148ff.

1   THE OLD LOGIC OF SOCIAL SCIENCE:
ACTION, REASONS, AND CAUSES

1   Carl Hempel, *Aspects of Scientific Explanation* (New York, 1965), p. 412.

2   William Dray, *Laws and Explanations in History* (Oxford, 1957); Charles Taylor, *The Explanation of Behavior* (New York, 1962). Both argue for distinctive, autonomous forms of explanation for human action.

3   Hempel, *Aspects of Scientific Explanation*, p. 236.

4   Karl Popper, quoted in Dray, *Laws and Explanations in History*, p. 28.

5   Hempel, *Aspects of Scientific Explanation*, p. 242.

6   Ibid., p. 472.

7   Ibid., p. 463.

8   Ibid., p. 471.

9   Ibid.

10 See, for example, the essays in parts 2 and 4 of *The Nature and Scope of Social Science*, ed. L. Krimmerman (New York, 1969).

11 Donald Davidson, "Actions, Reasons and Causes," in *Action and Events* (Oxford, 1978), p. 16.

12 Donald Davidson, "Freedom to Act," in *Action and Events*, p. 79.

13 Such a model of causation escapes the Davidsonian criticism made here. See the essays in *Probability and Causality*, ed. J. Fetzer (Dordrecht, 1988). For a more general probabilistic approach to the

philosophy of science that sees empirical confirmation as a non-deductive, "bootstrapping" affair, see Clark Glymour, *Theory and Evidence* (Princeton, 1980). I will not pursue this reaction to the breakdown of Hempelian naturalism in the philosophy of science, although it has enormous significance for more quantitative social sciences like econometrics and population studies. For an excellent overview of the problems with Hempel's deductive–nomological model and the many alternatives to it, see Wesley Salmon, *Four Decades of Scientific Explanation* (Minneapolis, 1989).

14 Nancy Cartwright, *How the Laws of Physics Lie* (Cambridge, 1983), p. 136.
15 Hempel, *Aspects of Scientific Explanation*, p. 472.
16 Ibid., p. 475.
17 Alexander Rosenberg, *Philosophy of Social Science* (Boulder, 1988), p. 44
18 Hempel, *Aspects of Scientific Explanation*, p. 481.
19 Taylor, *The Explanation of Behavior*, p. 9.
20 Talcott Parsons, *The Structure of Social Action* (New York, 1937). For different treatments of this aspect of Parsons' thought, see Jeffery Alexander, *Theoretical Logic in Sociology*, vol. 4 (Berkeley, 1984), chapters 1 and 2; and John Heritage, *Garfinkel and Ethnomethodology* (London, 1984), chapter 1.
21 Hempel, *Aspects of Scientific Explanation*, p. 465.
22 Parsons, *The Structure of Social Action*, p. 16.
23 Ibid., p. 58.
24 Ibid., p. 735.
25 Ibid., p. 730ff; for an analysis of the difficulties of this framework, see John Heritage, *Garfinkel and Ethnomethodology*, p. 10.
26 Parsons, *The Structure of Social Action*, p. 740.
27 Ibid., p. 64.
28 Jeffery Alexander, *Theoretical Logic*, vol. 4, p. 39.
29 This Freudian notion of internalization is developed most clearly in Talcott Parsons and Edward Shils, *Towards a General Theory of Action* (Cambridge, 1951).
30 Heritage, *Garfinkel and Ethnomethodology*, pp. 18–19.
31 Parsons, *The Structure of Social Action*, p. 729.
32 Alexander, *Theoretical Logic*, vol. 4, p. 75.
33 Talcott Parsons, *The Social System* (New York, 1951), p. 64; for a discussion of this problem, see Heritage, *Garfinkel and Ethno-methodology*, pp. 21–2.
34 See *The Theory of Social Action: the Correspondence of Alfred Schütz and Talcott Parsons* (Bloomington, 1978); Schütz argues this point repeatedly throughout his 1940 correspondence with Parsons.
35 Parsons, quoted in Alexander, *Theoretical Logic*, vol. 4, p. 41.
36 David Bloor, "Wittgenstein and Mannheim on the Sociology of Mathematics," *Studies in the History and Philosophy of Science* 4 (1973), p. 173; also, Bloor gives the same formulation in *Knowledge and Social Imagery* (London, 1976), pp. 4–5. In the latter, Bloor

elaborates the four "tenets" of the program as a causal, anti-normative approach: "1. It must be causal, that is concerned with the conditions which bring about belief and other states of knowledge." Bloor admits other types of causes than social ones. "2. It will be impartial with respect to truth or falsity, rationality or irrationality, success or failure." While Bloor says that both must be explained, in actual practice this requirement means that such considerations are bracketed. "3. It would be symmetrical in its style of explanation." As I discuss below, this "symmetry principle requires that true and false beliefs be explained in the same way. "4. It would be reflexive." Thus, sociology can itself be explained causally, although the case studies do not really reveal any such self-reflexivity about their own explanations.

37 David Bloor, *Knowledge and Social Imagery*, pp. 4–5, and numerous other instances.

38 David Bloor, "The Strengths of the Strong Programme," *Philosophy of the Social Sciences* 11, pp. 199–213, especially p. 213. Bloor is responding to criticism by Larry Laudan in the same issue, "The Pseudo-Science of Science?" Laudan also disputes whether the program has really explained science with science or even given causal explanations of beliefs at all, particularly in the absence of any general laws.

39 Barry Barnes and Steven Shapin, Introduction to *Natural Order: Historical Studies in Scientific Culture*, ed. B. Barnes and S. Shapin (Beverly Hills, 1979), p. 9.

40 Bloor, *Knowledge and Social Imagery*, pp. 4–5. Stephen Turner points out that Bloor still incoherently accepts participants' identification of their beliefs while rejecting their own explanations of them. As I argued earlier in the chapter, this same lack of awareness of interpretive indeterminacy is also present in Hempel's explanations of rational action. Turner goes on to show how the strong programme's approach does not compare favorably with Durkheim's more consistent macro-causal approach. "The difference can be put simply: Bloor rejects the participant's explanations of belief framed in teleological–rationalist terms, but he does not reject the participants' *identification* of beliefs; Durkheim bit the bullet and rejected both." See Turner, "Interpretive Charity, Durkheim and the 'Strong Programme,'" *Philosophy of the Social Sciences* 11, p. 232. Certainly, the identification of belief itself also counts as a belief.

41 Bloor, "Wittgenstein and Mannheim," p. 174. For a clear analysis of the (missing) epistemological arguments for the symmetry principle, see Paul Roth, *Meaning and Method in the Social Sciences* (Ithaca, 1987), p. 159ff.

42 Roth, *Meaning and Method*, especially the chapters on the programme's "voodoo epistemology."

43 See also Mary Hesse, "The Strong Thesis of the Sociology of Knowledge," in *Revolutions and Reconstructions in the Philosophy of*

Science (Bloomington, 1980), pp. 52–3, for a similar rejection of interest-based explanations and general laws. Other thorough criticisms of interest-based, causal explanations include Steve Woolgar, "Interests and Explanation in the Social Study of Science," *Social Studies of Science* 11 (1981), pp. 365–94; and Steven Yearley, "The Relationship Between Epistemological and Cognitive Interests: Some Ambiguities Underlying the Use of Interest Theory in the Study of Scientific Knowledge," *Studies in the History and Philosophy of Science* 13 (1982), pp. 353–88. Woolgar suggests that "interests" can still be used as "resources," something that I argue is incoherent as long as they are used in a causal-like manner, as in Shapin's study of phrenology analyzed below.

44 Paul Forman, "Weimar Culture, Causality, and Quantum Theory, 1918–1927: Adaptation by German Physicists and Mathematicians to a Hostile Intellectual Environment," in *Historical Studies in the Physical Sciences*, vol. 3, ed. R. McCormmach (Philadelphia, 1971), p. 62.

45 Ibid., p. 3.

46 Christopher Lawrence, "The Nervous System and Society in the Scottish Enlightenment," in *Natural Order*, pp. 19–40.

47 Ibid., p. 20.

48 Steven Shapin, "Homo Phrenologicus: Anthropological Perspectives on an Historical Problem," *Natural Order*, p. 55.

49 Shapin also explains phrenology non-causally as a "resource for cultural expression" (p. 63). In that case interests certainly cannot be said to have a causal role, since expression is entirely indeterminate; phrenology could express any number of things, or be used as a resource to express and to justify quite opposing interests.

50 Barry Barnes, *T. S. Kuhn and Social Science* (New York, 1982), pp. 9 and 76.

51 Jon Elster, *Nuts and Bolts for the Social Sciences* (Cambridge, 1989), p. 4.

52 Ibid., p. 10.

53 Robert K. Merton, *Social Theory and Social Structure* (New York, 1968), pp. 39–73.

54 Jack Douglas, *The Social Meaning of Suicide* (Princeton, 1967).

55 Emile Durkheim, *Rules of Sociological Method* (New York, 1967), pp. 52 and 132.

56 For a good account of the role such arguments play in Durkheim's *Suicide*, see Stephen Turner, *The Search for a Methodology of Social Science* (Dordrecht, 1986), p. 130ff.

57 Ibid., p. 139.

58 Douglas, *The Social Meaning of Suicide*, pp. 75–6.

59 Ian Hacking, "The Sociology of Knowledge about Child Abuse," *Nous* 22 (1988), pp. 53–63. We might also include statistics about "mental illness," poverty, crime, and other social ills. For an excellent account of the cultural construction of "drunk driving" as a

"public problem," see Joseph Gusfield, *The Culture of Public Problems: Drinking-Driving and the Symbolic Order* (Chicago, 1981). Gusfield points out the variety of ways in which the problem can be identified, causality imputed, responsibility distributed, and authoritative knowledge gathered and used. My point here is that this reflexive process of public and political choice in identifying and interpreting "problems" is a source of indeterminacy in causal explanation; Gusfield points out that the lack of awareness of such choices lends authority to technocrats who use social scientific knowledge.

60 Douglas, *The Social Meaning of Suicide*, p. 212.
61 Turner, "Interpretive Charity, Durkheim, and the 'Strong Programme,'" pp. 232–3.
62 For example, Thomas Cook and Donald Campbell, *Quasi-Experimentation* (New York, 1979), especially chapter 1.
63 Ibid., p. 6.
64 Hempel, *Aspects of Scientific Explanation*, p. 488.
65 Wesley Salmon, *Scientific Explanation and the Causal Structure of the World* (Princeton, 1984), p. 20.
66 Ibid., p. 22.

2 THE NEW LOGIC OF SOCIAL SCIENCE: RULES, RATIONALITY, AND EXPLANATION

1 Ludwig Wittgenstein, *Philosophical Investigations* (London, 1962), Section 208. This passage is the heart of what Saul Kripke calls "the Wittgensteinian paradox" about rules in *Wittgenstein on Rules and Private Language* (Cambridge, 1982). I construe it not so much as a paradox, but as a statement about the indeterminacy of rules in the sense discussed in my Introduction.
2 Peter Winch, *The Idea of a Social Science* (London, 1962), p. 72.
3 Ibid., p. 27. This passage is striking in that rules function to identify actions as the same actions, much as propositions were said to make sentences have the same meaning.
4 Ibid., p. 30.
5 Ibid., p. 60.
6 Ibid., p. 58.
7 Ibid., p. 52.
8 Alasdair MacIntyre, "The Idea of a Social Science," in *Against the Self-Images of the Age* (Notre Dame, 1969).
9 Winch, *The Idea of a Social Science*, p. 87.
10 Ibid., p. 89.
11 Ibid., p. 123.
12 Ibid., p. 92.
13 Alasdair MacIntyre, "The Intelligibility of Action," in *Rationality, Relativism, and the Human Sciences*, ed. J. Margolis, M. Krausz, and R. Burian (Dordrecht, 1986), pp. 78–9. Such an action is not prop-

erly governed by social rules of signalling (if such exist), as Winch
might respond. Rather, it is the product of a contingent negotiation
between the parties involved. Thus, it is not private, but also not
public in Winch's sense.

14 Robert Edgerton, *Rules, Exceptions and the Social Order* (Berkeley,
    1985), p. 2.
15 Ibid., p. 3.
16 In what follows I owe much to the explications of the various
    research programs in the following texts: Jon Elster, *Nuts and Bolts*
    (Cambridge, 1989), and his Introduction to *Rational Choice*, ed.
    J. Elster (New York, 1986), as well as Amartya Sen, "Rational
    Fools," in *Philosophy and Economic Theory*, ed. F. Hahn and
    M. Hollis (Oxford, 1979); John Heritage, *Garfinkel and Ethno-
    methodology* (Cambridge, 1984) and Harold Garfinkel, *Studies in
    Ethnomethodology* (Englewood Cliffs, 1967); Thomas McCarthy, *The
    Critical Theory of Jürgen Habermas* (Cambridge, Mass., 1979) and
    David Held, *Introduction to Critical Theory* (Berkeley, 1980).
17 For the relation between Hempel's account of rational action and
    decision theory, which is a sub-theory of rational choice theory, see
    Donald Davidson, "Hempel on Explaining Action," in *Essays on
    Actions and Events* (Oxford, 1980). The essay also shows why this
    view of rational choice theory as providing general laws clearly fails.
18 For a discussion of the history of the debate about measuring utility,
    see Alexander Rosenberg, *Sociobiology and the Preemption of Social
    Science* (Baltimore, 1980), pp. 55–61.
19 Elster, Introduction to *Rational Choice*, pp. 12–16.
20 See Rosenberg for a discussion of such "extremal" theories and their
    mathematics in *Sociobiology and the Preemption of Social Science*,
    pp. 81–4. Newtonian mechanics is also "extremal" because its ex-
    planations of a system "always minimize and maximize variables that
    reflect physically possible configurations of the system."
21 Ibid., p. 82.
22 Russell Hardin, *Collective Action* (Baltimore, 1982), p. 11.
23 Herbert Simon, *Models of Man* (New York, 1957). Simon develops
    the concept of "bounded rationality" to explain the behavior of
    administrators who cannot be perfect maximizers or act according to
    perfect information.
24 My reconstruction of this pattern is indebted to Elster's Introduction
    to *Rational Choice* and to his essay, "The Nature and Scope of
    Rational Choice Explanations" in *Action and Events*, ed. E. Lepore
    and B. McLaughlin (London, 1985).
25 This is the idea of Steven Jay Gould's well-known criticism of
    Darwinian explanations as Panglossian: that the organism represents
    the best of all possible biological worlds. Similarly, rational choice
    explanations make societies the most rational of all possible social
    worlds. This methodological artifact explains the theory's generally
    conservative orientation.

26 Jon Elster, *Sour Grapes* (Cambridge, 1982), p. 21.
27 Ibid., p. 24.
28 See Brian Berry, *Sociologists, Economists and Democracy* (Chicago, 1970), especially chapter 1, for one of the better discussions of applications of rational choice theory to politics, particularly voting.
29 Gary Becker, *The Economic Approach to Human Behavior* (Chicago, 1976), p. 8.
30 Ibid., p. 14.
31 Ibid., p. 10.
32 Rosenberg, *Sociobiology*, p. 87.
33 Becker, *Economic Approach*, p. 7.
34 Hardin, *Collective Action*, p. 14.
35 See many of the essays in *Judgment under Uncertainty* (Cambridge, 1982), ed. D. Kahneman, P. Slovic, and A. Tversky.
36 Sen, "Rational Fools," p. 102.
37 Ibid., p. 103.
38 See W. Sharrock and B. Anderson, *Ethnomethodology* (London, 1984), chapter 2. For example, Sharrock claims that ethnomethodology is a purely descriptive discipline that does not define its theories in terms of their explanatory power: "The failure to see this distinctive definition of theory has led many critics to make the quite misplaced allegation that ethnomethodology fails to account for or explain social life. It cannot fail to do that which it does not attempt" (p. 18). Such an argument is based on an extremely narrow conception of explanation. I argue that ethnomethodology is as much an explanatory program as the other two, and its theory of the reflexively accountable agent has explanatory power (although even its descriptive power is more limited than its advocates admit). In any case, this argument hardly defends ethnomethodology from the original charge, but grants it.
39 Garfinkel, *Studies in Ethnomethodology*, p. 67.
40 Ibid., p. 33.
41 Ibid., p. 3.
42 Ibid., pp. 33–4.
43 Ibid., p. 77.
44 See Bruno Latour and Steve Woolgar, *Laboratory Life* (Princeton, 1979). I shall return to the critical implications of the ethnomethodological description in chapter 5.
45 Harvey Sacks and Harold Garfinkel, "On Formal Structures of Practical Actions," in *Theoretical Sociology*, ed. J. McKinney and E. Tiryakian (New York, 1970), p. 140.
46 Heritage, *Garfinkel and Ethnomethodology*, p. 241.
47 See ibid., chapter 7.
48 Ibid., p. 196.
49 Garfinkel, *Studies in Ethnomethodology*, p. 33.
50 This claim is made repeatedly in Bruno Latour, *Science in Action* (Cambridge, Mass., 1987), especially in part 3. I shall consider this

claim, an implicit criticism of common sense realism and philosophical views of science, in chapter 5.

51 Jürgen Habermas, *The Theory of Communicative Action*, vol. 1 (Boston, 1984), p. 8.

52 For Habermas's most recent criticism of ethnomethodology, see ibid., pp. 124–32.

53 Ibid., p. 75.

54 Ibid., p. 88.

55 Ibid., p. 330.

56 The longest discussion of this idealization is Habermas's "Wahrheitstheorien," in *Wirklichkeit und Reflexion* (Pfullingen, 1973), p. 258. Here Habermas argues that "the ideal speech situation is neither an empirical phenomenon nor a mere construct, but rather an unavoidable supposition made in discourse. This supposition can, but need not, be counterfactual; but even if it is made counterfactually, it is a fiction that is operatively effective in the process of communication." I am trying to show the ways in which this idealization can figure in explanations of actual discourses. For a detailed discussion of this aspect of Habermas's theory, see Thomas McCarthy, *The Critical Theory of Jürgen Habermas*, pp. 305–10.

57 Jürgen Habermas, *Moral Consciousness and Communicative Action* (Cambridge, Mass., 1990), p. 202.

58 David Lewis, *Convention* (Cambridge, 1968), p. 105.

59 G.P. Baker and P.M.S. Hacker, *Language, Sense, and Nonsense* (London, 1984), p. 250.

60 Edgerton, *Rules, Exceptions and Social Order*, p. 26ff.

61 Lewis, *Convention*, p. 44.

62 Ibid., p. 58.

63 Elster makes a version of this argument in *Solomonic Judgements* (Cambridge, 1989).

64 See Robert Axelrod, *The Evolution of Cooperation* (New York, 1984), pp. 27–55. For a recent "Symposium on Norms in Moral and Social Theory" that emphasizes sophisticated rational choice explanations, see *Ethics* 100 (1990).

65 Edna Ullmann-Margalit, *The Emergence of Norms* (Oxford, 1977), p. 22.

66 Ibid., p. 134ff.

67 Heritage, *Garfinkel and Ethnomethodology*, p. 98.

68 Many philosophers use the term "practice" in this passive, rule-conforming sense, as when Rorty appeals to "practices" of justification that tell us "what our peers let us say." See Thomas McCarthy's criticisms of Rorty's "epistemological behaviorism" in "Social Practice without a Subject: The New Historicism," in *Reconstruction and Deconstruction in Philosophy* (Cambridge, Mass., 1991). While Garfinkel does provide a good criticism of the one-sided conformist models of rule following still prevalent in philosophy and social science, Edgerton shows that there are better accounts of the

contingent character of rules than ethnomethodology provides, and that its incautious statements about how rules do not regulate or proscribe behavior are simply empirically false.

69 See Heritage, *Garfinkel and Ethnomethodology*, p. 117.
70 Garfinkel, *Studies in Ethnomethodology*, p. 33.
71 Jürgen Habermas, *Moral Consciousness and Communicative Action* (Cambridge, Mass., 1990), p. 177.
72 Ibid., p. 178.
73 Habermas, *Theory of Communicative Action*, vol. 1, pp. 88–90.
74 Jürgen Habermas, *Moralbewusstsein und kommunikatives Handeln* (Frankfurt, 1983), p. 94. For a good discussion of this point, see Stephen White, *Recent Work of Jürgen Habermas* (Cambridge, 1988), p. 53.
75 See Jürgen Habermas, *Communication and the Evolution of Society* (Boston, 1978), pp. 64–5.
76 G.H. Mead, *Selected Writings* (New York, 1962), p. 104.

3   INTERPRETATION AND INDETERMINACY

1 See Clifford Geertz, "Thick Description," *The Interpretation of Cultures* (New York, 1973), pp. 3–30. For a thickly described sequence of actions, see his essay in the same volume, "Deep Play: Notes on a Balinese Cockfight," a model piece of interpretive social science.
2 Charles Taylor, "Interpretation and the Sciences of Man," *Collected Papers*, vol. 2 (Cambridge, 1985), pp. 15–57; P. Rabinow and W. Sullivan, eds, *Interpretive Social Science* (Berkeley, 1972); J. Bohman, D. Hiley, and R. Shusterman, eds, *The Interpretive Turn* (Ithaca, 1991).
3 For one of the better discussions of this practical side of interpretation related to the natural sciences, see Joseph Rouse, *Knowledge and Power* (Ithaca, 1988), especially chapter 6.
4 Hans-Georg Gadamer, *Truth and Method* (New York, 1974), p. 147ff.
5 John Searle, *Intentionality* (Cambridge, 1983), p. 158.
6 Taylor, "Interpretation and the Sciences of Man," p. 32.
7 See the papers on agency in Taylor, *Collected Papers*, vol. 1, (Cambridge, 1985).
8 Joseph Rouse and Mark Okrent hold that Taylor has committed the fallacy Kant identified as a paralogism: the inference to conclusions about the nature of an object from the concepts used to describe it. See Mark Okrent, "Hermeneutics, Transcendental Philosophy and Social Science," *Inquiry* 27 (1984), pp. 23–49; and Rouse, *Knowledge and Power*, chapter 6.
9 Anthony Giddens, *New Rules for Sociological Method* (Cambridge, 1973), p. 158.
10 The "double hermeneutic" comes from the analogy to texts, to symbolically pre-structured domains that are taken to be text ana-

logues. Taylor, Geertz and Ricoeur are all strongly influenced by this analogy. Like all analogies, the text analogy has its limits, particularly if we abandon the view that the purpose of the interpretation of a text is to discover what the author meant. In any case, the social sciences are concerned with multiple points of view as well as multiple theories, all of which supply different sources and kinds of evidence.

11 Taylor, "Interpretation and the Sciences of Man," p. 18.

12 Paul Roth, *Meaning and Method in the Social Sciences* (Ithaca, 1987), especially chapter 6 for a discussion of "meaning realism."

13 Jon Elster, Introduction to *Rational Choice* (New York, 1986), p. 11.

14 Alexander Rosenberg, *Philosophy of Social Science* (Boulder, 1988), p. 71.

15 See Alexander Rosenberg, *Sociobiology and the Preemption of Social Science* (Baltimore, 1980), p. 60ff.

16 Alasdair MacIntyre, "The Intelligibility of Action," in *Rationality, Relativism and the Human Sciences*, ed. J. Margolis, M. Krausz, and R. Burian (Dordrecht, 1986), p. 73.

17 Harold Garfinkel, *Studies in Ethnomethodology* (Englewood Cliffs, 1967), p. 33.

18 John Heritage, *Garfinkel and Ethnomethodology* (Cambridge, 1984), p. 261.

19 Taylor, "Interpretation and the Sciences of Man," p. 17.

20 Ibid.

21 Stanley Fish, *Is There a Text in the Class?* (Cambridge, Mass., 1980), p. 352; Hans-Georg Gadamer, *Truth and Method* (New York, 1982), p. 350. For a conceptual criticism of these claims, see Richard Shusterman, "Beneath Hermeneutics," in *The Interpretive Turn*. While Shusterman criticizes claims that interpretation is ubiquitous and universal, my target is contextualism. As I see it, the problem has more to do with how to understand the holistic epistemology of interpretation itself. Shusterman's epistemological point is to reject both holism and hermeneutic circularity by arguing that interpretations are based on prior or pre-interpretational evidence. My argument is that it is not necessary to make an appeal to such evidence to show that interpretations are based on evidential warrants. It is only necessary to understand the epistemological implications of the hermeneutic circle correctly.

22 Alexander Rosenberg puts it this way for an empiricist holism like Quine's: "If meanings are ultimately underdetermined by the evidence, the appeal to them cannot constitute knowledge of any kind empiricism would sanction" (Rosenberg, *Philosophy of Social Science*, p. 110). Paul Roth makes similar arguments in his paper in *The Interpretive Turn* and in his *Meaning and Method in the Social Sciences*. More hermeneutically oriented philosophers like Charles Taylor and Hubert Dreyfus make a similar point when they argue

that interpretation cannot produce knowledge of the sort the natural sciences would sanction. While many do formulate their own account of interpretation as a distinct form of knowledge, it is often by denying that it is "theoretical" knowledge, or by claiming that it must be based on insight and not evidence.

23 This position sketched here is adopted by Rorty in his arguments for "frank ethnocentrism": see Richard Rorty, "Solidarity or Objectivity?" in *Post-Analytic Philosophy*, ed. J. Rajchman and C. West (New York, 1984). Rorty argues that we must be "frank" about our inevitable ethnocentrism because Davidson's holism teaches us that there is no distinction between understanding and imposition. This argument for ethnocentrism is a good example of the ambiguities of holism: Davidson makes a weaker, non-skeptical argument, from which Rorty draws a stronger, more skeptical conclusion (see footnote 31). Clifford Geertz provides the weak holist response in his Tanner Lecture, "The Uses of Diversity," *Michigan Quarterly Review* 23 (1986), pp. 105–23. Geertz condemns Rorty's position for allowing "the easy comforts of merely being ourselves." Moreover, he challenges Rorty's empirical assumptions: "The social world does not divide at its joints into perspicuous we-s with whom we can empathize, however much we differ with them, and enigmatical they-s, with whom we cannot" (p. 112).

24 See Steve Woolgar, *Science: The Very Idea* (London, 1988), p. 107.

25 See Jonathan Culler, *On Deconstruction* (Ithaca, 1982), p. 102. A version of this same holistic argument informs such Derridean and deconstructive notions as "dissemination" and "the logic of the supplement."

26 James Clifford, "On Ethnographic Authority," in *The Predicament of Culture* (Cambridge, Mass., 1988), pp. 21–54.

27 Charles Taylor, "Interpretation and the Sciences of Man," p. 55. In this essay, Taylor argues that because interpretation cannot appeal to "brute data" as evidence, but only to other interpretations, "a hermeneutic science cannot but rely on insight" (p. 55). Such a science requires not publicly accessible evidence, as in the natural sciences, but "the sensibility and understanding necessary to make and comprehend the readings by which we can explain the reality concerned." Insight is "unformalizable," and the only possible form of verification, since Taylor asserts the limits on interpretation mean that evidence must eventually fail to resolve disputes. I want to show that if this is the case, it is not because of the holistic character of interpretation. Indeed, there is evidence enough within the hermeneutic circle.

28 Dreyfus argues repeatedly that one of the central insights of Heideggerian "practical holism" is to show why social science cannot have theories like those of the natural sciences. Citing Bourdieu, he criticizes Lévi-Strauss's formal theory of gift giving by claiming that such formal rules cannot replace the practical grasp of a whole

social background in which agents act. All these related arguments are brought together in "Why Current Studies of Human Capacities Can Never Be Made Scientific," *Berkeley Cognitive Science Report* 11, pp. 1–17. What Dreyfus calls "practical holism" is not necessarily skeptical in the philosophical sense, but rather an ambitious redescription of human knowledge in terms of skills and capacities. As his specific skeptical arguments show, not all theoretical knowledge can be redescribed in this way and must be shown to be "impossible" (such as theories of artificial intelligence). Joseph Rouse's "practical holism" developed in *Knowledge and Power* is ambiguous with regard to skepticism: his intentions are not skeptical at all. After his description of natural science in holistic terms, he judiciously suggests that his view "does not mean that science should be rejected, abandoned, or even necessarily modified in significant ways" (p. 208). Yet, he argues that we should not understand the transfer of scientific knowledge outside the laboratory as "an instantiation of universally valid knowledge claims" (p. 72); instead, the understanding that science produces is to be understood as "local knowledge." This claim does not follow from holism and does modify how science and theoretical knowledge is understood.

29 See Gadamer's debate with Habermas in *Hermeneutik oder Ideologiekritik?* (Frankfurt, 1975). Habermas's initial volley in the debate is reprinted in *Understanding and Social Inquiry*, eds F. Dallmayr and T. McCarthy (Notre Dame, 1977), pp. 335–63. My argument here is close to Habermas's in this debate.

30 A list of strong holists might include Derrida, Fish, Clifford, Woolgar, and Latour, and other post-modernists in various disciplines. A list of holist philosophers who make specific strong holistic inferences include Rorty, Dreyfus, Taylor, Rouse, Gadamer, and, more generally, many neo-Heideggerians and neo-Aristotelians. True to the second variety, these philosophers are not generally skeptical, and often take "weak holist" positions on other issues. Besides Latour's notion of a "network" as the limits of an activity's validity, Pierre Bourdieu's concept of a habitus, a set of unreflective dispositions that we are socialized into and become "variants" of is certainly a strong holist concept of Heideggerian inspiration; see Bourdieu, *Outline of a Theory of Practice* (Cambridge, 1977), p. 85ff; it is also an example of how, when strong holist concepts are employed empirically, they become highly dubious. I shall deal with this type of cultural explanation in chapter 4, since holism is here employed as part of an empirical theory of cultural reproduction. As in Latour's case, it is had only by impoverishing sociological explanation of social practice and agency. I will discuss Bourdieu in chapter 4 and Latour in chapter 5.

31 Weak holists include Searle, Davidson, Habermas, Geertz, and MacIntyre. An example of the resistance to skeptical inferences from anti-foundationalist, holistic premises comes at the end of Davidson's

"The Very Idea of a Conceptual Scheme," where he denies that holism requires giving up truth claims: "In giving up dependence on the concept of an uninterpreted reality, something outside of all schemes and science, we do not relinquish the notion of objective truth." See Donald Davidson, *Inquiries into Truth and Interpretation* (Oxford, 1985), p. 198. Like Rouse, MacIntyre is an ambiguous case: his notion of resolving cultural and epistemic crises by strong cross-contextual claims established in "the better argument" is a criterion typical of weak holism; his neo-Aristotelian insistence on submission to the authority of a practice reflects strong holism. For MacIntyre as "weak holist," see his essay in *After Philosophy*, eds K. Baynes, J. Bohman, and T. McCarthy (Cambridge, Mass., 1987), pp. 381–411, and my Introduction to it.

32   See Gadamer, *Truth and Method*, p. 147ff.

33   John Searle, *Intentionality*, p. 158.

34   Donald Davidson makes this weak holist argument in discussing Hempel's anti-holist explanations of intentional action when he argues that rational explanations cannot work for single actions but can work for identifying coherent patterns of actions; hence, they involve interpretation. See Davidson, "Hempel on Explaining Action," in *Essays on Action and Events* (Oxford, 1980), pp. 261–76.

35   Martin Heidegger, *Being and Time* (New York, 1962), p. 195.

36   As put by a practical holist, Joseph Rouse, as a gloss on Heidegger's notion of the hermeneutic circle; see *Knowledge and Power*, p. 67. What is most striking about this locution is the way it reifies our own interpretations and shared understandings. This view of our pre-reflective orientations explains why Rouse thinks that theoretical knowledge is "local" and context-dependent.

37   These claims are made by Rouse and Woolgar respectively.

38   Gadamer, *Truth and Method*, p. 238ff.

39   See Harold Garfinkel's criticism of Parsons' holistic concept of "internalization," in *Studies in Ethnomethodology*, p. 33ff. When used by strong holists and even some ethnomethodologists who talk of everyday practical knowledge, the skill metaphor, like all overly specific models of the variety of acts that make up interpretation, is seriously misleading as a general model of interpretation. At best, it generalizes one type of interpretation to all; at worst, it leads to the confusion of prereflective orientations and interpretations. Even if we are skillful at an activity, we could still be a "dope" about its conditions and constraints. Reflection has to have more epistemic content than "practical holism" sometimes seems to allow.

40   Kant, *Critique of Pure Reason*, A572. Kant does have limiting concepts, although they are inferred dialectically and not arrived at as a result of transcendental analysis: the concept of the noumena, which has no determinate content whatsoever. As Kant puts it, "The concept of the noumena is thus a merely limiting concept, the function of which is to curb the pretensions of sensibility; it is therefore only of negative employment" (B310). Strong holists are guilty not only

of an amphiboly, but also of confusing the positive and negative employment of limit concepts, leading to skepticism.

41 Strong holists dispute this view of reflective adjudication. When replacing epistemic accounts, they often appeal to practical forms of knowledge within interpretive limits, such as Gadamer's analysis of "phronesis" and Dreyfus's arguments for the superiority of "practical" over "theoretical" holism. See Hubert Dreyfus, "Holism and Hermeneutics," in *Hermeneutics and Praxis*, ed. R. Hollinger (Notre Dame, 1984), pp. 227–47. Practical holists see interpretation as "practical" in the sense of a skill and take Dilthey to be their main opponent, the founder of misleading theoretical and epistemological approaches to hermeneutics. I will defend Dilthey's approach at the end of this essay, but not his specific theory of interpretation. In his essay in *The Interpretive Turn* on Heidegger's scientific realism, Dreyfus goes beyond this discussion of practical holism and argues that the background enables some beliefs to be "decontextualized"; this is sufficient to establish the possibility of theoretical knowledge and a notion of truth not simply relative to social purposes.

42 Kant, B316. Some have argued that interpretive realists, like Charles Taylor, commit a paralogism, a false inference from the nature of the concepts describing a thing (interpretations) to the things themselves (interpreters). In any case, weak holists that accept the possibility of "correct" interpretations do not reify meanings in entities. It does not require anything of interpreters as metaphysical objects, but just agents with certain capacities to whom we stand in dialogical relationships. Further, it commits no paralogism, since its main point is not about human nature but about methodology: interpretation requires at least considering as evidence what meanings actions or expressions have for those who perform them, even if they are not ultimately accepted. Weak holists do not therefore privilege self-knowledge, but consider it to be part of the evidence grounding an interpretation.

43 Searle, *Intentionality*, p. 158,

44 Rouse claims this in *Power and Knowledge*, particularly chapter 4, entitled "Local Knowledge." It is hard not to see epistemic qualifiers like "local" as anything but skeptical; if they are not, Rouse needs to distinguish what he means by them more clearly from the obviously skeptical meanings they have for Woolgar and Latour, whom he quotes approvingly and without criticism throughout this chapter of his book.

45 MacIntyre uses this type of epistemological, weak holistic argument in his recent work, *Whose Justice? Whose Rationality?* (Notre Dame, 1988), but undercuts it with his historicism.

46 See the editors' Introduction to Rabinow and Sullivan, *Interpretive Social Science*; for an analysis of Geertz's interpretation as an explanatory narrative, see Paul Roth, "How Narratives Explain," *Social Research* 56 (1989), pp. 449–78.

47 Geertz, "Deep Play," *Interpretation of Cultures*, p. 417.

48 Ibid., p. 443.

49 For a good account of post-modernism in ethnography, see George Marcus and Michael Fisher, *Anthropology as Cultural Critique* (Chicago, 1986); also the collection of essays entitled *Writing Culture*, eds J. Clifford and G. Marcus (Berkeley, 1986), especially the essay by P. Rabinow, "Representations Are Social Facts."

50 See Paul Roth, "Ethnography without Tears," *Current Anthropology* 30 (1989), pp. 555–69 with responses from many post-modernist anthropologists, including James Clifford and Steven Tyler.

51 Vincent Crapanzano, "Hermes Dilemma," in *Writing Culture*, p. 72.

52 Clifford, *The Predicament of Culture*, p. 44.

53 Geertz, *Works and Lives* (Stanford, 1988), p. 144.

54 Wilhelm Dilthey, *Gesammelte Schriften*, vol. 5 (Stuttgart, 1956), p. 337.

55 See Woolgar, *Science: The Very Idea*, especially chapters 2 and 6.

56 Ibid., p. 92.

57 Ibid., p. 30. Besides my argument here for public as opposed to objective validity, Dreyfus's essay "Heidegger as Scientific Realist" in *The Interpretive Turn* (forthcoming) shows that the commitment to holism is entirely consistent with a belief in the context-independent status of scientific claims, even a form of realism.

58 Woolgar, *Science: The Very Idea*, p. 93.

59 Geertz, "Thick Description," pp. 14–15.

60 These essays are in Taylor's *Collected Papers*, vol. 2, pp. 116–33 and 134–51 respectively.

61 Ibid., pp. 125–6.

62 Jürgen Habermas, *Theory of Communicative Action*, vol. 1 (Boston, 1984), p. 103.

63 For a discussion of this distinction in Weber, see the beginning of chapter 5.

64 Donald Davidson, "Problems in the Explanation of Action," in *Metaphysics and Morality*, eds P. Pettit, J. Norman, and R. Sylvan (London, 1987), p. 47.

65 Donald Davidson, "Belief and Meaning," *Essays on Action and Events*, p. 153.

66 Donald Davidson, "The Very Idea of a Conceptual Scheme," in *Inquiries into Truth and Interpretation* (Oxford, 1983), pp. 183–98.

67 Donald Davidson, "The Method of Truth in Metaphysics," *Inquiries into Truth and Interpretation*, p. 199.

68 Davidson, "Problems in Explaining Action," p. 47.

69 Habermas, *Theory of Communicative Action*, vol. 1, pp. 107 and 111. See Kenneth Baynes for a clear analysis of this thesis, including a comparison with Davidson: "Rational Reconstruction and Social Criticism: Habermas's Model of Interpretive Social Science," *Philosophical Forum* 21 (1989–90), pp. 122–45. There are differences in our views on the relationship between Davidson and Habermas centering on the "principle of charity," which is not operative in

Habermas's work as a semantic principle. While both connect truth and interpretation, Davidson's transcendental argument works only by making it impossible to distinguish the imposition of norms from correct interpretation, and hence does not permit significant, specific differences in order to exclude differences so large as to make others' actions and utterances entirely unintelligible.

70 Davidson, "The Very Idea of a Conceptual Scheme," pp. 197–8.

71 For this sort of analysis of the problems of conflicting standards of rationality, see Paul Roth, *Meaning and Method in the Social Sciences*, especially chapters 6 and 9.

72 See Paul Veyne, *Did the Greeks Believe Their Myths?* (Chicago, 1986). If Veyne is correct, there are better and worse answers to the question of his title, although none of them are a simple "yes" or "no."

73 Habermas, *Theory of Communicative Action*, vol. 1, p. 108.

74 Ibid., p. 116.

75 Alasdair MacIntyre, "The Idea of a Social Science," in *Against the Self-Images of the Age* (Notre Dame, 1969), p. 228.

76 Habermas, *Communication and the Evolution of Society* (Boston, 1979), p. 120.

77 Habermas, *Theory of Communicative Action*, vol. 1, p. 43.

78 Ibid., pp. 43–74.

79 Ibid., p. 138.

80 Jürgen Habermas, *Moral Consciousness and Communicative Action* (Cambridge, Mass., 1990), p. 178.

81 Habermas calls these norm-related values or goods "structural conditions of the good life." Ibid., p. 202.

82 Ibid., p. 180.

83 Richard Rorty, "The Historiography of Philosophy: Four Genres," in *Philosophy in History*, eds R. Rorty, J.B. Schneewind, and Q. Skinner (Cambridge, 1984), p. 50.

84 Ibid.

85 See Geertz's Tanner Lecture, "The Uses of Diversity," *Michigan Quarterly Review* 23 (1986), pp. 105–23.

86 Stanley Fish, *Is There a Text in the Class?* p. 342.

4 THE MACRO–MICRO RELATION

1 Richard Lewontin, *The Genetic Basis of Evolutionary Change* (New York, 1974), p. 236. For a good account of non-deductive explanations of evolutionary change using concepts of selection and adaptation, see Elliot Sober, *The Nature of Selection* (Cambridge, Mass., 1985).

2 See Richard Miller, *Fact and Method* (Princeton, 1987), p. 122.

3 For a discussion of this problem with regard to classification in biology, see John Dupre, "The Disunity of Science," *Mind* 92 (1983), pp. 321–46.

4 Emile Durkheim, *Rules of Sociological Method* (New York, 1938), pp. 103–4; this rule is discussed throughout chapter 2. According to Durkheim, society is not a "mere sum of individuals."

5 Cited in Steven Lukes, "Methodological Individualism Reconsidered," in *Sociological Theory and Philosophical Analysis*, ed. D. Emmet and A. MacIntyre (New York, 1970), p. 76. This essay is an excellent discussion of the early phases of the debate in K. Popper and J.W.N. Watkins. See Karl Popper, *The Poverty of Historicism* (Boston, 1957); J.W.N. Watkins, "Ideal Types and Historical Explanations," in *Readings in Philosophy of Science*, ed. H. Feigl and M. Broadbeck (New York, 1953), pp. 72–43. Also see *The Nature and Scope of Social Science*, ed. L. Krimmerman (New York, 1969), especially part 7.

6 Durkheim, *Rules of Sociological Method*, p. 18.

7 Jon Elster, *Making Sense of Marx* (Cambridge, 1985), p. 5.

8 Ernst Nagel, *The Structure of Science* (New York, 1961), pp. 520–46. According to Nagel, functionalist explanations can be empirically useful only if they are based on descriptions "precise enough to identify unambiguously the states which are supposed to be maintained in the social system" (p. 530). He also defends the use of teleological explanations for "directively organized systems" (p. 422), and sees "no good reason" to reject them outright.

9 Arthur Danto, *Narration and Knowledge* (New York, 1985), pp. 257–84.

10 See Louis Dumont, *Essays on Individualism: Modern Ideology in Anthropological Perspective* (Chicago, 1986).

11 See the essays in *The Micro–Macro Link*, ed. J. Alexander, B. Giesen, R. Münch, and N. Smelser (Berkeley, 1987), especially the introductory essay by Alexander and Giesen, "From Reduction to Linkage."

12 For a demonstration of the ubiquity of functionalist explanations in many sciences and a defense of their empirical validity in the social sciences, see Michael Faia, *The Strategy and Tactics of Dynamic Functionalism* (Cambridge, 1986).

13 Robert Merton, "Manifest and Latent Functions," in *Social Theory and Social Structure* (New York, 1968), pp. 73–138; Arthur Stinchcomb, *Constructing Social Theory* (New York, 1968), pp. 78–100; Jon Elster, *Explaining Technical Change* (Cambridge, 1983), pp. 49–68.

14 Merton, "Manifest and Latent Functions," p. 85.

15 Durkheim, *Rules of Sociological Method*, p. 90. Durkheim continues, "The uses which it serves presuppose the specific properties characterizing it but do not create them. The need we have of things cannot give them existence, nor can it confer their specific nature upon them."

16 Merton, "Manifest and Latent Functions," p. 88.

17 Elster, *Making Sense of Marx*, p. 28.

18 Andrew Levine, Elliot Sober, and Erik Olin Wright develop this

relation as one type of token, where functional explanations are explanations of a type whose realizations need not be token identical. While the type-token relation is too indefinite, supervenience requires that the non-functional properties be such that they are related to the functional ones. See their "Marxism and Methodological Individualism," *New Left Review* 162 (1987), pp. 67–84. The sort of relation that I have in mind is like that between structure and function. As Nagel in *The Structure of Science* puts the same point in a different context, "Anatomical structure does not logically determine function, though as a matter of contingent fact the specific anatomical structure possessed by an organism does set bounds on the kinds of activities in which the organism can engage. And conversely, the pattern of behavior exhibited by an organism does not logically imply a unique anatomical structure, though in point of fact an organism manifests specific modes of activity only when its parts possess a determinate anatomical structure of a definite kind" (p. 428).

19 Elster, *Explaining Technical Change*, p. 57.
20 Ibid., pp. 57–8.
21 Ibid., p. 59.
22 This is true because of the transitivity of relations of supervenience: if A is supervenient on B (so that whenever B, therefore A; but not A, therefore B), and B on C, then A is supervenient upon C as well. In this admittedly technical discussion, I simply want to establish the possibility of a variety of interrelated levels of explanation, so long as connections between them can be established. These connections do not warrant reductionism.
23 Mary Douglas, *How Institutions Think* (Syracuse, 1984), p. 34.
24 Ibid., p. 39.
25 Ibid., p. 43.
26 Levine, Sober, and Wright, "Marxism and Methodological Individualism," p. 77.
27 Ibid., p. 80. The authors call their position neither a radical holist nor a methological individualist one, but "anti-reductionism." The indeterminacy of micro-reductions of relations of supervenience demands such a view simply as a matter of explanatory adequacy.
28 See, for example, J. Craig Jenkins, "Resource Mobilization and Social Movements," *American Journal of Sociology* 82 (1977), pp. 1212–41. The analysis of social movements follows the pattern of rational choice, emphasizing opportunities, membership recruitment, and resources as opposed to symbolic meanings and solidarity. Movements have an "entrepreneurial" nature, garnering and investing power and resources. For a comparative discussion of various approaches to social movements, including resource mobilization and the theory of communicative action, see Jean Cohen, "Strategy and Identity: New Theoretical Paradigms and Contemporary Social Movements," *Social Research* 52 (1985), pp. 662–716.

29 A classic case of an individualist explanation of cooperation that simply presupposes a stable macro-context is Robert Axelrod, *The Evolution of Cooperation* (New York, 1984). In this work, Axelrod uses the formal model of an iterated prisoners' dilemma situation (simulated in a computer tournament between competing strategies ranging from nasty to nice) to explain the emergence of such behavior over time; however, this model already presupposes what it is trying to prove by simply assuming that interaction will not break down. While the model has some *post hoc* value, it is not strictly speaking an explanation of cooperation, since it begs the question.

30 Durkheim, *Rules of Sociological Method*, all taken from chapter 2.

31 For an excellent analysis of the ambiguities of Durkheim's view of social facts, see Stephen Lukes, *Emile Durkheim* (New York, 1973), pp. 11–15.

32 Durkheim, *The Division of Labor*, as cited by Lukes, p. 145.

33 Ibid.

34 See Danto's discussion of the debate about this example taken from Maurice Mandelbaum's "Societal Facts" in *Narration and Knowledge*, pp. 270–5.

35 Pierre Bourdieu, *An Outline of a Theory of Practice* (Cambridge, 1977), p. 85.

36 Ibid., p. 72.

37 Ibid., p. 214.

38 Ibid., pp. 20–1.

39 Ibid., p. 76.

40 Ibid., p. 77.

41 Elster, *Sour Grapes* (Cambridge, 1983), p. 126ff.

42 Jürgen Habermas, *Theory of Communicative Action* (Boston, 1987), vol. 2, pp. 198–9, and also p. 130.

43 Pierre Bourdieu, *Distinction: A Social Critique of the Judgement of Taste* (Cambridge, 1984), especially part 3.

44 As noted in chapter 3, Searle describes the background in the same way in *Intentionality* (Cambridge, 1985), p. 158.

45 Harold Garfinkel, *Studies in Ethnomethodology* (Englewood Cliffs, 1967), pp. 66–7.

46 H. Garfinkel and H. Sacks, "On the Formal Structure of Practical Action," in *Theoretical Sociology*, ed. J. McKinney and E. Tiryakian (New York, 1970), p. 358. A "member" is therefore not an empirical concept at all and does not designate real people who have biographies and identities.

47 A. Cicourel, *Cognitive Sociology* (New York, 1973), p. 224.

48 See Jon Elster, *Cement of Society* (Cambridge, 1989). Social practices that have no real benefits and obvious disadvantages are, however, quite effective counter-examples to rational choice assumptions of maximization; other phenomena that cannot be explained on this assumption might be addictive behavior, collective action, and most political behavior generally.

49 David Lockwood, "Social Integration and System Integration," in *Explorations in Social Change*, ed. G.K. Zollschan and W. Hirsch (Boston, 1964); for a good discussion of the relation between Lockwood's distinction and Marxian social theory, see Alex Callinicos, *Making History* (Ithaca, 1988), chapter 2.

50 I am here following Giddens' discussion of structure in general. See Anthony Giddens, *Central Problems in Social Theory* (Berkeley, 1979).

51 Giddens, *Central Problems in Social Theory* (Berkeley, 1979), pp. 61–2.

52 Lockwood, "Social Integration and System Integration," p. 245.

53 This passage is, of course, from Marx's autobiographical preface to *The Critique of Political Economy* (New York, 1967).

54 Miller, *Fact and Method*, p. 147ff.

55 Lockwood, "Social Integration and System Integration," p. 245.

56 See Karl Marx, *Capital*, vol. 1 (New York, 1967), especially chapter 25, which describes technical innovation as crucial to the accumulation of capital.

57 Daniel Little, *The Scientific Marx* (Minneapolis, 1986), pp. 132–3. This book is an excellent treatment of *Capital* from a rational choice perspective.

58 James S. Coleman, "Micro-Foundations and Macro-Social Behavior," in *The Micro-Macro Link*, p. 160. Coleman does give cases of collective actions for which institutions are not required, albeit unorganized ones like escape panics (p. 172).

59 See Parsons, "Some Problems of General Theory in Sociology," in *Theoretical Sociology*, pp. 40–1.

60 For a closer analysis of this view of reification, see my "System and Lifeworld," *Philosophy and Social Criticism* 13 (1990), pp. 381–402.

61 For Habermas's reply to such criticisms of his use of systems in the theory of communicative action, see his "Entgegnungen," *Kommunikatives Handeln* (Frankfurt, 1986), pp. 377–8.

62 Habermas, *Theory of Communicative Action*, vol. 2, p. 259.

63 Ibid., p. 258.

64 See Nancy Fraser, *Unruly Practices* (Minneapolis, 1989), especially her essay "What's Critical about Critical Theory?"

65 Max Weber, *From Max Weber* (New York, 1946), p. 78.

66 Max Weber, *Economy and Society*, vol. 3, p. 973. For a discussion of Weber on bureaucracy, see Anthony Giddens, *Capitalism and Modern Social Theory* (Cambridge, 1971), p. 159ff.

67 Habermas, *Theory of Communicative Action*, vol. 2, p. 307.

68 Weber, *Economy and Society*, vol. 2, p. 1402.

69 Empirical studies do not bear out the ceaseless expansion of bureaucracy, especially with regard to the efficiency of centralization. See Randall Collins, *Conflict Sociology* (New York, 1971), p. 472ff.

70 Garfinkel, *Studies in Ethnomethodology*, pp. 186–207.

71 Collins, *Conflict Sociology*, p. 286. Herbert Simon originated this line of research into "bounded rationality" in administrative decision

making. See Herbert Simon, *Models of Man: Social and Rational* (New York, 1957), pp. 196–206.
72 See Amos Tversky and Daniel Kahneman, "Judgment under Uncertainty: Heuristics and Biases," in *Judgment under Uncertainty*, ed. D. Kahneman, P. Slovic, and A. Tversky (Cambridge, 1982), pp. 3–20.
73 Habermas, *Theory of Communicative Action*, vol. 2, p. 260.
74 Ibid., p. 271.
75 Ibid., p. 196.
76 Ibid., p. 372.
77 Habermas, *Philosophical Discourse of Modernity* (Cambridge, Mass., 1987), p. 361. His most pessimistic essay to date is "The New Obscurity," in *Philosophy and Social Criticism* 12 (1986), pp. 1–18.

5 CRITICISM AND EXPLANATION

1 Quine's two dogmas are: first, the distinction between conceptual and empirical statements; and, second, reductionism, the belief that all meaningful statements can be reduced to some statement, all terms of which refer to immediate experience. See W.V.O. Quine, "Two Dogmas of Empiricism," in *From a Logical Point of View* (New York, 1953), pp. 20–46.
2 Alexander Rosenberg effectively uses some Davidsonian arguments against the pretensions of rational choice theory and sociobiology in his *Sociobiology and the Preemption of Social Science* (Baltimore, 1980); similarly, Paul Roth uses Quinean assumptions to show that most dilemmas about relativism revolve around pseudoproblems in his *Meaning and Method in the Social Sciences* (Ithaca, 1987).
3 This similarityy in their views of the role of values in science holds despite Hempel's strident criticisms of Weber's view of rational explanation. See Max Weber, "The Meaning of 'Ethical Neutrality' in Economics and the Social Sciences," *The Methodology of the Social Sciences* (New York, 1949), pp. 1–49; for Hempel's criticism of Weber's notion of an interpretive and subjective component to rational explanations, see *Aspects of Scientific Explanation* (New York, 1965), p. 241ff.
4 See Donald Levine, *Flight from Ambiguity* (Chicago, 1985); and Steven Kahlberg, "Max Weber's Types of Rationality," *American Journal of Sociology* 85 (1980), pp. 1145–79.
5 Weber, "Value Neutrality," in *Methodology of the Social Sciences*, p. 37ff.
6 Ibid., p. 22.
7 See A.K. Sen, *Poverty and Famines* (Oxford, 1981).
8 Max Weber, "Politics as a Vocation," in *From Max Weber* (New York, 1946), p. 123ff. Weber argues that ends cannot ultimately be justified, because they are only justified by other ends, and so on;

infinite regress in justification means that there is no ultimate justification for values. This questionable philosophical argument has
enormous implications for his analysis of certain social phenomena,
in particular, politics. It is questionable insofar as it does not consider obvious ways out of the difficulty, such as rational procedures
that do not determine unique substantive outcomes.

9   For an alternative, less decisionistic view of Weber, see Donald
    Levine. *Flight from Ambiguity*, chapter 8.
10 Weber, *Methodology of the Social Sciences*, p. 60.
11 See Seyla Benhabib, *Critique, Norm and Utopia* (New York, 1986),
    especially chapters 1–4, for a good discussion of the different phases
    and models of Marx's project.
12 The best instance of a fairly complete and non-reductive explanation
    of ideology in Marx is *The Eighteenth Brumaire* (New York, 1963);
    the point of this essay is to show the active formation of an ideology
    of nationalism that explains the rise of Bonaparte, whom Marx
    regarded as an absurd, repetitive figure of the French historical
    imagination.
13 See Paul Ricoeur, *Lectures on Ideology and Utopia* (New York, 1986)
    for a good comparative treatment of Mannheim and Marx.
14 Karl Mannheim, *Ideology and Utopia* (New York, 1936), p. 59.
15 Brian Fay, *Critical Social Science* (Ithaca, 1987), p. 23.
16 For several of Marx's lists of what things are ideological, see *The
    German Ideology* (New York, 1970), p. 53ff.
17 Marx contrasts his theories to those of Adam Smith in this way in
    several passages, including *Capital*, vol. 3 (New York, 1967), p. 830.
    Smith's theories are false for Marx, but still scientific.
18 This is Walzer's own example in *The Company of Critics* (New York,
    1989), p. 11.
19 See David Braybrooke, *Philosophy of Social Science* (Englewood Cliffs,
    1987) for arguments which also dispute claims for the unique char-
    acter of critical social science, especially in chapter 4.
20 Max Horkheimer, *Critical Theory* (New York, 1982), pp. 244–6.
21 For criticisms of this view, see Amartya Sen, *On Ethics and Econ-
    omics* (New York, 1987), chapter 1; and Alexander Rosenberg,
    Philosophy of Social Science (Boulder, 1988), p. 178.
22 Marx, *The German Ideology*, p. 47.
23 Jon Elster, *Sour Grapes* (Cambridge, 1983), p. 141.
24 Jon Elster, *Making Sense of Marx* (Cambridge, 1985), p. 474.
25 See Richard Nisbett and Lee Ross, *Human Inference: Strategies and
    Shortcomings of Social Judgment* (Englewood Cliffs, 1980) for a
    social psychology of the widespread tendencies of human beings to
    form similar false beliefs.
26 Elster, *Sour Grapes*, p. 124.
27 Elster, *Sour Grapes*, p. 24. In general, Elster sides with Weber in his
    disagreements with Marx about the necessary role of rationality in
    explanations of social beliefs.

28 Elster, *Making Sense of Marx*, p. 474; he makes similar claims in *Sour Grapes*, p. 14.

29 Nisbett and Ross, *Human Inference*, p. 250.

30 See Sandra Harding, *The Science Question in Feminism* (Ithaca, 1986) especially chapters 1 and 2.

31 Elster, *Sour Grapes*, p. 140ff.

32 For perhaps the best example of this strand, see James M. Buchanan, *The Limits of Liberty* (Chicago, 1975). Buchanan seeks to limit the coercive power of the state, while recognizing the necessity of "public goods," including legal order; both are governed by norms of contract and the value of individual freedom. Amartya Sen's work shows that these commitments might have stronger egalitarian implications concerning social welfare than Buchanan admits.

33 William Riker, *Liberalism against Populism* (San Francisco, 1982).

34 For a discussion of the implication of this theorem for politics, see Brian Berry, *Sociologists, Economists and Democracy* (New York, 1970), chapter 5.

35 Mancur Olson, *The Logic of Collective Action* (Cambridge, 1962). The solution for Olson is side-payments or "selective incentives," pay-offs given to those who participate. However, such payments take resources, and rational agents participate only if organizations can muster them. The problem of collective action has given rise to a whole direction of research in social movements inspired by rational choice theory called "resource mobilization theory." Alternative explanations emphasize the role of norms, symbols, and other features of social identity to explain people's prevalent collective behavior.

36 For a good empirical refutation of this view, see George Quattrone and Amos Tversky, "Self-Deception and the Voter's Illusion," in *The Multiple Self*, ed, J. Elster (Cambridge, 1985), pp. 35–58.

37 H. Garfinkel, *Studies in Ethnomethodology* (Englewood Cliffs, 1967), pp. 133–4.

38 Melvin Pollner, *Mundane Reasoning* (Cambridge, 1987), p. 69ff.

39 One of many examples of the growing number of ethnomethodological studies of science is Michael Lynch, *Art and Artifact in Laboratory Science* (London, 1984). I focus on Latour and Woolgar's work primarily because it has had a wider impact. Lynch's work is more strictly ethnomethodological, and he criticizes Latour and Woolgar for being too "disengaged" in their ethnographic method. See Lynch, "Technical Work and Critical Inquiry: Investigations in the Scientific Laboratory," *Social Studies of Science* 12 (1982), pp. 499–533.

40 Edmund Husserl, *Ideas* (New York, 1931), pp. 147–8.

41 Bruno Latour and Steve Woolgar, *Laboratory Life: The Construction of Scientific Facts* (Princeton, 1986), p. 157. For the analogy to vitalism: "Our position is not unlike the opponents of vitalism in nineteenth century biology. No matter what progress was made by biologists to explain life on purely mechanistic and materialistic

terms, some aspects remained unexplained" (p. 168). The only resistance to their approach, they claim, is the unjustified belief in "something peculiar and mysterious which materialist and constructivist explanations" supposedly cannot grasp. In what follows, I will argue that their explanations are not successful on their own terms and that social *and* normative accounts are much more successful as explanations.

42   Ibid., p. 105. Latour and Woolgar argue here that understanding facts as constructed "would obviously hinder any attempt to implement what has been called the 'strong programme' in the sociology of science."

43   Steve Woolgar, *Science: The Very Idea* (London, 1988), especially chapter 2.

44   Ibid., p. 84.

45   Latour and Woolgar, *Laboratory Life*, p. 29.

46   Ibid., p. 29. This is surely an odd methodology for ethnographers of any kind to espouse.

47   Bruno Latour, *Science in Action* (Cambridge, 1987), p. 36.

48   Woolgar, *Science: The Very Idea*, p. 63. According to Woolgar, norms are "resources" for evaluating others' claims and defending one's own. Similarly, citing the work of others is not part of the mutual search for truth, but an appeal to the tribal authority, the "trusted story tellers" who help the scientist to establish "community membership." The objectivity of a "discovery" is demystified by analyzing how it results from the embedding of a new claim in many other older ones, with the "cumulative effect of citing more and more people who similarly recognize the object being claimed" (p. 76).

49   Latour, *Science in Action*, p. 32.

50   Ibid., p. 70.

51   Latour and Woolgar, *Laboratory Life*, p. 254. This quotation is taken from a response to critics printed as an appendix to the second edition of the book. Once again, the Durkheimian problem of agents' self-descriptions emerges in the impoverished nominalist strategies of the sociology of science, which obviously conflict with those descriptions.

52   For a similar criticism, see Ronald Giere, *Explaining Science* (Chicago, 1988), p. 127. Giere shows that detailed account of the *ad hoc* character of scientific research can be given a more comprehensive treatment within a realist rather than a nominalist perspective. Such an approach does not exclude treating knowledge as social activity. See his chapter on realism and the sociology of science entitled "Realism in the Laboratory."

53   Woolgar, *Science: The Very Idea*, p. 108.

54   Helen Longino, *Science as Social Knowledge* (Princeton, 1990). She calls for the establishment of "oppositional science," which would produce theories that would be the product of a more inclusive scientific community. Such a theory would be better relative to a

particular purpose: "It is better not as measured against some independently accessible reality, but as measured against the cognitive
needs of a genuinely democratic community" (p. 214). Creating this
new political reality is the task that an adequate criticism of Galileo's statement discussed here sets; but in the absence of such norms,
Latour and Woolgar's anthropology of science is neither critical nor
practical. For another normative and democratic view like Longino's,
see Evelyn Fox Keller, *Reflections on Gender and Science* (New Haven,
1985), especially the essays in part 3; she sees democratic, gender-
free science as the goal of a practical and cognitive transformation
of how we look at nature and ourselves.

55 In a famous passage from *The German Ideology*, Marx did regard
language as "practical consciousness," but his discussion makes it
clear that he thought of language as externalizing and objectivating
activity on the same model of labor and production.

56 For a definition of distorted communication, see Habermas, "On
Systematically Distorted Communication," *Inquiry* 13 (1970), pp. 205–
18.

57 This view is still present even in Habermas's most recent writings on
the subject; see *The Theory of Communicative Action*, vol. 1, p. 332.

58 Some critics argue that Habermas's theory of speech, or "formal
pragmatics," cannot be made critical; see Seyla Benhabib, *Norm,
Critique, Utopia* (New York, 1986), p. 325ff.

59 Habermas, *Theory of Communicative Action*, vol. 2, p. 63.

60 Ibid., vol. 1, p. 226.

61 For a fuller treatment of these issues, see my "Ideology, Communication and Democratic Theory," *American Political Science Review*
84 (1990), pp. 93–104. For a more expository treatment of
Habermas's view of democracy, see my "Habermas's Cognitivist
Conception of Democracy," in *Knowledge and Politics*, ed. M. Dascal
and O. Gruengard (Boulder, 1988), pp. 264–89.

62 Peter Bachrach and Morton Baratz, *Power and Poverty* (Oxford,
1970).

63 For an analysis of this type of speech, see my "The Perlocutions and
Illocutions of the Social Critic," *Philosophy and Rhetoric* 21 (1987),
pp. 185–204.

64 For Habermas's longest discussion of this purpose of criticism, see
Theory and Practice (Boston, 1973), especially the Introduction.

65 Clifford Geertz, *Local Knowledge* (New York, 1983), p. 57.

66 Ibid., p. 58.

67 Michael Walzer, *Interpretation and Social Criticism* (Cambridge,
Mass., 1986), p. 60.

68 Ibid., p. 30.

69 Walzer, *The Company of Critics*, p. x.

70 See Eric Hobsbawn's discussion of the reception of the *Manifesto in
The Age of Capital* (New York, 1975), p. 110.

71 For an analysis of these possibilities focusing on continuities between

the Enlightenment, the Reformation, and European socialism, see Robert Wuthnow, *Communities of Discourse* (Princeton, 1990).

72 South Africa provides a good test case and the poet Breyten Breytenbach is supposed to support Walzer's claim that even Afrikaner culture supports critics. I find Johnny Clegg's recognition of the necessity of a multicultural identity in this context much more convincing than any insistence that the Afrikaners are "a people" (although Breytenbach himself once urged that South Africans "decompose together"). Clegg recognizes the need for a much greater distance to overcome apartheid.

73 Habermas, *Legitimation Crisis* (Boston, 1973), p. 2.

74 Ibid., p. 3.

75 See Seyla Benhabib, *Critique, Norm, and Utopia*, p. 126ff.

76 Marx, *Capital*, vol. 3, p. 830.

77 Sometimes Marx also seems committed to the false view that crises are "inevitable" by some teleological necessity, although he clearly recognizes that an exploitative social system can last for centuries if agents do not change it through self-conscious, collective effort, as was the case in many empires.

78 Jürgen Habermas, *Communication and the Evolution of Society* (Boston, 1979), p. 97.

79 Ibid., p. 124.

80 Habermas, *Legitimation Crisis*, p. 4.

81 Raymond Geuss, *The Idea of a Critical Theory* (Cambridge, 1981), p. 78.

82 Ibid., p. 79.

83 This account of power and its relation to the "human sciences" is developed most clearly in Michel Foucault, *The History of Sexuality*, vol. 1 (New York, 1980), and in the interviews in *Power/Knowledge* (New York, 1980).

84 Walzer, *The Company of Critics*, p. 232.

CONCLUSION PHILOSOPHY AND THE SOCIAL SCIENCES

1 For a discussion of more recent criticisms of the Kantian notion of philosophy, see our Editors' Introduction to K. Baynes, J. Bohman, and T. McCarthy, eds, *After Philosophy* (Cambridge, Mass., 1987). On the relation of philosophy to the social sciences (especially as it is developed by the Frankfurt School), see my "Critical Theory as Metaphilosophy," *Metaphilosophy* 13 (1990) pp. 239–52.

2 For a whole range of arguments for this conclusion, see Jürgen Habermas, *The Theory of Communicative Action*, vol. 1 (Boston, 1984), p. 2ff.

3 See Jürgen Habermas, *Communication and the Evolution of Society* (Boston, 1979), p. 8ff.

4 Max Horkheimer, *Critical Theory* (New York, 1972), p. 202.
5 Herbert Marcuse, *Negations* (Boston, 1969), p. 152.
6 Such a critical and practical sociology of science could help create both oppositional sciences and counter-institutions that are genuinely governed by democratic norms. But this practical project makes sense only if the sciences count as knowledge because they are concerned to test currently held beliefs and create discursive conditions that formally suspend relations of power. Apart from the context of such clear practical goals, the theory of ideology contributes little. For an articulation of such a critical–practical perspective with regard to scientific institutions and beliefs, see Helen Longino's discussion of ideology in *Science as Social Knowledge* (Princeton, 1990).
7 Here, too, the simple rejection of morality as such blunts both the practical and critical edge of social theory. As Horkheimer put it, "Morality cannot be completely rejected by materialism as pure ideology, in the sense of false consciousness." See Max Horkheimer, *Kritische Theorie* (Frankfurt, 1977), p. 77. Similarly, Habermas argues that moral beliefs are not merely epiphenomena, but are the very "pacemakers" of social learning and change. See Habermas, *Communication and the Evolution of Society*, p. 96. Habermas makes clear that a theory oriented to emancipatory change needs a normative orientation.
8 Both Weber and Habermas argue that these institutions can be changed to make modern life more rational.

Index